Ambedkar's Vision of Economic Development for India

AF755202

This book discusses Ambedkar's engagements with the issues of social justice, economic development and caste enclosures. It highlights his significant contributions in the field of trade, public finance and monetary economics, Indian agriculture, education, among others, and examines their relevance in contemporary India.

The volume analyses the basic theoretical conceptions in Ambedkar's writings which attributed a key role to industrialisation, favoured economic planning and progressive labour laws. It reaffirms these theories and illustrates that focus on social and economic democracy promotes productivity, equitable distribution of wealth and an inclusive society. Through an analysis of Ambedkar's interdisciplinary works, the book discusses issues of rural poverty, lagging infrastructure growth, the persistence of an exploitative ruling class and the economic and social marginalisation of the downtrodden which are still relevant today. Further, it offers solutions for a restructuring of the society under democratic principles which would recognise the basic right of all to social dignity, and devise means to insure against social and economic insecurity.

Insightful and authoritative, this volume will be of great interest to students and researchers of economics, sociology, development studies and social exclusion.

Gummadi Sridevi is an Associate Professor at School of Economics, University of Hyderabad, Hyderabad. She has completed collaborative research projects supported by ICSSR on climate change, food security and education. She's currently working on a collaborative ICSSR-IMPRESS major research project on Commons. Her research areas cover a wide range of issues relating to food security, health, gender, climate change and economics of discrimination. She has published articles in various journals and edited volumes. She has 13 years of teaching experience at the University of Hyderabad. She has been teaching courses such as economics of discrimination, international trade and payments, microeconomics and mathematical economics.

Ambedkar's Vision of Economic Development for India

Edited by Gummadi Sridevi

Routledge
Taylor & Francis Group
LONDON AND NEW YORK

First published 2020
by Routledge
2 Park Square, Milton Park, Abingdon, Oxon OX14 4RN

and by Routledge
52 Vanderbilt Avenue, New York, NY 10017

Routledge is an imprint of the Taylor & Francis Group, an informa business

© 2020 selection and editorial matter, Gummadi Sridevi; individual chapters, the contributors

The right of Gummadi Sridevi to be identified as the author of the editorial material, and of the authors for their individual chapters, has been asserted in accordance with sections 77 and 78 of the Copyright, Designs and Patents Act 1988.

All rights reserved. No part of this book may be reprinted or reproduced or utilised in any form or by any electronic, mechanical, or other means, now known or hereafter invented, including photocopying and recording, or in any information storage or retrieval system, without permission in writing from the publishers.

Trademark notice: Product or corporate names may be trademarks or registered trademarks, and are used only for identification and explanation without intent to infringe.

British Library Cataloguing-in-Publication Data
A catalogue record for this book is available from the British Library

Library of Congress Cataloging-in-Publication Data
A catalog record for this book has been requested

ISBN: 978-0-8153-8216-4 (hbk)

ISBN: 978-0-367-50863-0 (pbk)

ISBN: 978-1-003-05157-2 (ebk)

Typeset in Sabon
by Apex CoVantage, LLC

Contents

Figures

Tables

Contributors

Ajaya Kumar Naik is currently working in a multinational consulting firm. He has more than 15 years of research experience in the fields of social discrimination, labor market, poverty and inequality. Earlier he worked as associate fellow at Indian Institute of Dalit studies, New Delhi for six years. As a former full-time consultant in the National Commission for Enterprises in the Unorganized Sector (NCEUS), he was associated with the task force "Definitional and Statistical Issues related to Informal Economy". Besides this he has worked at Indian Institute of Public administration, Institute of applied manpower research in different capacities.

Anand Teltumbde is a writer, columnist, social activist and educationist. He has Bachelor of Engineering (Mechanical) from VNIT, Nagpur; PGDM (IIM, Ahmedabad), Ph.D (Management). He served as Executive Director at Bharat Petroleum Corporation Ltd. and Managing Director and CEO at Petronet India Ltd. He also handled important assignments in Nigeria, Kenya, Tanzania and China. He has worked on many important industry and government committees and was a member of the study group on Petroleum Deregulation in 1995. He has taught at various management institutes and published more than 20 research papers in reputed international journals in the areas of production research, ergonomics, information technology and business strategy. He has actively participated in movements of unorganised and workers in informal sectors, and more than 100 fact-finding missions in the incidents of civil rights violations and communal crimes. As a noted public intellectual, he has delivered scores of public speeches on issues of public interests and education. He was also the editor of, *Thinagi (The Spark)*, a Marathi working class monthly – and has served on the editorial boards of *Samaj Prabodhan Patrika, Vidrohi* and other progressive magazines. He has pioneered a critique of neoliberal globalisation in India from a viewpoint of downtrodden people with a book (Marathi) published in 1995 and thereafter numerous papers, pamphlets and articles. He received many prestigious awards and recognitions such as Vikas Ratna, Ambedkar

Centenary Award (UK), Ram Manohar Lohia Centenary Award, Maharashtra Foundation (USA) Award for Social Work (2008) and Maharashtra Foundation (USA) Award (2010) for the book- *Samrajyavadvirodh ani Jati Vinash*. He teaches Management at the Goa Institute of Management (GIM).

Chandrani Dutta has a Ph.D from Centre for the Study of Regional Development (CSRD), School of Social Sciences, Jawaharlal Nehru University (JNU), New Delhi. She has been working on the status of development of Dalits in selected states of India and is currently working on the areas interface of gender/ethnicity, caste and urban exclusion. Her areas of interests are in the field of marginal communities living in slums, contemporary urban policies. Earlier she was associated with Indian Institute of Dalit Studies, New Delhi as Assistant Professor. She is currently an independent social science researcher.

Dontha Prashanth is currently a Research Scholar at School of Economics, University of Hyderabad. His areas of interest Agricultural Economics, Development Economics, Economics of Caste and Discrimination and Economic History. He works on contemplating caste in changing economic relations in particular relation to its relevance in the context of land, labour and the course of economic development.

Gayatri Nair is Assistant Professor, Sociology, Department of Social Sciences and Humanities, Indraprashta Institute of Information Technology (IIITD), New Delhi. She has studied in Delhi, Mumbai and Pune and has completed her M.Phil and Ph.D from Jawaharlal Nehru University. Her doctoral research explored contestations for rights on urban commons, specifically the fisheries, in the context of a capitalist transformation. She teaches courses on the sociology of public policy and urbanisation. She also offers a policy area concentration on urbanisation. Her research interests lie in the interstices of urbanisation and social conflict with a focus on its impact on labour. She is also interested in studies related to popular culture specifically related to questions of caste and gender. She has previously taught sociology at Kamla Nehru College, University of Delhi and sociology and women and gender studies at the Symbiosis School for Liberal Arts, Pune. She is currently teaching these courses: Urban Identities and Governance; Civil Society, New Social Movements and Public Policy; and Urbanization and Development (Offered at the Development Studies Programme).

G. Nancharaiah is currently Emeritus Professor at School of Economics, University of Hyderabad, Hyderabad and Chairman, IV State Finance Commission, Amaravati, Andhra Pradesh. He was ICSSR National Fellow during 2015–17 at School of Economics, University of Hyderabad, Hyderabad and Emeritus Professor at Babasaheb Bhimrao Ambedkar Central University, Lucknow. He served as a Head of the Department of

Economics and Dean, School of Social Sciences and School of Economics at University of Hyderabad. He was Vice-Chancellor of Babasaheb Bhimrao Ambedkar Central University, Lucknow for five years from 2002 to 2007. He was a Fulbright scholar under Indo-US Exchange Programme and worked at University of California, Berkeley, USA in 1990. He has served as the chairman and member on the boards and research councils of many universities. He has been working in the areas of international economics, agricultural economics, developmental economics, economics of discrimination and Dr. Ambedkar's economic thought. He authored the book, *Land and Caste* (1988) and edited *Economic Reforms and Rural Development in India* (2003). He has published monographs in the areas of trade and has contributed research articles to reputed national and international journals.

K. Laxminarayana is currently Professor at the School of Economics, University of Hyderabad. He has been teaching post-graduate students for about 26 years in the areas of political economy of development, agricultural economics, economics of education and Indian political economy of caste and class. He has guided many M.Phil. and Ph.D. students. He has been extensively working on the Right to Education Act and also working on a project that deals on education among private and public schools.

Khalil Shaha holds a Ph.D in Economics and is currently incharge of Databank at Institute for Social and Economic Change (ISEC), Bangalore. He has more than ten years of research experience and worked as a member of the research team in the studies sponsored by Ministry of Agriculture and Farmers' Welfare, Government of India, Competition Commission of India (CCI), Food and Agriculture Organisation (FAO), United Nations and Government of Karnataka. He has published a good number of research papers in edited books and national and international journals on issues related to terms of trade, regional agricultural development, agricultural production and prices, market imperfections and farm sector distress, land, poverty, agricultural labour, common pool resources and BRICS.

Malathy Duraisamy is Professor and Head, Department of Humanities and Social Sciences, Indian Institute of Technology, Madras. She is a member of the Institutional Review Board, YRG CARE, Chennai (2003 onwards) and Member of the Senate at NITT (since 2008) and NITK (since 2013). She has completed six sponsored research projects funded by agencies such as The Rockefeller Foundation, USA, UNDP, NCAER & Planning Commission GOI, ICSSR, TN State DPEP and SSA. She has published in various highly reputed national and international journals. Her research interests include labour economics, economics of human resources (education, health, migration), technical education and manpower, gender discrimination, industrial economics, and banking and financial economics.

Matta Srinivas is currently pursuing his Ph.D. titled "Market Discrimination in MSME: An Empirical Study of Scheduled Caste Entrepreneurship" in School of Economics at University of Hyderabad. He has double masters degree in Commerce and Economics from Osmania University, Hyderabad and Annamalai University, Tamilnadu respectively. His areas of interests are finance, development economics, and caste discrimination.

Nitin Tagade is Assistant Professor at the Department of Economics, Savitribai Phule Pune University, Pune. He obtained his Ph.D. from the Institute for Social and Economic Change, Bangalore and worked as an assistant professor at the Indian Institute of Dalit Studies, New Delhi. His work has been mainly in the areas of development economics, inequality and economics of discrimination. He has published several articles in journals and edited books on the issues of food security, poverty, inequality, employment and land policy.

P. Duraisamy is currently Vice-Chancellor at University of Madras, Chepauk in Chennai. He had served for over 28 years at the University of Madras (1986–2014) and was a professor for over 21 years. Subsequently he was Sir Sarvepalli Radhakrishnan National Fellow of the Indian Council of Social Science Research (ICSSR) and affiliated to the Madras Institute of Development Studies, Chennai (2014–2016). Prof. Duraisamy was a member/convenor of several important National level Committees of the UGC, NAAC, MHRD and Planning Commission. His areas of specialisation and interest are economics of education, especially higher education, health, labour, macroeconomics, applied econometrics, political choice and voting behaviour. He was also involved in the preparation of policy document by the National Commission for Macroeconomics and Health, Ministry of Health and Family Welfare, GoI. To his credit more than 70 research articles published in international journals with 'A' level and impact factors, and he is on editorial boards of various journals.

Patturi Balaji is currently pursuing a Ph.D. at the School of Economics at University of Hyderabad. He pursued M.Phil from Centre for Development Studies, Trivandrum, Kerala (affiliated to Jawaharlal Nehru University, New Delhi) in June 2013. He has participated in workshops and presented papers in various seminars and also published research papers on issues related to poverty, food security, health trade and reproductive tourism.

R. Radhakrishna is currently Chairman, Centre for Economic and Social Studies (CESS), Hyderabad and Chairperson, Madras Institute of Development Studies, Chennai. He was Director of the Indira Gandhi Institute of Development Research (IGIDR) in Mumbai and Vice-Chancellor of Andhra University, Visakhapatnam. He taught and pursued research at Sardar Patel Institute of Economics and Social Research, Ahmedabad, and at the University of Hyderabad. He was the Member Secretary, ICSSR and was the Director, Centre for Economic and Social Studies, Hyderabad. He was a consultant to international organizations like ADB, FAO, World Bank and UNDP and UNESCO. He was a member of several government committees including the Expert Group on Estimation of Proportion and Number of Poor (Lakdawala Committee), Planning Commission, Government of India, 1989–93, Working Group for the Revision of the Current Series of Wholesale Price Index Numbers, Ministry of Industry, Government of India, 1993, among others. He has published several books/monographs in the areas of consumer demand, food security, labour and poverty studies and has contributed to reputed national and international journals.

R. S. Deshpande is currently Honorary Visiting Professor at the Institute for Social and Economic Change (ISEC), Bangalore. He was a Rajiv Gandhi National Fellow at the Indian Council of Social Science Research (ICSSR), and previously Director of ISEC. Dr. Deshpande holds a Bachelor of Science, and Masters' Degree with a Ph.D. in Economics. His specialisations include agricultural development policy, watershed development, political economy of agrarian changes, WTO – Agriculture & Trade, rural policy and poverty, economics of drought-prone areas and rain-fed regions, economics of irrigation, economics of caste, policy analysis and applied econometrics. He is a recipient of PNASF Gold Medal for his contributions to agricultural policy and Sir M Visvesvaraya Global Leadership Award in Karnataka for Excellence in Education. He was the sole architect of Karnataka's Agricultural Policy 2006 and Chairperson of Mission Group on Agriculture and Rural Development of Govt. of Karnataka. He has many books and research papers. His books include *Agrarian Crisis and Farmer Suicides*, *Where Water Seeps: NGOs and Farmers' Movements in India*, and *Moon in the Mirror: Farmers and MSP in Karnataka*.

R. Thirunavukkarasu is Assistant Professor in the Department of Sociology, School of Social Sciences at University of Hyderabad, Hyderabad. His areas of interest include nation and nationalism, political sociology of caste and social movements.

Sukhadeo Thorat is Emeritus Professor in Economics at the Jawaharlal Nehru University and Chairman ISEC, Bangalore. Former Chairman of the Indian Council of Social Science Research (ICSSR), and University Grants commission (UGC) New Delhi, India. He has received many awards for public service for marginalized groups, minorities and education including the Padmashree from Government of India, the Mother Teresa International Award and the Dr. Ambedkar Chetna Award. His research focuses on problems of excluded groups, socially inclusive growth, poverty, agricultural growth in dry agriculture, caste and economic discrimination, labour market discrimination, impact of economic discrimination on poverty and marginalization, economic ideas of Babasaheb Ambedkar and higher education. He has published extensively on these subjects.

He was the member of "Equality Group" that worked in the villages. He has published in various Indian and International journals.

Tajuddin Md. is Post-Doctoral Fellow at Council for Social Development (CSD), Hyderabad, Telangana, India. He is a doctorate in regional studies, University of Hyderabad and post-graduate from Department of Political Science, University of Hyderabad. His areas of interest are food security, migration and education. He has published papers in peer-reviewed journals.

Y. Sreenivasulu is a faculty member at the Center for Economic and Social Studies (CESS), Hyderabad. Rural labour market, rural land market, rural migration and agrarian economy have been his areas of research interest. He has published articles in various reputed journals and presented papers in professional seminars. He has participated in international advanced professional training programmes like Managing Global Governance (MGG) and International Futures (IF) in Germany. He interned at the migrant department at the International Labour Organization (ILO), Geneva, Switzerland.

Foreword

Lord Mayanard John M. Keynes had proposed to Chamberlain Commission (1913) a State Bank for India which would combine the Central Bank and Commercial Bank functions. First World War broke out before any action was taken on it. Later, appearing before the Hilton Young Commission (1925), Dr. Ambedkar differed with Lord Keynes and was in favour of a Central Bank (Reserve Bank). Similarly, Dr. Ambedkar argued in favour of a gold standard as opposed to the suggestion by Lord J.M. Keynes, who preferred gold exchange standard. On Centre-State financial relations, Dr. Ambedkar argued that under a sound administrative system, each political unit should be able to finance its expenditure from its resources. In a way, his doctoral theses in London and Columbia addressed the burning issues of the day, and even now of contemporary interest, namely, price stability and fiscal responsibility. That he was one of the eminent economists of India at that time and that he contributed to economic thinking and policy even early in his life is often masked by his subsequent historic contributions in many other fields.

His vision of economic development of India and his contributions in the area of political economy have received less attention than other aspects of his life. This book titled "Ambedkar's Vision of Economic Development in India" fills this gap in our perception of Dr. Ambedkar's contribution to the development of our country. The book captures his scholarly work, his contribution and the extent to which his vision has been fulfilled.

This book should inspire people to recognise many aspects of Dr. Ambedkar, some of which remain largely unappreciated. He was without doubt a statesman with courage and a visionary with a purpose – to serve the downtrodden. He actually set the standards with which we, Indians, can measure our performance both as a nation and as an economy. It will be enlightening to recall what he said in the Constituent Assembly and introspect where we are.

In his last address to the Constituent Assembly (November 25, 1949), he said:

> I came into the Constituent Assembly with no greater aspiration than to safeguard the interests of the Scheduled Castes.

Dr. Ambedkar was courageously unapologetic about his unwavering orientation towards the downtrodden. He added:

> I am grateful to the Constituent Assembly and the Drafting Committee for reposing in me so much trust and confidence and to have chosen me as their instrument and given me this opportunity of serving the country.

Dr. Ambedkar had the wisdom, vision and sagacity to earn the gratitude of the nation, as the principal architect of the Constitution of India and one of the founding fathers of the Republic of India.

While introducing the Draft Constitution in the Constituent Assembly, he laid out the essentials of our form of government.

> The Parliamentary system differs from a non-Parliamentary system in as much as the former is more responsible than the latter but they also differ as to the time and agency for assessment of their responsibility.

Dr. Ambedkar went on to say:

> The daily assessment is done by members of Parliament, through questions, Resolutions, No-confidence motions, Adjournment motions and Debates on Addresses. Periodic assessment is done by the Electorate at the time of the election which may take place every five years or earlier. The Daily assessment of responsibility which is not available under the American system is, it is felt far more effective than the periodic assessment and far more necessary in a country like India. The Draft Constitution in recommending the Parliamentary system of Executive has preferred more responsibility to more stability.

We have elections every five years, giving stability. What is our record recently, of the responsibility? Where are the debates and addresses on our Parliament and legislatures?

On the federation, Dr. Ambedkar while introducing the draft said:

> The Draft Constitution is, Federal Constitution inasmuch as it establishes what may be called a Dual Polity. This Dual Polity under the proposed Constitution will consist of the Union at the Centre and the States at the Periphery each endowed with sovereign powers to be exercised in the field assigned to them respectively, by the Constitution.

In recognition of shared sovereign powers, Pandit Nehru was writing periodic letters to Chief Ministers on several issues including global developments, wars and national planning. Periodic consultations between the Prime Minister and Chief Ministers were in order. Of late, Chief Ministers get from Union Ministers more of advice on what they should do or not do, and little information on what the Union is doing.

Are we ignoring what Dr. Ambedkar said about Centre and States being co-equal? He said:

> As to the relation between the Centre and the States, it is necessary to bear in mind the fundamental principle on which it rests. The basic principle of Federalism is that the Legislative and Executive authority is partitioned between the Centre and the States not by any law to be made by the Centre but by the constitution itself. This is what Constitution does. The States under our Constitution are in no way dependent upon the Centre for their legislative or executive authority. The Centre and the States are co-equal in this matter.

What did Dr. Ambedkar expect from political parties? In his last lecture, to the Constituent Assembly, he said the following:

> The Constitution can provide only the organs of State such as the Legislature, the Executive and the Judiciary. The factors on which the working of those organs of the State depends on the people and the political parties they will set up as their instruments to carry out their wishes and their politics. Who can say how the people of India and their parties will behave?

Can we now say that our political parties are doing a satisfactory job? The legislatures are virtually non functional. Public servants may be removed or at least punished for not doing their work, but not our legislators. The executive has lost the trust of people at large in terms of impartiality and incorruptibility. The judiciary at the highest level has brought into public domain the differences out into the streets. What are the people doing about the state of affairs?

How about Satyagraha that political leader and some others practice, day-in and day-out? That could threaten our democracy, warned Dr. Ambedkar in his last address to the Constituent Assembly.

> A study of the Buddhist Bhikshu Sanghas discloses that not only there were Parliaments–for the Sanghas were nothing but Parliaments–but the Sanghas knew and observed all the rules of Parliamentary Procedure known to modern times. They had rules regarding seating arrangements, rules regarding Motions, Resolutions, Quorum, Whip, Counting of Votes, Voting by Ballot, Censure Motion, Regularization, Res Judicata, etc. Although these rules of Parliamentary Procedure were applied by the Buddha to the meetings of the Sanghas, he must have borrowed them from the rules of the Political Assemblies functioning in the country in his time.

> If we wish to maintain democracy not merely in form, but also in fact, what must we do? The first thing in my judgement we must do is to hold fast to constitutional methods of achieving our social and economic objectives. It means we must abandon the bloody methods of revolution. It means that we must abandon the method of civil disobedience, non-cooperation and Satyagraha.

We have had the good fortune of several great leaders – some at the Union level and some at the state level. We observe holidays in their memory, erect statues and, in some cases, erect temples. Dr. Ambedkar warned us on this also in his last address.

> The second thing we must do is to observe the caution which John Stuart Mill has given to all who are interested in the maintenance of democracy, namely, not "to lay their liberties at the feet of even a great man, or to trust him with powers which enable him to subvert their institutions." There is nothing wrong in being grateful to great men who have rendered life-long services to the country. But there are limits to gratefulness. As has been well said by the Irish Patriot Daniel O'Connell, 'no man can be grateful at the cost of his honour, no woman can be grateful at the cost of her chastity and no nation can be grateful at the cost of its liberty.

In one of his most important observations, towards the end of his address, Dr. Ambedkar said:

> On the 26th of January 1950, we are going to enter into a life of contradictions. In politics we will have equality and in social and economic life we will have inequality. In Politics we will be recognizing the principle of one man one vote and one vote one value. In our social and economic life, we shall, by reason of our social and economic structure, continue to deny the principle of one man one value. How long shall we continue to live this life of contradictions? How long shall we continue to deny equality in our social and economic life? If we continue to deny it for long, we will do so only by putting our political democracy in peril.

The world has only recently become actually aware of the need to resolve contradictions in equality in different spheres of life. We in India have been forewarned 70 years ago by Dr. Ambedkar.

> We must remove this contradiction at the earliest possible moment or else those who suffer from inequality will blow up the structure of political democracy which this Assembly has so laboriously built up.

What have we done so far?

Ambedkar was a man of courage. Till his death at the age of 65, he worked to bring about not just equality, but also fraternity and liberty in legal, social, economic and political spheres. With his wisdom, vision, and sagacity, he earned the gratitude of the nation.

The book is in some ways a tribute to Dr. Ambedkar, the prescient statesman, *sans pareil*.

Dr. Y. Venugopal Reddy
(Former Governor, Reserve Bank of India)
(Former Chairperson, Fourteenth Finance Commission, Govt. of India)

Preface

Dr. B. R. Ambedkar was one of the early economists of the country who advocated for the development of society with a blend of modernization of the economy coupled with socio-economic development of all sections of the society. The solutions offered by Dr. Ambedkar are practically relevant to the Indian economy even in the 21st century. Dr. Ambedkar's approach to understanding the economy by decoding the ill-effects of social systems offered a theorisation on the effects of the caste system in India. Caste was defined as an endogamous unit, which divides labourers not labour in a graded hierarchy in vertical order by placing one caste above another. The division of labour, as argued by Smith, should originate from an individual's disposition to work in a certain occupation, which further leads to innovation.

Dr. Ambedkar's view on division of labour appears to be consistent with Smith's proposition, where he argues:

> Social and individual efficiency requires us to develop the capacity of an individual to the point of competency to choose and to make his own career. This principle is violated in the Caste System, in so far as it involves an attempt to appoint tasks to individuals in advance – selected not on the basis of trained original capacities, but on that of the social status of the parents.
>
> (BAWS, 1979, Vol. 1, pg. 47)

According to Dr. Ambedkar, such a system of gradation of labour in watertight compartments preventing mobility of labour is a cause for much of the unemployment, as society moves towards modernisation/capitalisation and industrialisation. Preventing labour to flow freely from one occupation to another creates surplus labour in one occupation while causing scarcity in another. The presence of surplus labour disguises the persistence of unemployment, where more labour is engaged in an economic activity which requires a lesser proportion of labour, which, in turn, entails a lesser proportion of wages.

In India, a large proportion of labour force is engaged in agriculture. Agriculture is largely characterised by problems of heavy dependence (wherein a higher proportion constitutes female labour) coupled with fragmentation of land holdings. Niti Aayog (2016) problematises such heavy dependence on agriculture, and, in particular, phases out the need for driving out dependent population from agriculture to non-agricultural occupations. Ambedkar was the first among modern economists of the world, who identified problems of heavy dependence on agriculture in India, to suggest industrialisation as a means to squeeze out surplus labour within agriculture.

Ambedkar (1918) had pointed out the problems of fragmentation of land holdings leading to increased costs on supervision and cultivation. This made it impossible for mechanisation in agriculture which can effectively reduce costs of cultivation. The problems of inadequacy of capital in agriculture with increasing costs and unprofitable avenues through mechanisation hindered by fragmentation of land are still a reality in modern times. He advocated for a transformation from traditional dependence on occupational structures to a modernised economy for an improved standard of living. Dr. Ambedkar's vision for such transformation was a broader concept, which envisaged conversion of labour engaged in agrarian and menial occupations, broadly categorised as unskilled labour, to skilled labour by way of state intervention in imparting education. Ambedkar gave importance to the spread of technical education enabling greater employment opportunities to a vast majority, as the economy tends to move on the path of growth and development. He envisioned the importance of imparting technical education and skill development in absorbing unskilled unemployed labour to be utilised in the process of modernisation of the economy. However, Dr. Ambedkar was also cautious while propounding the idea of modernisation and industrialisation. He stood for creation of wealth and transfer of excessive labour from unproductive sectors to productive ones, and at the same time, he proposed that industrial development and subsequent creation of wealth must be distributed in a socially desirable level. To quote:

> It will not be enough to make industrial development of India as our goal. We shall have to agree that any such industrial development shall be maintained at a socially desirable level. It will not be enough to bend our energies for the production of more wealth in India. We shall have to agree not merely to recognise the basic right of all Indians to share in that wealth as a means for a decent and dignified existence but to devise ways and means to ensure him against insecurity.
>
> (BAWS, 1991, Vol. 10, pg. 105)

Dr. Ambedkar's economic propositions were multi-dimensional in nature and fit into the frame of both growth and development; for by development, he meant development for all. Being the Labour Member of the Viceroy Council, he had enacted the minimum wages for labour act and introduced maternity benefit schemes to reduce tensions between state, employer and employee. In settlement of disputes, he proposed tripartite settlements by involving employer, employee and state. His conception of labour was something that goes beyond the frame of securing fair conditions of work while insisting that labour wants fair conditions of life.

The debates of Dr. Ambedkar in the Bombay Legislative Council on Budget sessions mark his views on fair conditions of life. His views on public finance carried a visionary approach of laying down a formidable future of the economy and a long-term development of the country.

The advocacy of Ambedkar, in allocating a higher share of the budget towards the aim of imparting education and enabling education to be state-sponsored, underlies a vision to create human capital which becomes the engine of long-term growth for the economy. The creation of human capital leads to innovation in industry and scientific advancement, resulting in a forward leap for the economy. His views on imparting technical and scientific education have transgressed beyond the times of war as stressed by him during his tenure as Labour Member of Viceroy Council. To quote:

> No plan for the future development of the country can be deemed to be complete which does not provide for technical and scientific training. This is the age of Machine and it is only those countries in which technical and scientific training has risen to the highest pitch that will survive in the struggle that will commence when the war is over, for maintaining decent standards of living for their people.
>
> (BAWS, 1991, Vol. 10, pg. 181)

Dr. Ambedkar was a staunch supporter of the system of progressive taxation, which aimed at collection of taxes for the welfare of citizens. In the Bombay Legislative Assembly, he (BAWS, Vol. 2) spoke:

> Why do we have progressive income-tax? Why don't we tax all people alike? The reason why we tax the rich at a higher rate and the poor at a lower rate is that the taxable capacity of the two is different. In a case like that equality would produce the greatest inequity.
>
> (BAWS, 1982, Vol. 02, pg. 230)

His approach to essential services for the survival of humankind included sickness insurance, old-age pensions, maternity benefits, unemployment benefit and premature death benefits to dependents. He had categorically maintained that a budgetary provision on the aforementioned services along with education, public health, medical relief and water supply would ensure a decent standard of living.

Dr. Ambedkar is also hailed as a founder of India's Modern Water Policy which included proposals on construction of dams, setting up Central Water Commission. He opined:

> Man (Woman) suffers more from lack of water than from excess of it. Water being the wealth of the people and its distribution uncertain, the

> correct approach was not to complain about nature but to conserve water. If conservation of water was mandatory from the point of view of public good, then obviously the plan of embankments was a wrong plan . . . The appropriate approach was to Dam Rivers at various points to conserve water permanently in reservoirs.
>
> (CWC, 1993, p. 53)

The proposal for construction of dams was aimed at both conservation of water and generating multi-purpose utilities such as generation of electricity and irrigation.

Dr. Ambedkar's approach to economic development was both modern and inclusive, aimed at ushering growth and distributing the benefits of growth thus accumulated. Dr. B. R. Ambedkar's famous quote in the Parliament while adopting constitution of India explains the vision of a society embedded in the principles of socio-economic equality. To quote:

> On the social plane, we have in India a society based on the principle of graded inequality which we have a society in which there are some who have immense wealth against many who live in abject poverty. . . . How long shall we continue to deny equality in social and economic life? If we continue it for long, we will do so only by putting out political democracy in peril. We must remove this contradiction at the earliest possible moment or else those who suffer from inequality will blow up the structure of political democracy which this assembly has so laboriously built up.

His vision against an unequal society is echoed by World Bank, while formulating the Sustainable Development Goals in ending poverty, where SDG's articulates that growing inequality would become detrimental to economic growth and becomes a vehicle for increasing socio-political tensions undermining social cohesion which would in turn drive instability and conflicts. The speech of Dr. B. R. Ambedkar in Constituent Assembly on 25th November 1949 sums up his vision of Indian economy to be inclusive and at the same time stands as a warning against the dangers of perpetuating inequality. Dr. B. R. Ambedkar's thoughts become highly relevant in present context where inequalities on socio-economic plane are a reality of present times. The present edited book is the outcome of the special lectures/papers presented at a national seminar on "Dr. B. R. Ambedkar's vision of Economic Development in India" in the context of 125th birth anniversary celebrations of Dr. B. R. Ambedkar organized at the School of Economics, University of Hyderabad. This edited book is brought out to analyze Dr. Ambedkar's views on caste and its economic implications, fiscal system, exchange rate and trade, Indian agriculture, education, development of women and marginalized sections (i.e., SC/ST/OBC/Minorities), and thus elaborately presenting his views on the plan of economic development and examining their contemporary relevance for India. It also fills the gap of absence of interpretation of the works of Dr. B. R. Ambedkar in relation to the problems that persist in the society.

Reference

Ambedkar, B. R. (1918). Small Holdings in India and Their Remedies. *Journal of Indian Economic Society*, 1, 1900–1945.

Ayog, N. I. T. I. (2016). *Annual Report*. Government of India. http://niti.gov.in/sites/default/files/2018-12/AnnualReport_16-17_ENGLISH.pdf

Central Water Commission (CWC). (1993). *Ambedkar's Contribution to Water Resources Development*, p. 53. New Delhi: Central Water Commission.

Dr. Babasaheb Ambedkar Writings and Speeches (BAWS). (1979). Vol. 1, p. 47. Maharashtra, India: Government of Maharashtra.

Dr. Babasaheb Ambedkar Writings and Speeches (BAWS). (1982). Vol. 2, p. 230. Maharashtra, India: Government of Maharashtra.

Dr. Babasaheb Ambedkar Writings and Speeches (BAWS). (1991). Vol. 10, p. 105. Maharashtra, India: Government of Maharashtra.

Dr. Babasaheb Ambedkar Writings and Speeches (BAWS). (1991). Vol. 10, p. 181. Maharashtra, India: Government of Maharashtra.

Acknowledgements

Ambedkar is a giant when it comes to political philosophy and policies especially for the underprivileged. However, very little is known and discussed about his far-fetched economic thoughts. Ambedkar's deeper understanding of the ontology of his contemporary society and immense epistemological clarity on how to build a fair and just society influenced his economic thinking, different from the mainstream economic ideas. His ideas of inclusiveness, rather than the injustice of exclusion, influenced me in my research. I feel satisfied and at the same time immensely indebted to many who helped me bring out this edited volume on Ambedkar's economic thoughts, influence and applications.

This edited book could not have been carried out without the financial and administrative support of Indian Council for Social Science Research (ICSSR). I am grateful to ICSSR, New Delhi.

I express my heartfelt gratitude to all the paper contributors for encouraging and supporting me in bringing out this edited volume.

My sincere appreciation and personal gratitude to Dr. Y. V. Reddy for taking his time in writing a thought-provoking foreword to the book. I express my gratitude to the University of Hyderabad administration; faculty colleagues and office staff of School of Economics; Dr. K. Y. Ratnam, Coordinator, Centre for Ambedkar studies; Prof. S. Galab, Director, Centre for Economic and Social Studies, Begumpet, Hyderabad and the office staff of School of Economics for extending all possible support. I also thank Routledge for all the cooperation in carrying out this edited book.

A very special thanks to Matta Srinivas, Patturi Balaji and Dontha Prashanth who helped me at various stages of this volume's evolution. The seeds of this volume was sown while we ideated and organized a conference on Ambedkar's economic thoughts at University of Hyderabad.

I couldn't have accomplished this without the support of my family and friends Dhanalaxmi Gummadi, Samhita, Madhu, Vidya, Sanju, Vijju as well as Amal and Priya, who all stood like pillars at various difficult phases. My heartfelt thanks to all of them.

G. Sridevi

Part I

Ambedkar's economic thought

1 Dr. B. R. Ambedkar's vision of economic development of India and its relevance

G. Nancharaiah

Ambedkar believed that the state has a crucial role to play in restructuring society under democratic polity and the foundations of our democracy would be feeble and shaky if social and economic democracy are sidelined and the emphasis is put solely on political democracy. Dr. Ambedkar opined that existing social and economic institutions, particularly caste and land tenure systems in India were not conducive for accelerating economic development with social justice. He emphasized the need for removing social and economic inequalities as a pre-condition for a stable democracy which secures for its citizens justice and rapid economic development.

After the attainment of independence, India adopted the national economic policy with the primary objective of growth with justice. Self-reliance was one of the important objectives of planning besides expansion of employment and removal of poverty. India, like other developing countries, had given priority to import substitution as an effective means of industrialization. The state was expected to steer the engine of growth and the public sector was assigned a crucial role in the process of industrial development. All basic and heavy industries were supposed to be under the control of the public sector. The emphasis was more on aid than on exports. But by mid-sixties, the problem of foreign exchange became very acute due to drought and war with Pakistan. The policy was changed to export promotion while continuing import substitution which has been synonymously viewed as self-reliance. Then several measures to boost exports had been initiated by the Government of India in the form of subsidies to exports and the rupee was devalued by about 57.5 percent in June 1966 (Sen, 1986, p. 132). Despite various incentives given to the exporting industry and protection to the import-competing industry in the form of tariffs and other controls on imports during 1961–1991, there was a negative trade gap which constituted about 3 percent of GDP on average. With the balance of payments problem becoming very serious in 1991 and added difficulties due to the Gulf War, this period was described as the 1991 economic crisis. Since 1991, the economic policy of India has been liberalized with an emphasis on privatization and globalization. There has been a shift in the Indian economic policy from state-oriented development strategy to market-oriented development leaving decisions of production and distribution to market signals. But this new economic policy became controversial as it failed at the global level, particularly in case of some Latin American and African countries.

In this context, the views of Dr. Ambedkar on various aspects of Indian economy merit serious discussion. This paper attempts to analyse Dr. Ambedkar's views on caste and its economic implications, monetary and fiscal systems, exchange rate and trade, Indian agriculture, education, and his plan of economic development as well as examines their relevance for contemporary India.

Caste and its economic implications

Ambedkar argued that caste system as an economic organization did not result in efficiency (Govt. of Maharashtra, 1979, pp. 50–58). It does not represent a division of labour on the following grounds.

Caste is not merely the division of labour. It is also a division of labourers. It is hierarchical. The division of labourers is graded one above the other. Civilized society undoubtedly needs this division of labour. But in no civilized society is division of labour accompanied by this unnatural division of labourers into water-tight compartments. In no other country is the division of labour accompanied by the gradation of labourers.

The division of labour represented by the caste system is not spontaneous. It is not based on natural aptitudes. Social and individual efficiency requires development of capacity of an individual to the point of competency to choose and make his own career. This is violated in the caste system to the extent that it involves an attempt to assign tasks to individuals in advance, not on the basis of trained original capacities, but on the basis of the social status of parents. This is positively pernicious from the point of view of economic development which is a dynamic phenomenon. The industry is never static and undergoes rapid changes. An individual must be free to choose his occupation compatible with such change. Otherwise, it becomes very difficult for him to gain his livelihood. If a Hindu is seen starving rather than taking to new occupation not assigned to his caste, the reason is to be found in the caste. Thus, by not permitting readjustment of occupations, castes become a direct cause of much of the unemployment existing in the country.

Caste system as a form of division of labour suffers from another serious defect as it is based on the dogma of predestination. Individual preference has no place in it. And certain occupations assigned by caste system are degraded and people engaged in such occupations are treated as a defiling group and are put through the social stigma of untouchability. As a result, people engaged in such occupations are provoked to aversion and their inconstant desire to avoid and escape from such occupations. In a system under which neither men's hearts nor minds are at their work, there cannot be any efficiency. "As an economic organization Caste is therefore a harmful institution, in as much as, it involves the subordination of man's natural powers and inclinations to the exigencies of social rules," (Ambedkar, 1979a, pp. 47–48).

Untouchability, which is the by-product of the caste system, is not only a form of social discrimination but also a source of economic exploitation. Untouchables are made to live in the outskirts of the village and physically segregated from the mainstream of life (Govt. of Maharashtra, 1989, p. 21). They are assigned occupations which are unclean and filthy and forced to remain in the same occupations. The untouchables are denied right to education. They are denied the right of owning land and the right of bargaining wages. They have to perform a number of duties in villages without any remuneration (Govt. of Maharashtra, 1990, p. 94). Ambedkar observed that untouchability is more than a religious system. It is also an economic system worse than slavery. Untouchability as an economic system permits exploitation without obligation. Untouchability is not only a system of unmitigated economic exploitation but is also a system of uncontrolled economic exploitation (Govt. of Maharashtra, 1989, pp. 61–87).

In view of the above reasons, Ambedkar argued that there was a need of annihilating caste so that there was no contradiction between socio-economic conditions, existing in the Indian society and political democracy. Ambedkar, in his speech delivered to the Constituent Assembly on November 25, 1949, referred to this contradiction, that is, equality in politics and inequality in social and economic life, which the country was going to enter upon after the inauguration of the new constitution on January 26, 1950. Ambedkar said:

> How long shall we continue to live this life of contradictions? How long shall we continue to deny equality in our social and economic life? If we continue to deny it for long, we will do so only by putting our political democracy in peril. We must remove this contradiction at the earliest possible moment or else those who suffer from inequality will blow up the structure of political democracy which is Assembly has to laboriously built up.

Dr. Ambedkar's views on fiscal and monetary system and trade in colonial India and their contemporary relevance[1]

Following the proposition of Adam Smith that the finances of a country are to be judged from the viewpoint of developmental expenditure, Ambedkar condemned the entire fiscal system of the East India Company. He quotes (Govt. of Maharashtra, 1989, pp. 31–32) Mr. Martin who says:

> As the territorial acquisitions of the company expanded the revenue increased with more than a commensurate increase of expenditure. The cost of government by Europeans, the growth of standing army in each province and other sources of legitimate or illegitimate expenses

> swallowing up all the anticipated surplus and leaving nothing for the development of the resources of the country or even for the maintenance of the roads, canals and other public works constructed by native rulers.

From the data on gross revenue and gross expenditure during 1792–1793 to 1857–1858, Ambedkar inferred that there were 32 years of surpluses and 14 years of deficit and there was a surplus of £32 million during these 46 years. But this money was neither saved nor devoted to the works of irrigation or other works of improvement in India. It went as a continuous tribute to England to pay dividends to the Company's shareholders and, as the flow of money from India was not sufficient to pay the dividends, there was an increasing debt called "the public debt of India". The public debt of India at least under company's rule was entirely the creation of war. The entire heavy load of the debt of the East India Company amounting to £69,473,484 – mostly on-productive was placed on the shoulders of the poverty-stricken natives who had no voice in the doings of the Company. Ambedkar said that this large size of debt was the result of mismanagement and extravagance of the East India Company and was one of the important reasons why discussions about direct assumption of the government of India by the Crown even before the mutiny of 1857 took place (Ibid, p. 37).

Dr. Ambedkar, in his work *Evolution of the Provincial Finance in British India*, examined the fiscal policy adopted by the Government of India and financial relationship between imperial and provincial governments during 1833–1919, (Ibid, p. 73). The imperial system of government was necessarily accompanied by the imperial system of finance from 1833. Dr. Ambedkar observed that the imperial system of the government suffered from financial inadequacy and chronic deficits from 1834–1835 to 1857–1858 and it was only occasionally that finance ministers were successful in restoring equilibrium and avoiding the hour of crisis. He ascribed it to an unsound fiscal policy. The test of sound finance does not merely consist in being capable of raising the requisite amount of revenue as the mode of raising revenue had tremendous implications for the stability and productivity of the economy. He (Ibid, p. 73) wrote,

> It is too obvious to be denied that a tax system by its unequal incidence may cause social upheavals just as by its unwise incidence on trade and industry it may impoverish society by setting out of gear its economic mechanism and technique and eventually beggar the state by impairing the productive powers of the society. The wealth of society is the only patrimony on which the state can draw, and the state that damages it, cannot but end in damaging itself.

He also further said that the system of imperial finance established in India was an example of it.

Land tax was one of the important taxes of the imperial system. On the basis of the theory that, from time immemorial, land was regarded as a property of the state and the cultivator was not the proprietor but only the occupier, land tax had been imposed irrespective of the question of necessity or justice. Enhancement of land tax in India has also been justified on the basis of the theory of physiocracy. Dr. Ambedkar observed that heavy rates of taxation on any species of industry absorbing the whole or nearly the whole of its profits are ruinous and impolitic. He calculated the ratio of land revenue to the total revenues of India for the year 1792–1793 to 1841–1842 and came to the conclusion that land tax was so heavy that the system of tax prevailing in India might well have been called a near approach to the single tax system (Ibid, p. 74).

He also opined that while land tax prevented prosperity of the agricultural industry, customs taxes hampered manufactures of the country. There were internal customs and external customs, and both were injurious to trade and industry. The internal customs were made of transit and town duties. The country was divided into a number of small customs areas for the purpose of transit duties. Commodities which crossed the customs areas were liable to duty. The transit duties hampered trade which in turn crippled the growth of manufacturing industry. The town duties which formed a part of internal customs duties worked towards de-urbanization (Ibid, pp. 75–76).

Under those depressed conditions, the Indian industry was called upon to meet the external competition. But the external duties could not be said to have given any protection to the country because tariff was based on political rather than economic considerations. The Indian import tariff was varied not with the nature of imports, but with the origin of imports. Goods from England as well as goods shipped on English bottoms were charged at half the rate of what goods of foreign origin shipped on foreign bottoms were charged. Moreover, British goods were allowed into India at lower rates than what the Indian goods had to pay under the internal customs, and this was done when England was prohibiting, by high tariff, the entry of Indian-made goods and India-built ships. The Indian industry also suffered from heavy export duties. Thus, the customs laws, internal and external, blockaded trade and hampered industry (Ibid, p. 77).

Ambedkar also commented that justice in taxation under the imperial regime was conspicuous by its absence.

> The landlords who passed their lives in conspicuous consumption and vicarious leisure on the earnings of the poor tenants, or the many European civil servants who fattened themselves on pay and pickings, were supremely exempted from any contribution towards, the maintenance of the government, whose main activities were directed towards the maintenance of pomp and privilege. On the other hand, the salt tax and the moturpha[2] and other oppressive taxes continued to harass the industrious poor.
>
> (Ibid, p. 78)

Because of this injurious revenue system, the taxpaying capacity of people decayed and as a result, the imperial government was unable to make both ends meet.

The tax system – based on the unit of land – taxes the poor man who had one acre of land and the landlord owning hundreds of acres, without realizing vast income disparities between them, at a uniform rate produces glaring inequity of treatment between rich and poor. Similarly, the salt tax was an example of the oppressive tax system. The pernicious character of the salt tax was urged as a sufficient ground for its elimination from the revenue system of India. But the government not only refused to accept the demand, it increased the salt tax rate in the 1887–1888 budget to meet the increased deficit while income tax of 1886 left untouched the incomes of the Bengal Jamindars and the Assam tea planters and the Talukdars of Oudh (Ibid, p. 230).

Ambedkar further examined how revenues raised through such injurious taxes were expended. He found that during 1809–1857, military expenditure accounted for more than half of the total revenues and it represented a dead weight on the scanty resources of India. It did not benefit the population, which contributed to the revenue of the state either from the point of public utility or private employment. Scales of salaries of European and natives were so grossly unequal that on average a European drew more salary than the salaries of four natives put together.

He also observed that education formed no part of the expenditure, incurred and useful public works were lamentably few (Ibid, p. 83). Dr. Ambedkar concluded that the collapse of the imperial system was due to a faulty fiscal system marked by injurious taxes and unproductive and extravagant expenditure (Ibid, p. 88).

Dr. Ambedkar's view on exchange rate and trade

Dr. Ambedkar's view on exchange rate and trade can be understood from his work on the problem of the rupee. Dr. Ambedkar analysed the relationship between exchange rate and external trade in his book, *The Problem of Rupee*.[3] The par of exchange between any two countries will be stable if they employ the same metal functioning as their standard money. On the other hand, there cannot be fixed par of exchange between two countries having different metals as their currency standards. In that case, their exchange is governed by the relative values of gold and silver and fluctuates as their relative values change. The gold-silver exchange which was stable before 1873 between England and India fluctuated widely after 1873. Sterling rupee exchange which was a reflection of gold-silver exchange was also fluctuating after 1873. One reason was demonetization of silver as standard money medium by the principal countries of the world due to the agitation for uniformity of weights, measures and coinages, and the other was a great increase in the production of silver compared to gold (Ibid, pp. 397–403).

There was a continuous fall in the exchange rate due to the decline in the relative value of silver in terms of gold, and it increased the burden of those which had the obligation to pay in terms of gold. Amongst such, Ambedkar said, the most heavily charged was the Government of India as it had the obligation to make certain payments to England in terms of gold. But silver being the sole legal tender money, the revenues of India were in silver (Ibid, p. 416).

The burden of these gold payments increased due to growth in their magnitude and also due to a fall in the exchange rate during 1875–1892. The excess amount required due to the fall in the exchange rate raised from Rs. 41,13,723 to Rs. 6,54,52,999. The government of India enforced a policy of high taxes and rigid economy to meet this increased burden. The rates of duty on imported spirit and the excise duties on spirits were not only raised in 1890 but afterwards added to in every province (Ibid, p. 417). The yield of the taxes and duties levied increased from Rs. 10,72,30,000 in 1882–83 to Rs. 16,18,20,000 in 1892–1893. This entire additional burden was due to the enhanced cost of meeting the gold payments due to a fall in the exchange rate (Ibid, p. 417). Despite these measures the government was in financial difficulties throughout the period of falling exchange rate and could not find any money for undertaking public works. The government also inaugurated a policy of "extra-ordinary public works" financed by the public. Such finance could not be offered by Indian public who were poor and did not have any savings. India resorted to external borrowings. But foreigners were also reluctant to invest in the rupee securities due to fall in the value of silver in terms of gold (Ibid, p. 419).

But the fall in the exchange rate had a different effect on the trade and industry, and it was flourishing compared to the affairs of the Government of India. The exports increased from Rs. 5,75,56,951 in 1870–71 to Rs. 11,14,60,278 in 1891–1892 and imports rose from Rs. 3,99,13,942 to Rs. 8,41,55,045 during the same period. Not only was the trade increasing, but the nature of trade was also changing. India, which was a primary exporting country before 1870, started exporting manufactures also. There was 43 percent increase in the exports of manufactures during 1879–1892. Jute and cotton industries showed rapid advances. After 1870, farming also tended to be more and more market-oriented. During the same period, England which was on the gold standard tended to be at a standstill (Ibid, pp. 426–430).

There was also a common notion that the bounty arising from export trade due to fall in the exchange rate was a gain to the whole nation. But Ambedkar observed that the bounty was felt because the prices of all goods and services in India did not move uniformly in the same direction. General prices during 1873–1893 had fallen in England, but wages had not fallen to the same extent. Prices had risen in India but wages had not risen to the same extent during the same period (Ibid, p. 437). The Indian producer got bounty because he did not have to pay a higher wage although the price of his product had risen. The falling exchange rate might have acted as a motivating force to export more. But it did so by bringing about changes in the distribution of wealth in the society. In case of India where prices were rising it was the wage earner who suffered. The fall of exchange insofar as it was a gain, registered a loss to a large section of the Indian people with fixed incomes (Ibid, p. 439). He (Ibid, pp. 632–633) quotes:

> Now the class that suffers is the poor labour class which pays the bounty to the richer or the business class. Such transference of wealth from 'the poor to the rich' can never be in the general interest of the country. I therefore strongly oppose the higher prices and low exchange, and a righteous government should not be party to such a clandestine picking of the pockets of the poor class in the country.

Ambedkar explained domestic prices in terms of excess creation of currency under gold exchange standard. From the point of view of economic stability, he preferred the gold standard to gold exchange standard as the discretion of the currency issue was not regulated under gold exchange standard. The progress of trade depends on the stability of exchange. To maintain exchange rate stability, Ambedkar suggested, that since all important countries in the world had moved towards gold standard, the silver standard countries should abandon silver and move in favour of gold or the gold and silver standard countries have to establish fixed ratio of exchange so as to make the two metals into a common standard of value (Ibid, p. 445).

From the above analysis, the following can be inferred. The important reasons for the fall of the East India Company and imperial system were government extravagance, unproductive expenditure, public debt, and injurious tax system. Due to extravagance, the East India Company could not spend on developmental works. The fiscal policy of the government would be sound when the tax policy is not only elastic but also just. And government must control its unproductive expenditure while expending more on progressive works like roads, irrigation, education, etc. There was also much scope in raising the revenues of the government by introducing agricultural income tax instead of land tax which is based on the unit of land at a uniform rate. Indirect taxes, particularly salt tax, whose demand is very inelastic, should be completely exempt from state revenue.

It also follows from the above analysis that, according to Ambedkar, a fall in the exchange rate – that is currency depreciation – leads to a rise in prices, thereby causing redistribution of income in favour of the business class at the cost of the working class, whose wages will not rise in proportion to the price rise. As the growth of trade and industry depends on economic stability, there is a strong need of controlling exchange rate fluctuations within limits. He preferred the gold standard to gold exchange standard from the point of economic stability.

Relevance

When we compare the 1991 economic crisis and subsequent policy changes in fiscal monetary management in India, we find some similarities and differences between fiscal and monetary problems analysed by Dr. Ambedkar particularly during 1833–1919.

In 1991 as well, there was an economic crisis because of the huge trade gap, rising exchange rate, raising prices and alarming external debt. To overcome this, the Government of India initiated devaluation of rupee by about 22 percent in terms of dollar and sterling. Though there was a need for correcting exchange rate by taking into consideration relative purchasing power of currencies, devaluation cannot solve the problem permanently as it, in Ambedkar's view, causes inflation. After 1991, the Government of India liberalized to large extent duties on imports, as a result, the negative trade gap was about Rs. 31,467 crores in 2001–2002 (EPW, 2003, p. 6). It is to be noted here that when there was an increased payment burden during 1869–1889, the Government of Colonial India raised import duties. Under the new economic policy, public expenditure on infrastructure, education and other development activities was also reduced particularly in the early 1990s. But Ambedkar suggested increased expenditure on these items while reducing unproductive expenditure. Ambedkar believed that trade and industry should be encouraged with price stability but not through exchange rate instability. Foreign investment would not flow unless there were exchange rate and price stability. The Government of India can mobilize necessary revenues to solve the problem of deficit finance through agricultural income tax as suggested by Dr. Ambedkar.

Dr. Ambedkar's views on Indian agricultural development

Indian agriculture has been characterised by a large number of scattered, marginal, and small holdings. As per 2010–2011 agricultural censuses, 85.01 percent of the operational holdings are marginal and small holdings account for 44.58 percent of the total area under cultivation. Marginal holdings alone constitute 67 percent of total operational holdings but control only 22.5 percent of the total operated area while the top five percent of the total holdings account for more than 31.79 percent of total area under cultivation (Agriculture Census Division, 2014, p. 6).

There was a good deal of debate on the size of the holding and productivity in Indian agriculture. The debate was initiated by A. K. Sen (1962) in his paper "An Aspect of Indian Agriculture". He stated, on the basis of farm management survey, that by and large productivity per acre decreased with the size of holding (Sen, 1962, p. 243). This debate continued in the post green revolution period as well. It was observed by C. H. Hanumantha Rao and some other economists that the earlier find of inverse relationship under traditional technology no longer holds with the adoption of new technology (Hanumantha Rao, 1980, p. 147). However, recently the inverse relationship between farm size and productivity in Indian agriculture has been established by many studies.

In this context, it is interesting to note that Dr. Ambedkar in his paper on small holdings in India and their remedies (1918) initiated the discussion on the size of the holding and its effects on productivity in Indian agriculture and examined the various methods of dealing with the problem of small holdings, which were fragmented. He also proposed state ownership of agriculture and collective farming in his book *States and Minorities* (1979b) as the soundest remedy for the problems of Indian agriculture and fostering industrialization.

An attempt is made to analyse the views of Dr. Ambedkar on the relationship between the size of the holding and its effects on productivity in Indian agriculture, and to examine the possible implications of Dr. Ambedkar's proposal of state ownership of agriculture and collective farming as a remedy for the problems of Indian agriculture.

Consolidation

The problem of consolidation raises the two following issues: (1) how to unite such small and scattered holdings given the existing ones, and (2) once consolidated how to perpetuate them at that size. Subdivision of land involves what is called the fragmentation of land as the heirs, instead of sharing the lands by survey numbers, claim to share in each survey number, thus causing fragmentation. Though fragmentation does subserve the ends of distributive justice, it renders farming in India considerably inefficient and it increases the cost of production. To overcome the problems of fragmentation, the process of consolidation is to be strengthened. He examined the proposals made by R.B.C. (Report of the Committee appointed to make proposals on the consolidation of small and scattered holdings in the Baroda State in 1917, Govt. of Maharashtra, 1979, p. 456) Prof. Jevons and Keatinge, then Director of Agriculture, Bombay Presidency. Ambedkar observed that the principles for consolidation advocated by R.B.C. and Prof. Jevons are almost the same and so is their procedure for carrying it out. Keatinge proposed the one-man rule of succession for the preservation of consolidated holdings while R.B.C. proposed the same only when a division of land results in uneconomic holdings. In R.B.C. scheme the other disposed heirs get compensation while Keatinge's scheme does not provide any compensation.

Enlargement

Enlargement of holdings is as important as their consolidation and it is also desired that holdings should be economic holdings. But it is believed that large holding is somehow economic. In the words of Jevons, economic holding is one which produces enough for a farmer to sustain a higher standard of living. According to R.B.C., economic holding must be of such a size as having regard to the local conditions of soil, village, etc., necessary to keep fully engaged and support one family. According to Keatinge, an economic holding is a holding which allows a man the chance of producing sufficient to support himself and his family in reasonable comfort, after paying his necessary expenses (Govt. of Maharashtra, 1979, p. 466).

Dr. Ambedkar critically examined the above definitions of "economic holding" and argued that these definitions view economic holding from the standpoint of consumption rather than of production. Consumption is not the correct standard to judge the economic character of holdings. In obedience to the social custom, a farmer has to support all labour corps at his disposal, although some portion of this labour corps is superfluous. Many of the farm enterprises may be declared as failures when a farm could not support all family members, even though some could not be productively used, as per the criterion of consumption standards. A true economic relation can subsist only between the total out-turn and the investments and as long as pays for investments, no farm enterprise would be closed even if it could not support all family members. It follows that economic holding is to be viewed in terms of production rather than consumption. Although production is for consumption, it is for those who help to produce (Ibid, p. 466).

An ideal proportion ought to subsist among the various factors combined, though the ideal will vary with changes in the proportions. The factor proportions would change depending on the elasticity of substitution. Thus, Ambedkar was of the opinion that if agriculture has to be treated as economic enterprise then, by itself, there could be no such thing as small or large. To a farmer, a holding may be small or large depending upon other factors at his disposal. The mere size of the land is empty of all economic connotations and hence it could not be said that a large holding is an economic holding, while a small holding is uneconomic. It is the right or wrong proportion of other factors of production to a unit of land that renders the latter economic or uneconomic. Thus, a small farm may be as economic as a large farm; for economy does not depend upon the size of the land but upon the due proportions, among all the factors, including land (Ibid, p. 468). The size of the holding should be allowed to change in response to changes in the equipment a farmer has, to make it an economic holding ensuring efficient cultivation. Hence, the size of a holding can be large and yet not economic. Therefore, Dr. Ambedkar argues that the proposal of enlarging the existing holdings as a remedy to the ills of Indian agriculture can be entertained only if it is shown that farms have diminished in size while the agricultural stock has increased in amount (Ibid, p. 470).

He argued on the basis of some studies (Table 1.1) that there was a deterioration in the agricultural equipment during 1898–1910.

In the light of the above facts, Dr. Ambedkar argues that existing holdings are uneconomic, not however in the sense that they are too small, but they

Table 1.1 Change in the Agricultural Equipment During 1898 to 1910 in Baroda State

Year	*Plough*	*Carts*	*Plough Cattles*	*Other Domestics*
1898	1,75,989	–	4,15,089	5,70,517
1910	1,51,664	68,946	3,34,801	5,09,416

Source: Govt. of Maharashtra, Dr. Babasaheb Ambedkar Writings and Speeches, Vol. I, 1979, p. 471

are too large. There is a need for increasing agricultural stock and implements which in turn necessitate enlarged holdings which will be economic holdings as well. Consequently, the remedy for the ills of agriculture in India is not, primarily, in the matter of enlarging holdings but in the matter of increasing capital and capital goods (stock of agricultural implements) (Ibid, p. 472).

He strongly believed that the evils of small holdings in India are not fundamental, but they are derived from the parent evil of mal-adjustment in their social economy. He also explained how we suffered from bad social economy (Ibid, p. 472). He showed that little land was cultivated in proportion to the population in India on the basis of the data presented and argued that a large part of the agricultural population is superfluous and idle.

Dr. Ambedkar argued that out of the total population of 254 million in 1881, nearly two-thirds were agricultural and as per estimate allowing one-third to be taken up, we can safely say that a population of equal magnitude was lying idle instead of performing any sort of productive labour. With the increasing ruralisation of India and a continually decreasing proportion of land under cultivation, the volume of idle labour must have increased to an enormous extent. He also argued that increased pressure on land was the chief cause of subdivision of land.

He did not agree with the view that the law of inheritance causes subdivision of land. Naturally, the population that has little else to prefer to agriculture will try to invoke every possible cause to get a piece of land however small. It is not, therefore, the law of inheritance that is the evil but it is the high pressure on land which brings it into operation. Thus the universal prevalence of small farms of petit culture is due to this enormous pressure on land (Ibid, p. 474).

He draws the distinction between idle labour and idle capital and explains the effects of idle labour. Capital exists but labour lives. That is to say capital, when idle, does not earn but does not also consume much to keep itself. But labour, earning or not, consumes in order to live. Idle labour is, therefore, a calamity: for if it cannot live by production as it should, it will live by predation as it must. Instead of contributing to our national dividend it is eating up what little there is of it. Thus depression of national dividend is another important effect of idle labour. Since a large portion of our society makes little current effort due to the existence of idle labour, there can be no surplus and hence no capital which is nothing but a crystallized surplus. Thus he argued that our bad social economy was responsible for the ills of our agriculture and our entire dependence on agriculture leads to small and scattered farms and the existence of idle labour makes ours a county without capital (Ibid, p. 475).

He further explained how the remedies suggested above for consolidation and enlargement under the existing social economy are bound to fail. They are bound to give raising the army of landless and disposed men which is neither cheerful from the individual point of view nor agreeable from the national point of view. If agriculture is made capitalist, it aggravates the evils by adding to our stock of idle labour, for capitalist agriculture will not need as many hands as are now required by our present-day methods of cultivation.

According to Ambedkar, the remedy is to shift this labour to non-agricultural channels of production where it can be productively used. When it is productively employed, it ceases to live by predation as it does today and will not only earn to keep itself but will give us a surplus and more surplus is more capital. This means industrialization of India is the soundest remedy for the agricultural problems of India (Ibid, p. 477).

Industrialization reduces pressure on agriculture and increases the amount of capital goods which will forcibly create the economic necessity of enlarging the holding. By legislation, we will get some economic holding at the cost of many social ills. But by industrialization, a large economic holding will force itself upon us a pure gain. While he was sure of industrialization as an effective remedy for enlargement, and it will be the most effective barrier against sub-division and fragmentation, he realized that industrialization will not be a sufficient remedy for consolidation. But it will facilitate consolidation by lessening the premium on land. "Thus, if small and scattered holdings are the ills from which our agriculture is suffering, to cure it of them is undeniably to industrialize" (Ibid, p. 479).

From the above analysis, it follows that efficient production requires the ideal combination of all other factors of production to a unit of land. It is the right or wrong proportion of factors of production to a unit of land that renders the latter as economic or uneconomic. The mere size of land holding is empty of all economic connotations and hence it could not be said that a large holding is economic while a small one's not. As farm equipment a farmer has changes, the size of the farm should also be allowed to change to make it an economic holding, ensuring efficient production.

Under the existing conditions of social economy, Dr. Ambedkar observed, the proposed remedies of either one-man rule of succession or expansion of capital for enlarging and consolidating are bound to fail as they would add to the existing idle labour. Therefore, the remedy is to shift idle labour to non-agricultural channels of production. This means industrialization of India is the soundest remedy for the agricultural problems in India. Industrialization, while reducing the pressure on land, increases the amount of capital which will, in turn, create the large economic holding and foster industrial development. However, Ambedkar proposed collectivization of agriculture in 1947 for solving the problems of Indian Agriculture.

The views of Dr. Ambedkar on education

Dr. Ambedkar opines that education is an important instrument of bringing social change and for the emancipation of Dalits. Education enables depressed classes to fight against injustice, exploitation, and oppression.

Ambedkar observes that the object of primary education is to see that every child that enters the portals of a primary school does leave it only at a stage when he becomes literate and continues to be literate throughout the rest of his life. But if we take the statistics, we find that out of every 100 children that enter a primary school, only 18 reach the fourth standard; the rest of them, that is to say, 82 out of every 100, relapse into the state of illiteracy. He argues that unless we spend sufficient amount of money, to see that every child that enters a school reaches the fourth standard, what we have already spent upon him is of no purpose what so ever (Govt. of Maharashtra, Vol. II 1982, p. 39).

Ambedkar pleads in the Bombay Legislative Council that we should at least spend on education the same amount that we take from the people in the form of excise revenue. The amount of expenditure that we incur per individual in this presidency on education is only 14 annas, but the amount of money that we recover in the form of excise revenue is Rs. 2–2–9 (Rs. 2.17) (Govt. of Maharashtra, 1982, p. 39).

He strongly opposes the commercialization of education. He opined (Govt. of Maharashtra, 1982, pp. 40–41):

> Education is something which ought to be brought within the reach of every one. The Education Department is not a department which can be treated on the basis of quid pro quo. Education ought to be cheapened in all possible ways and to the greatest possible extent.

He urges this plea because he feels that we are arriving at a stage when the lower orders of society are just getting into the high schools, middle schools, and colleges.

He also explains the great comparative disparity in the educational advancement of the different classes in the Bombay presidency with the help of census report. The census report of the Bombay presidency has divided the total population into four different classes. The first class is called "advanced Hindus"; the second class is called "intermediate Hindus", and it includes those people who for political purposes have now been designated as non-Brahmins i.e., Marathas and allied castes.

There is a third class called "the backward classes" which includes the depressed classes, Hill Tribes and the Criminal Tribes. Then, we have the fourth class which covers the Mahomedans. Bearing these divisions in mind, one sees a great disparity in the comparative advancement of these different communities in the matter of education. Comparing these classes of people, according to the order in which they stand on the basis of population and according to the order in which they stand on the educational progress, it is found that the intermediate classes, namely, non-Brahmins, who are first in order on the basis of population, are third in college education, third in secondary education, and third in primary education. The backward classes, who are second in order of population, are the fourth in the order of college education, fourth in order of secondary education, and fourth in order of primary education. The Mahomedans, who are third in order of population, are second in the order of college education, second in the order of secondary education, and second in order of primary education. The advanced Hindus, who are fourth in order of population, are the first in order of college education, first in order of secondary education, and first in order of primary education.

He emphasizes that this country is composed of different communities and all these communities are unequal in their status and progress. He argues that if they are to be brought to the level of equality then the only remedy is to adopt the principle of inequality and to give favoured treatment to those who are below the level (Ibid, p. 42):

> There are some I know who object to this and adhere to the principle of equality of treatment. But I say the Government has done well in applying this principle to the Mahomedans. For I honestly believe that equality of treatment to people who are unequal is simply another name for indifferentism and neglect. My only complaint is that Government has not yet thought fit to apply this principle to the backward classes. Economically speaking or socially speaking, backward classes are handicapped in a manner in which no other community is handicapped. I, therefore, think that the principle of favoured treatment must be adopted in their case.

No community, however, intellectually advanced it may be, can be the guardians of other communities. Every access must be given to every grade of modern education to the communities which are educationally backward, in order that they may realize their rights and liabilities of citizenship, and secondly, in order that every access may be given to these communities, it is absolutely necessary, under the present circumstances, that special representation should be provided for them (Govt. of Maharashtra, 1982, pp. 50–52).

One of the fundamental functions of the university is to provide facilities for bringing the highest education to the doors of the needy and the poor. The university cannot justify its existence if it merely deals with the problems of examinations and the granting of degrees (Govt. of Maharashtra, 1982, pp. 61–62).

Backward classes have come to realize that after all education is the greatest material benefit for which they can fight. We may forego material benefits, we may forego material benefits of civilization, but we cannot forego our right and opportunity to reap the benefit of the highest education to the fullest extent. Backward classes have just realized that without education their existence is not safe. The number of the nominated seats should be increased for ensuring adequate representation of the backward classes (Govt. of Maharashtra, 1982, p. 62).

Dr. Ambedkar founded the People's Education Society on July 8, 1945 for promoting the educational development of people from scheduled castes, in general, and scheduled tribes, in particular. Under the auspices of this society, he started the Siddhartha College at Bombay on June 20, 1946. It was named after Buddha as he stood for social, intellectual, and political freedom. The society was also founded at the Milind College at Aurangabad and its foundation stone laid by Dr. Rajendra Prasad in September 1951. King Milind was a great Buddhist scholar. Both of these colleges have grown in strength and stature over the years. The society started many more such institutions at various places. The colleges were open to students of all castes and creeds. The main criterion for appointment of teachers in these colleges was merit only (Shahare, 1991, pp. 137–138).

Dr. Ambedkar's plan of economic development

Dr. B. R. Ambedkar presented his plan of economic development in his book *States and Minorities* (1979b), emphasizing state socialism in important fields of economic life. State socialism proposed by Dr. Ambedkar has the following salient features (Govt. of Maharashtra, 1979, pp. 411–412).

Industries which are key industries or which may be declared to be key industries shall be owned and run by the State. Industries which are not key industries but which are basic industries shall be owned by the state and shall be run by the state or by a corporation established by the state. Insurance shall be the monopoly of the state and that the state shall compel every adult citizen to take out a life insurance policy commensurate with his wages as may be prescribed by the legislature. The agricultural industry shall be state industry. The state shall acquire the subsisting rights in such industries; insurance and agricultural lands held by private individuals, whether as owners, tenants or mortgages and pay them compensation in the form of debenture equal to the value of his or her right in the land. The state shall also determine how and when the debenture holder shall be entitled to claim cash payment. The debenture shall be transferable and inheritable property but neither the debenture holder nor the transferee from the original holder nor his heir shall be entitled to claim the return of the land or enter in any industrial concern acquired by the state or be entitled to deal with it in any way. The debenture-holder shall be entitled to interest on his debenture as such rate as may be defined by law, to be paid by the state in cash or in kind as the state may deem it fit. Agricultural industry shall be organized on the following basis:

The state shall divide the land acquired into farms of standard size and let out the farm for cultivation to residents of the village as tenants (made up of a group of families) to cultivate on the following conditions:

1 The farm shall be cultivated as a collective farm.
2 The farm shall be cultivated in accordance with rules and directions issued by the government.
3 The tenants shall share among themselves, in the manner prescribed, the producer of the farm left after, the payment of the charges properly liveable on the farm.
4 The land shall be let out to villagers without distinction of caste or creed and in such manner that there will be no landlord, no tenant, and no landless labour.
5 It shall be the obligation of the state to finance the cultivation of the collective farms by the supply of water, drought animals, implements, manure, seeds etc.
6 The state shall be entitled to
7 Levy the following charges on the produce of the farm:
8 A portion for land revenue,
9 A portion to pay debenture holders, and
10 A portion to pay for the use of capital goods supplied, and
11 To prescribe penalties against the tenants who break the conditions of tenancy or wilfully neglect to make the best use of the means of cultivation offered by the state or otherwise act prejudicially to the scheme of collective farming.
12 The scheme shall be brought into operation as early as possible but in no case shall the period extend beyond the tenth year from the date of the constitution coming into operation.

Thus he proposed state ownership of agriculture with a collectivized method of cultivation and modified form of state socialism in the field Industry.

Dr. Ambedkar also proposed that the above scheme of state socialism should not be left to the will of the legislature and it should be established by the law of constitution so that it will be beyond the reach of a parliamentary majority to suspend, amend, or abrogate it. This guarantees state socialism while retaining parliamentary democracy. "It is only by this that one can achieve the triple objects namely, establish socialism, retain parliamentary democracy and avoid dictatorship". Dr. Ambedkar also believed that his plan of state socialism was essential for rapid industrialization, increasing productivity without closing every avenue to the private sector and also for distributing wealth equitably (Ibid, p. 408). Further, Dr. Ambedkar also argued that if democracy was to live up to its principle of one man one value, it was essential to define both the economic structure as well as the political structure of society by the Law of Constitution. But the same could not be incorporated under fundamental rights as part of the Constitution as it was not agreed in the Constituent Assembly. However, the Indian Constitution clearly laid down in the Directive Principles that the state should secure a social order where justice – social, economic, and political – shall inform all institutions of life.

The relevance of collective farming

It is true that to solve the problems of agriculture collective farms under State control had been adopted in the USSR. This gave security of employment and a minimum income to agricultural labourers as well as solving the problems of inequality in the distribution of wealth and income. Through this system, the basic problem of rural poverty was solved. The congress agrarian reforms committee under the chairmanship of J.C. Kumarappa (1949) rejected the concept of capitalist farming as the form of agricultural organization on the ground that it would deprive the agriculturists of their rights in land and turn them into mere wages earners. It would also create the problem of disposal personnel. It was held that peasant farming would be the most appropriate form of cultivation above the basic holding, but the smaller holding should be brought under the scheme of cooperative farming. It was also held that collective farming would be more suitable for development of reclaimed wastelands on which landless labourers could be settled (Haque and Sirohi, 1986, p. 100). This was further supported by the debate on farm size and productivity, initiated by A. K. Sen who writes (Sen, 1962, p. 246), "for example, if a large cooperative farm operates on a non-wage family labour basis, there is nothing in our observation to indicate that it will have to lower output per acre". But cooperative farming did not materialize, although family based peasant farming was adopted in India. Through land reform intermediaries could be abolished, but land concentration persists and it is the most important reason for the existence of higher incidence of rural poverty despite tremendous increase in food production due to green revolution.

In India, large chunks of agricultural labourers come from depressed sections which suffer from social discrimination and economic exploitation. The condition of agricultural labourers was worse, particularly on the eve of independence, and collectivization would have definitely solved their basic problem of poverty had we opted for collectivization of farms. However, collective farming under state control was subjected to much criticism after the collapse of communism in Eastern Europe, particularly in USSR, and subsequent shift to market-oriented strategies of development became inevitable. It was pointed out that when minimum needs were met by State in a regime of collective farming, State used to make decisions regarding what to produce and how to produce irrespective of cost considerations without involving farmers in the decision making. This was one of the reasons for the failure of State farming. It is true that agriculture requires personal attention which is lacking in State farming. It implies that productivity suffers due to lack of personal attention and incentive to produce more. This means that collective farming under State helps in solving basic problems of poverty initially but it may not lead to increased productivity. Personal attention and incentives to produce more are ensured in the case of family-based peasant farming above a basic limit. But collective farming is better suited in the case of marginal farms, which constitute more than 60 percent of agricultural holdings but control only about 20 percent of the area under cultivation in India. Consequently, State should take the responsibility of supplying necessary capital and other inputs.

Thus, it follows from the above analysis of Dr. Ambedkar's perspective of development that State has to play a very active and crucial role in accelerating educational development and economic growth with justice through democratic methods. The foundation of democracy would be feeble and shaky if the contradictions between political democracy, enshrined in the constitution, and social and economic inequalities, existing in our society, are not resolved.

Now let us look at the present socio-economic conditions in India. The percentage of people below the poverty line was estimated by the planning commission as 21.9 percent at all India level in 2011–2012 (Planning Commission, 2013, p. 2). It was reported that 48.9 percent of the workforce depends on agriculture and its allied sectors, and agriculture contributes to 17.5 percent of the total GDP (Ministry of Finance, 2016, p. 98). As per the 2011 population census, 68.86 percent of the total population live in rural areas (Office of the Registrar General of India., 2011). According to the 2010–2011 agricultural census 67 percent marginal holdings account for about 22.5 percent of the total area under cultivation, while the top five percent of total holdings account for 31.79 percent of total area under cultivation (Agriculture Census Division, 2014). The distribution of land remains skewed despite land reforms. This is mostly responsible for social tensions in rural India. In addition to economic inequalities, the Indian society is characterized by social inequalities, due to caste. Moreover, 26.6 percent of the total population is illiterate, as per 2011 census.

Hence, given the stage and structure of the Indian economy, Dr. Ambedkar's vision of economic development – which emphasizes an active State role in bringing the desired change in socio-economic institutions to accelerate growth with justice – is relevant.

Notes

1 The required information is drawn on: (1) "Administration and Finance of the East India Company", (2) "Evolution of Provincial Finance in British India", (3) "The Problem of Rupee", (4) and other relevant works of Dr. Ambedkar. Ambedkar

dealt with the finances of East India Company in his work "Administration and Finance of the East India Company".

2 A tax on trades and occupations embracing weavers, carpenters, all workers in metals, all salesmen (whether possessing shops which are taxed separately), or vending by the roadside, etc., some paying imports on their tools, others for permission to sell, extending to the most trifling articles of trade and the cheapest tools machines can employ, the cost of which frequently exceeded six times over by the moturpha under which the use of them is permitted (Dr. Ambedkar, Writing and Speeches; Vol. 6 1989, p. 78).

3 Exchange rate was defined as the number of units of foreign currency to be obtained for one unit of Indian currency. However, at present, exchange rate is defined as number of units of domestic currency to be paid for one unit of foreign currency.

References

Agriculture Census Division. (2014). *Agriculture Census in India (2010–2011)*. All India Report on Number and Area of Operational Holdings, Department of Agriculture & Co-operation, Ministry of Agriculture, Govt. of India.

All India Congress Committee. (1949). *Report of the Congress Agrarian Reforms Committee*. Madras: Madras Publishing House.

Ambedkar, B. R. (1918). Small Holdings in India and Their Remedies. *Journal of Indian Economic Society*, 1, 1900–1945.

Ambedkar, B. R. (1979a). Annihilation of Caste. In B. R. Ambedkar (Ed.), *Dr. Babasaheb Ambedkar Writings and Speeches*, Vol. 1, pp. 23–96. Maharashtra, India: Government of Maharashtra.

Ambedkar, B. R. (1979b). States and Minorities. In B. R. Ambedkar (Ed.), *Dr. Babasaheb Ambedkar Writings and Speeches*, Vol. 1, pp. 137–204. Maharashtra, India: Government of Maharashtra.

EPW Research Foundation. (2003). Current Statistics. *Economic and Political Weekly*, 38(1), p. 6.

Govt. of Maharashtra. (1979). *Dr. Babasaheb Ambedkar: Writings and Speeches*, Vol. 1. Bombay.

Govt. of Maharashtra. (1982). *Dr. Babasaheb Ambedkar: Writings and Speeches*, Vol. 2. Bombay.

Govt. of Maharashtra. (1989). *Dr. Babasaheb Ambedkar: Writings and Speeches*, Vol. 6. Bombay.

Govt. of Maharashtra. (1990). *Dr. Babasaheb Ambedkar: Writings and Speeches*, Vol. 9. Bombay.

Hanumantha Rao, C. H. (1980). *Technological Change and Institutional Change in India*. New Delhi: Macmillan & Co.

Haque, T. and Sirohi, A. S. (1986). *Agrarian Reforms and Institutional Changes in India*. Concept Publishing Company.

Ministry of Finance. (2016). *Economic Survey 2015–16*. New Delhi: Government of India.

Office of the Registrar General of India. (2011). *Census of India (2011)*. New Delhi: Government of India.

Planning Commission. (2013). *Press Note on Poverty Estimates, 2011–12* (No. id: 5421). New Delhi.

Sen, A. K. (1962). An Aspect of Indian Agriculture. *Economic Weekly*, 14(4), pp. 243–246.
Sen, P. (1986). The 1966 Devaluation in India: A Reappraisal. *Economic and Political Weekly*, 21(30).
Shahare, M. L. (1991). Dr. B. R. Ambedkar: An Eminent Educationist. In Sudarshan Agarwal (Ed.), *Dr. B.R. Ambedkar, the Man and His Message: A Commemorative Volume*. Prentice-Hall.

2 Ambedkar's thought on economic development and poverty alleviation

Sukhadeo Thorat

Introduction

During 1915 to 1925, Ambedkar made significant contributions in the field of public finance and monetary economics, almost all of which were academic requirements for advanced studies at Columbia University and the University of London. After the 1920s, the main themes of his writings switched to other disciplines.[1] Nevertheless, he continued to express views on economic issues not only as an academic economist but also as a policy-maker, in the Bombay Legislative Assembly and the Constituent Assembly, as a Labour Minister in the Central Cabinet from 1942 to 1946, and as a Member of Parliament and a Minister until 1956. His economic writings covered a wide range of inter-related issues, including economic development and planning, the capitalist system, alternative economic systems, and the economics of the caste system.

Ambedkar's three major writings on economic issues appeared in 1920s. While they generally bear the mark of a neo-classical perspective, they also show both his identification with the working classes and a harsh critique of imperialism (Omvedt, 1994). After 1930, there is a gradual change and a heightening of economic radicalism that came in 1946. In this chapter, I propose to highlight Ambedkar's views on economic development, economic planning, including agricultural development, water resource development, the labour problem, and alternative economic systems.

Economic development

In 1918, Ambedkar participated in an academic debate on the problem of small holdings, to which he contributed a thought-provoking paper (Ambedkar, 1918). Although this paper focuses on the problem of small holdings, Ambedkar placed the analysis in a much broader theoretical framework of economic development. The paper begins with a discussion on small holdings, goes on to an economic analysis of agricultural backwardness, and ends with industrial development as the solution to the problem of agricultural development, in general, and of small farmers, in particular. The paper, thus, laid a theoretical and policy framework for general economic development.

The underlying assumption in academic discussion was that small and scattered landholdings were economically inefficient. The issue was how to consolidate small and scattered holdings and to maintain them at an economically viable level. The solution put forward by academic economists comprised two methods: the voluntary exchange of owned land to reduce parcelling and increase the size of holdings; and compulsory consolidation of farms by the government, including restricted sale of the right of occupancy. Whether the restriction should be compulsory or voluntary was to be decided on the principle of "economic holding," to be fixed on the basis of acreage of land owned. The lower land ceiling was to be "a parcel of land necessary to keep fully engaged and support one family," or a "holding which allows a man the chance of producing sufficient to support himself and his family in reasonable comfort, after paying his necessary expenses" (Ambedkar, 1918). The solution was found in administrative and legal measures and treated the consolidation of holdings as a practical problem.

Ambedkar approached the issue differently. For him, the issue was essentially economic, and not legal or administrative. He differed from others on two important grounds: the definition of economic holding and the economic principles determining the size of holdings (and, hence, the solution of their enlargement). While others viewed an economic holding from the standpoint of consumption rather than production, Ambedkar looked at the issue of small size holding from the standpoint of economics of production. Ambedkar maintained that true economic relations could subsist only between total out-turn and investment. If out-turn paid for all the investment, no producer would think of closing his/her farm. The farm was, thus, a paying economic unit in terms of production, and not consumption. Production, in turn, was not governed by land alone but was the result of a combination of land, capital, and labour. It was the proportion of other factors of production to a unit of land, and not only the amount of land, that rendered a piece of land economical or uneconomical. A small farm might be as economical as a large farm.

According to Ambedkar, the problem of small holdings was not fundamental but derived from the parent evil of maladjustment in the social economy. A household with a small holding was unable to acquire and use some factors of production in the right combination. While there was too little capital (in the form of capital goods and implements) and land, the supply of labour was in excess. Being in short supply, land and capital were relatively expensive compared to labour and, hence, became major constraints for the population. The solution was to increase capital in the form of goods and implements and reduce the use of labour by siphoning off the surplus labour to non-agricultural production. This would, at one stroke, lessen the pressure on land in India. Besides, the remaining labour would be productively employed and would produce a surplus; and since surplus is capital, it could be invested in agriculture. In short, Ambedkar saw industrialisation as the soundest remedy for India's agricultural problems. Besides leading to an increase in labour productivity and capital investment in agriculture, it would create the economic necessity of enlarging landholding. By doing away with the premium on land, industrialisation would leave few occasions for subdivision and fragmentation. As an indirect consequence of industrialisation, the problem of agriculture would be curbed.

Thus, the problem of agricultural backwardness (of which the issue of small farms was a part) was essentially due to deficiency of material capital in relation to land and labour. Low capital accumulation was due to low capacity to save, which, in turn, was the result of low productivity and income from agriculture. The solution to agricultural development lay in improving the productivity of land and labour, increasing the farm income of cultivating households, and expanding the domestic capacity to save for productive investment. The way out was an inter-sectoral transfer of labour from agriculture to industry. This was expected to increase productivity and, hence, the income of labour in both agriculture and industry. The reduced pressure of population would encourage the enlargement of farm size by reducing the premium on land. The availability of implements and a more flexible supply of land for cultivation would thus provide the opportunity for optimum use of resources in production.[2]

Economic planning: the post-war economic (reconstruction) plan (1942–1946)

Ambedkar's entry into the Central Cabinet as member-in-charge of the labour (and also irrigation and power) portfolio in 1942 coincided with the formulation and implementation of the post-war plan for India's reconstruction and economic development. Such a plan was necessary to overcome some urgent post-war problems pertaining to the rehabilitation of defence personnel and the conversion of industry from the requirements of war to those of peace. Unlike the war-affected countries of Europe and Asia, in India the plan was not confined to measures for rehabilitation but included plans for economic development. In fact, this plan marks the beginning of a systematic, all-India economic planning by the central government. Not only did the policies and plans conceived and implemented from 1942 to 1944 have an impact on the type of economic regime that India adopted at independence, but many of these plans continued and became a permanent feature of India's economic development.

As a member of the Central Cabinet, Ambedkar was also a member of the Reconstruction Committee of the Council, the highest body set up to decide the objectives and policies of the plan. In addition, he was President of the Policy Committee set up to improve the condition of labour and develop irrigation and electric power (Ambedkar, 1943a). He contributed significantly to the formulation of the general objectives of the plan and the specific policies for labour, irrigation, and electric power development.

A perusal of Ambedkar's writings and discussions during 1942–1946 allows us to understand his thinking about economic planning for India. Ambedkar (Government of India, 1944) argued that:

> The problem of post-war reconstruction in India is essentially different from the problem of reconstruction in other war-affected countries because for them the problem of reconstruction is a problem of rehabilitation of industries which were destroyed in war. The problem of reconstruction in India, on the other hand, is mainly of the industrialisation of India as distinguished from the rehabilitation of industry.

Based on the theoretical framework developed in the paper of 1918, he emphasised the need for industrialisation in support of overall economic development as well as for the development of the agricultural sector. Poverty in India, according to him, was due entirely to the dependence upon agriculture alone. Agriculture failed to produce sufficient food to feed the people. The roots were to be found in the maladjustment of the social economy (Ambedkar, Times of India, 1943):

> India is caught between two sides of pincers, the one side of which is progressive pressure of population and the other is limited availability of land in relation to its needs. The result is that at the end of each decade we are left with negative balance of population and production and a constant squeezing to standard of living and poverty. The population pressure is giving rise to an army of landless and dispersed families as well. It can be stopped when agriculture is made profitable. Nothing can open possibilities of making agriculture profitable except a serious drive in favour of industrialisation. For it is industrialisation alone which can drain away excess of population into gainful employment other than agriculture.

In the government, therefore, Ambedkar emphasised the need for industrial development in order to gain increased agricultural productivity and income. The policy prescriptions based on theoretical formulations conceived in 1918 were restated in 1943 and eventually incorporated in the objectives of the post-war reconstruction plan. The section on general objectives, which relates to the sectoral dimension, reads:

> Agriculture is and will remain India's primary industry but the present imbalanced economy has to be rectified by intensive development of the country's industries so that both agriculture and industry may develop side by side. That will enable the pressure of population on the land to be relieved and will also provide the means required for the provision of better amenities.

Infrastructure such as roads, communication and transport services, irrigation, and electric power, in the development of which Ambedkar had played a pioneering role, was treated as a prerequisite for industrial development. It was believed that this infrastructure would bring a relatively higher (annual) rate of growth in industrial production and employment and help absorb the surplus labour from agriculture. In the Policy Committee on Public Works and Electric Power, Ambedkar asked, "Why do we want cheap and abundant electricity? The answer is that without cheap and abundant electricity no effort for industrialisation of India can succeed" (Ambedkar, 1943b).

Water and power development

The central government policy with regard to water resources and hydroelectric power development was evolved and given a definite shape under Ambedkar's tenure as Minister for Labour (and Irrigation and Power) between 1942 and 1946.[3] It began as part of the reconstruction plan and later on became a long-term policy of the Central Government. These efforts by Ambedkar and the Labour Department resulted in the emergence of an all-India policy for the development of the country's "water and electric power resources," the creation of an administrative apparatus and technical bodies at the centre to assist the states in developing irrigation and electric power resources, the initiation of such important present-day river valley projects as the Damodar River Valley project and the Hirakud project; and, for the first time, the development of an electric power policy. The key elements of the new water policy were a multipurpose approach to water resources development on the basis of river basins, the concept of a river valley authority, and the creation of technical expert bodies at the Centre to promote the development of water and power resources.

In a conference on the development of the rivers of Orissa, Ambedkar expressed his views about the conservation and use of water resources. Criticising the recommendations made by various committees, from the first one in 1872 to the Orissa Flood Advisory Committee of 1945, he (1945b, p. 304) observed:

> With all respect to the members of these committees, I am sorry to say that they did not bring the right approach to bear on the problem. They were influenced by the idea that water in excessive quantity was an evil, that when water comes in excessive quantity what needs to be done is to let it run into the sea in an orderly flow. Both these views are now regarded as grave misconceptions, as positively dangerous from the point of view of the good of the people.

Man suffers more from lack of water than from excess of it, Ambedkar said. Nature is not only niggardly in the amount of water it gives but also erratic in its distribution, alternating between drought and storm. This could not change the fact that water is wealth. Water being the wealth of the people and its distribution uncertain, the correct approach was not to complain about nature but to conserve water (1945b, pp. 304–306).

In the earlier approach, since excess water was considered a major problem, the remedy suggested had a single purpose: to control floods. Ambedkar differed with those who believed in this approach. He observed that "if conservation of water was mandatory from the point of view of public good, then obviously the plan of embankments was a wrong plan. It was a means which does not subserve the end, namely conservation of water, and must, therefore, be abandoned." The appropriate approach, according to him, was the one adopted by some developed countries: "to dam rivers at various points to conserve water permanently in reservoirs" and put it to multipurpose use. Besides irrigation, such reservoirs could be used for generating electric power and navigation. Ambedkar particularly emphasised the use of rivers for navigation. In the Conference on Orissa Rivers (8 November 1945), he observed:

> Navigation in India has had a very chequered history. During the rule of the East India Company, provision for internal navigation occupied a very prominent part in the public works budget of the Company's government. Many of the navigation canals we have in India today are remnants of that policy. The railways came later, and for a time the policy was to have both railway and canal navigation. By 1857, there arose a great controversy in which the issue was railway versus canals. The battle for canals was fought bravely by the late Sir Arthur Cotton . . . Unfortunately, supporters of railways won.
>
> (Ambedkar, 1945a)

Ambedkar (1945a, p. 223) added:

> I am not quite happy about this victory of railway over canals. Much more annoying is the opinion of supporters of railways that canals must go because they do not pay without knowing that if the canals do not pay it is because their capacity to pay has been terribly mutilated by leaving them uncompleted. I am sure that internal navigation cannot be neglected in the way in which it has been in the past. We ought to borrow a leaf from Germany and Russia in this matter and not only revive reconstruction of our old canals but make new ones also and not to sacrifice them to the exigencies of railways.

The storage scheme that Ambedkar proposed would provide not only irrigation and electricity but also a long line of internal navigation. He believed that the multipurpose use of water would convert the forces of evil into powers of good. He subsequently emphasised this perspective for projects on the Damodar, Mahanadi, Sone, and other inter-state rivers. The Sone Valley Project, for example, was a multipurpose river management scheme.

Its purpose was not only canal irrigation and perennial hydroelectric power, but also increased utilisation of such power for agricultural development (such as for pumping from tube wells), increased fertility achieved by dewatering water-logged areas, cheap power for industrial development, and improved flood control. Opening the Conference on Sone Valley in March 1945, Ambedkar highlighted the scheme's importance to the economic development of UP, Bihar, and parts of other states. He emphasised that for the possibilities of the scheme to be fully exploited the approach must be regional rather than local. In the conferences on the Mahanadi and Sone rivers as well, Ambedkar urged the participants to adopt a regional approach (CWC, 1993).

In the Conference on the river Sone, Ambedkar emphasised that to the necessity of taking a regional rather than a local approach meant that ultimately there must be an agreement to set up an appropriate organisation to which they would give certain powers, the principal of which would be to supply the bulk of electricity and water for irrigation and navigation.[4] The systematic steps towards the introduction of the concept of a River Valley Authority for projects on interstate rivers and the creation of two technical-expert bodies at the Centre, namely the Central Waterways, Irrigation and Navigation Commission, and the Central Technical Power Board, were attempts to provide technical advice for the multipurpose development of water resources on a regional basis. Ambedkar made this clear in the first Calcutta Conference (3 January 1944):

> as a preliminary step for securing the best use of water resources of the country the Government of India have created a central organisation, called the Central Technical Power Board, and are contemplating to create another to be called the Central Waterways, Irrigation and Navigation Commission. The objects which have led to setting up of these two organisations are to advise the Provinces on how their water resources can be best utilised and how a project can be made to serve purposes other than irrigation.
>
> (Ambedkar, 1945c)

At the same conference, Ambedkar expounded the nature of the new water policy. It is not far from true to say that so far there has been an absence of a positive all-India policy for the development of water resources. There has not been enough realisation that our policy for waterways must be a multipurpose policy so as to include the provision for irrigation electrification and navigation. The government of India is very much alive to the disadvantage arising from the present state of affairs and wishes to take steps to evolve a policy which will utilise the water resources to the purposes which they are made to serve in other countries.

Multipurpose use of water resources for the regional development of the entire river valley basin was the key element of the new water policy. The adoption of the concept of a River Valley Authority (to overcome the jurisdictional problem on interstate rivers) and the creation of two technical expert bodies at the Centre were means to achieve this objective.

Economic planning and labour

Aware of the limitations of a capitalistic economic system under parliamentary democracy in ensuring economic security to the masses, Ambedkar argued for an important place for labour and the depressed classes in the planned economic development of the country. He was particularly concerned that the government should not only develop programmes but translate them into terms that the common man could understand: peace, housing, clothing, education, good health and, above all, the right to work with dignity. The State could not be content merely with securing fair conditions of work for labour but should strive to secure fair conditions of life as well. Great responsibility lay on the State to provide the poor with facilities for individuals to grow according to their needs. In order to do that, the government could not be laissez-faire but would have to use a system of control.

Influenced by Ambedkar's view and facilitated by the Labour Government in Britain during the 1940s, labour was accorded an important place in the post-war development plan, elucidated in the objective of the post-war economic development, to quote the declared objective, which was declared:

> to raise the standard of living of the people as a whole and to ensure employment for all. To that end, the purchasing power of the people was to be increased, improvement in the efficiency and consequently the productivity of labour on the one hand and simultaneous development and reorganisation of agriculture and industries and services on the other.
> (CWC, 1993)

Provisions to make labour more productive (to raise agricultural and industrial productivity) included free or subsidised education up to age 14, medical relief, water supply, and other public utility services, including electric power. This would improve the health and efficiency of labour. Other goals included fairer wages, maternity and sickness benefits, and holidays. Many of these schemes were undertaken by the Labour Department while Ambedkar was President of the Policy Committee on labour.

Labour policy

In addition to the water and power policy, significant measures were taken to deal with the problems of labour during Ambedkar's tenure as labour member from 1942 to 1946. Ambedkar's labour policy goals were threefold: 1) Providing safeguards and social security measures to workers; 2) Giving equal opportunity to workers and employers to participate in formulating labour policy, and strengthening the labour movement by introducing compulsory recognition of trade unions; and 3) Establishing the machinery for enforcing labour laws and settling disputes. The mechanism evolved to achieve these purposes included: (1) Setting up the Indian Labour Conference and Standing Labour Committee; (2) Enactment of labour laws; (3) Establishment of the Chief Labour Commissioner's organisation; (4) Appointment of the Labour Investigative Committee; (5) Machinery for fixing minimum wages; (6) Standing orders in industrial employment; and (7) Recognition of trade unions. These efforts to protect and promote the interests of labour and the working class made a significant impact on the labour movement and industrial relations of India.

Economic planning and scheduled castes

In Ambedkar's view, the Schedules Castes and depressed classes needed to be treated as a separate entity in the planning exercise, and this provision was incorporated in the Plan objectives. The Plan documents stated that:

> One of the objectives of the government would be to take steps to ameliorate the condition of the Scheduled Castes and backward classes. Care must be taken to see that social amenities such as education, public health, water supply, housing, which are meant to be provided under the plan, work especially for the benefit of such classes and that the handicap of ignorance and poverty under which they now labour is offset by special concessions in the shape of educational facilities, grant, scholarships, hostels, improved water supply and similar measures. It would be the special responsibility of the government to see that early measures are taken to remove the handicap of these classes and help them to raise their level to that of their more fortunate fellow citizens. The provision of full employment, as well as various measures of social security contemplated under the section of labour, would also automatically benefit the backward and the depressed classes.[5]

Besides labour, the central government's irrigation and electric power policy of 1942–1944 also reflected this view of Ambedkar's, about the place of the poor in the country's development. He urged policy-makers to incorporate measures in the irrigation development policy to benefit the poor and oppressed section of society.

Ambedkar was in favour of improvement in production efficiency. But, like Jawaharlal Nehru, he was not merely a growth-maximiser (of national income). He did talk about letting the national income grow large enough before an adequate standard of living could be provided for all. At the same time, he was concerned about the distribution of national income to the common man. In 1943, Ambedkar (1943b) underlined that:

> It will not be enough to make industrial development of India as a goal. We shall have to agree that any such industrial development shall be maintained at a socially desirable level. It will not be enough to bend our energies for the production of more wealth in India. We shall have to agree not merely to recognise the basic right of all Indians to share in that wealth as a means for a decent and dignified existence, but devise ways and means to insure him against insecurity.

This view was emphasised in formulating India's irrigation and hydroelectric policy. In October 1943, in his presidential address to the Policy Committee on electric power, Ambedkar said:

> Why do we want cheap and abundant electricity in India? . . . Without cheap and abundant electricity no effort for the industrialisation of India can succeed. . . .Why is industrialisation necessary? . . . We want industrialisation of India as the surest means to rescue the people from the eternal cycle of poverty in which they are caught. Industrialisation of India must, therefore, be grappled with immediately.
>
> (Dr. B. R. Ambedkar, 1943a)

He went on to add that India would have to tackle the problem of electricity in an earnest, statesman-like manner, thinking in terms of human life and not in terms of competing claims of the central and provincial governments.

A similar vehemence was to be accorded to the development of irrigation. In his presidential address to the Conference on Multipurpose Development of Damodar Valley, Ambedkar (1945a) stressed that:

> The Centre expects the Provinces to bear in mind the absolute necessity of ensuring that the benefits of the project get ultimately right down to the grass roots i.e., everyone living in the valley and some of those in the vicinity, all have their share in the prosperity which the project should bring. This, in my view, is essential and for this reason we want the establishment of some agency early enough so that that agency can set about planning at once in a manner in which its essential and ultimate objective can be secured.

The limits of capitalism, and alternative economic frameworks

The preceding sections cover the period until the late 1940s. In that period, Ambedkar attributed a key role to industrialisation, and favoured economic planning (particularly in infrastructure and the social service sector), progressive labour laws, and a focus on labour and the downtrodden. The theoretical arguments for industrialisation were developed within the framework of mainstream economics, assuming a private economy or capitalist organisation. Prior to the 1940s Ambedkar emphasised industrialisation as a progressive agenda but said nothing about its being organised under the public sector, except for his insistence on state or public ownership and/or distribution of electric power and social services.

Between the mid-1930s and the late 1940s, Ambedkar's position changed, to an economic radicalism that criticised capitalism and advocated a dominant role for the state, the abolition of feudalistic land tenure systems like *Khoti* and *Mahar Vatan*, distribution of land, cultivation by cooperative and collective farms, and production and distribution of electric power under State ownership and control. Again, Ambedkar proposed these measures assuming the inevitability of capitalist organisation (although occasionally he showed a preference for socialism). There was no serious alternative economic framework during these years. The precise statement of an alternative radical economic and political framework making a departure from the earlier position came in *States and Minorities*, written as a memorandum to the Constitutional Assembly in 1948. This book calls for "State socialism": nationalisation of basic and key industries, insurance, and agricultural land, the land to be worked in collective farms by peasants treated as tenants of the state. For the first time, Ambedkar explained his preference for having industrialisation and agriculture under the State; he also explained the need for economic planning, a stronger role for the state, and special safeguards against social and economic discrimination of socially deprived classes. Providing a justification for State socialism, Ambedkar (1947) stated:

> The main purpose behind it is to put an obligation on the state to plan the economic life of the people on lines which would lead to the highest point of productivity without closing the avenues to private enterprise and also provide for equitable distribution of wealth. The Plan set out proposes state ownership in agriculture with a collectivised method of cultivation and a modified form of State socialism in the field of industry. It places squarely on the shoulders of the State the obligation to supply capital necessary for agriculture as well as industry . . . State socialism is essential for rapid industrialisation of India. Private enterprise cannot do it and if it did, it would produce those inequalities of wealth which private capitalism has produced in Europe and which should be a warning to India.

In the case of agriculture, unlike the 1930s and 1940s, when Ambedkar argued for land distribution and tenancy rights, he now argued that:

> Consolidation of holdings and tenancy legislation are worse than useless. They cannot bring about prosperity in agriculture. Neither consolidation nor tenancy legislation can be of any help to the 60 million untouchables who are just landless labourers . . . Only collective farms on the lines set out in the proposal can help them.
>
> (Ambedkar, 1947)

Ambedkar's criticism of capitalism was mainly drawn from Marx, with whom he was in basic agreement. Writing in 1956, Ambedkar observed (Dr. B. R. Ambedkar, Buddha or Karl Marx, 1987):

> What remains of Karl Marx is a residue of fire, small but still very important. The residue in my view consists of four items:
>
> - The function of philosophy is to reconstruct the world and not to waste its time in explaining the origin of the world.
> - That there is a conflict of interest between class and class.
> - That private ownership of property brings powers to one class and sorrow to another through exploitation.
> - That it is necessary for the good of society that sorrow be removed by abolition of private property.

Taking the surviving points from the Marxist creed, Ambedkar built up a case for socialism. Ambedkar (1947) argued that in a social economy based on private enterprise and personal gain, both the unemployed and the employed must relinquish their rights and subject themselves to being governed by a private employer:

> For the unemployed persons fear of starvation, the fear of losing house, fear of being compelled to take children away from school, the fear of having to be on public charity are the factors too strong to permit a man to stand out for his fundamental rights. The poor are thus compelled to relinquish their fundamental rights for the sake of securing the privilege to work and subsist.

Writing about the safeguards suggested by the constitutionalists, Ambedkar observed that:

> If the State refrains from intervention in private affairs economic and social, the residue is liberty. But . . . to whom and for whom is this liberty. Obviously, this liberty is liberty to the landlord to increase rents, for capitalists to increase hours of work and reduce the rate of wages . . . In other words, what is called liberty from the control of State is another name for the dictatorship of the private employers.

Ambedkar was critical of most democratic governments, which impose arbitrary restraints in the political domain and invoke the power of legislature to restrain more powerful individuals from imposing arbitrary restraints on the less powerful in the economic field. Ambedkar favoured an economic system where not only the power of the government to impose arbitrary restraints was limited, but also that of more powerful individuals. This would be achieved by minimising their control in the economic life of the people.

In responding to the resolution related to the "aims and objectives" of the future constitution of India moved by Jawaharlal Nehru on 13 December 1946, as a member of the Constitutional Assembly – argued for a socialistic economic framework for India (Loksabha, 1946):

> I should have expected . . . the Resolution to state in most explicit terms that in order that there may be social and economic justice in the country, that there would be nationalisation of industry and nationalisation of land. I do not understand how it could be possible for any future government which believes in doing justice, socially, economically and politically, unless its economy is a socialistic economy.

However, Ambedkar was aware of the constraints on acceptability of the proposal by the Constitutional Assembly. He, therefore, pushed only as far as he could go. He continued and observed, "Therefore, personally although I have no objective to the enunciation of these propositions, the resolution is to my mind, somewhat disappointing. I am however prepared to leave this subject where it is with the observation I have made" (Loksabha, 1946). As on some other occasions, such as the Poona Pact, Ambedkar had to adjust his position on this issue as well.

Notes

1 Dr. Ambedkar's principal academic works on public finance and currency between 1915 and 1925 included his MA dissertation (1915), his PhD dissertation (1925), and his DSC dissertation (1923). The underlying causes of structural backwardness were, first, an acute deficiency of material capital, which prevented the introduction of more productive technologies; second, the low capacity to save, which could be raised by means of suitable fiscal and monetary policies; and, third, the fact that agriculture was subject to diminishing returns. Industrialisation would allow surplus labour, currently underemployed in agriculture, to be more productively employed in industries that operated according to increasing returns to scale (Chakravarty, 1998, p. 40).

2 The 10th meeting of Reconstruction Committee of Council held on September 11, 1944 which discussed the objective of the plan, recorded that there was a case for treating the Scheduled Castes and Depressed Classes as a separate entity for the purpose of planning. Honourable member of Labour, Dr. Ambedkar said that he would like to suggest certain amendments on these lines. (Minutes of the 19th meeting, 11 September 1944, Reconstruction Committee of the Council, 2/10/121, 1945.8.)
(ii) Reconstruction Committee of Council, Post-War Development Policy, Draft Report, 1944, File No. 1(4) p. 45, Finance Department, Planning Division.

3 Between 1943 and 1945, Dr. Ambedkar addressed conferences on Post-War Development of Electric Power in India, 25 October 1943; Damodar Valley Scheme, First Calcutta Conference, 3 January 1945; Post-War Electric Development, 2 February 1945; Multi-Purpose Development of Damodar Valley, Second Calcutta Conference, 23 August 1945; and Multi-Purpose Plan for Development of Orissa Rivers, 3 November 1945.

4 Proceedings of a meeting held on 10 March 1945 to discuss certain proposals regarding the development of Sone Valley, File No. D.W./IRI/336-p/45, Finance Department, Planning Branch.

5 Between 1943 and 1945, Dr. Ambedkar addressed conferences on Post-War Development of Electric Power in India, 25 October 1943; Damodar Valley Scheme, First Calcutta Conference, 3 January 1945; Post-War Electric Development, 2 February 1945; Multi-Purpose Development of Damodar Valley, Second Calcutta Conference, 23 August 1945; and Multi-Purpose Plan for Development of Orissa Rivers, 3 November 1945.

References

Ambedkar, B. R. (1915). "Administration and Finance of the East India Company." Submitted in partial fulfilment of the requirements of the degree of Master of Arts.

Ambedkar, B. R. (1918). "Small Holdings in India and Their Remedies." *Journal of Indian Economic Society*, 1, 1900–1945.

Ambedkar, B. R. (1923). *Problem of the Rupee: Its Origin and Its Solution*. London: PS King and Sons.

Ambedkar, B. R. (1925). *The Evolution of Provincial Finance in British India*. King.

Ambedkar, B. R. (1943a). "Post War Development of Electric Power in India." Indian Information, 15 November.

Ambedkar, B. R. (1943b). "First Session Plenary Labour." Indian Information, 15 July 1944.

Ambedkar, B. R. (1945a). "Multipurpose Development of the Damodar Valley, 23 August 1945." Indian Information, 10 October.

Ambedkar, B. R. (1945b). "Multi-Purpose Plan for Development of Orissa Rivers." Presidential Speech, 8 November 1945. Indian Information, 15 December.

Ambedkar, B. R. (1945c). "Damodar Valley Scheme Calcutta Conference, 1 February 1945." Indian Information.

Ambedkar, B. R. (1945d) "Dr. Ambedkar on Social Security." Indian Information, 15 September.

Ambedkar, B. R. (1947). "States and Minorities." In *Writing and Speeches of Dr. Ambedkar* (Vol. 1). Education Department, Government of Maharashtra.

Ambedkar, B. R. (1987). "Buddha or Karl Marx." In B. R. Ambedkar (Ed.), *Dr. Babasaheb Ambedkar Writings and Speeches* (Vol. 3, p. 444). Government of Maharashatra.

Central Water Commission (CWC). (1993). *Ambedkar's Contribution to Water Resources Development*. New Delhi: Central Water Commission.

Chakravarty, S. (1998). "Development Planning: The Indian Experience." OUP Catalogue.

Government of India. (1944). "Reconstruction Committee of Council (1944)." Record of the First Meeting of the Policy Committee No. 3C (Public Works and Electric Power), held at Delhi on 23 September 1943. Magazine, Government of India, File No. 1(4): 45.

Loksabha. (1946). *Constituent Assembly of India Debates (Proceedings): Volume I*. New Delhi: Lok Sabha.

Omvedt, G. (1994). *Dalits and the Democratic Revolution: Dr. Ambedkar and the Dalit Movement in Colonial India*. India: Sage Publications.

Times of India. (1943). "Urgency of Industrialisation of India." 26 October.

3 Dr. Ambedkar

Inter-disciplinarian with commitment

R. S. Deshpande and Khalil Shaha

Introduction

Not many social scientists traverse across disciplines, with a focused objective and demonstrating complete authority across disciplines. During those days the disciplinary walls in social sciences were being created and perpetuated so strongly that even angels dare not break these obstacles. Social scientists breaking these stockades require a different thinking process and inborn talent of challenging and breaking the irrationally created barriers by the academic society. Dr. Babasaheb Ambedkar demonstrated this inimitable quality of crushing these artificially created barricades in the society and also in academics. He traversed across disciplines like sociology, social anthropology, monetary economics, public finance, Indology, law, labour, and political science. Rarely do we come across a social scientist like him who can negotiate with ease of a swan through the maze of different disciplines and provide original out of box thinking. Dr. Ambedkar was a revolutionary attacker on the barricades like an angry lion, bringing in new paradigms. Undoubtedly, he was a first rate economist and an accomplished social scientist with minute understanding of the problems of the society. Through the fresh ideas he provided the most needed turning points in the thinking process in that area of knowledge. These turning point ideas have been discussed by many but we should realize that these ideas were articulated by him even before the world's best thinkers could even think of them. Mostly all the new ideas originated in the closed door of a single subject discipline (often in the West) and rarely peeked out of the disciplinary borders. In the process of commercialisation of knowledge, these generated power houses in the respective subject domains, the emerging specialists got compartmentalised and fortified to protect power equations. This process originated in the western world and cumulatively reinforced by disciplinary satraps. That led to the usage of "social sciences" as a plural concept and the understanding of the problems of society also became compartmentalised and prejudiced by the subject boundaries. Dr. Ambedkar was an exception in this regard. He did not care the artificially construed imaginary boundaries, as he was a revolutionary and refused to fall in these enclosures. As we said above, he was one of those rare social scientists, who traversed with ease in the entire field of social sciences that included subjects that include: anthropology, sociology, political science, economics, law, development theory, agricultural economics, religion studies, monetary economics, legal studies and Oriental studies. We might have erred in leaving some of the areas because of his vast span of thinking is absolutely difficult to comprehend. We are attempting here to understand Dr. Ambedkar as an economist with a unique thinking process that was far ahead of his times and innovatory in its content.

Unfortunately, despite the originator of many important ideas, through his writings, Dr. Ambedkar did not enter the portals of classrooms in any of the universities or colleges in any of the subjects that he handled? Was this phenomenon incidental or deliberate? There is enough room to believe that such omissions were deliberate and attempts to side-track the views were blatant. We are well aware that comprehending Dr. Ambedkar as an economist from today's standpoint is a difficult task. Today we find in the field of economics four strong established currents. The first strand includes those who use complex mathematics or statistics in order to decipher and comment on complex social realities. *Mathematicalisation* of economics has become the order of the day and largely the Noble prizes are in favour of these complex economists. Second group consists of economists with strong ideological leaning establishing their identity through some specific ideological framework and most preferred structures are Marxian or the Open Market Capitalist framework. It is difficult to argue or contradict such groups and reality is unreachable in the discussions with them sometimes since these are diagonally placed groups for any analytical issue. The third group is that of empiricist wherein, a large amount of data is churned in order to get to the axioms in social reality. These economists only reiterate the ground situations supported by a few statistical tools and techniques. The last strand is that of the intellectuals who navigate through by-lanes of different conceptual constructs from among the branches of social sciences and arrive at a distilled theoretical knowledge. This is the rarest group and has very thin membership today. During Dr. Ambedkar's time onwards the earlier three groups were quite prevalent but a small number of researchers preferred the fourth group (these included: J. C. Kumarappa, Justice M. G. Ranade, Dadabhai Nauroji etc.). But there was a significant difference between Dr. Ambedkar and his contemporaries even during those days. Being a revolutionary and pluralistic economist Dr. Ambedkar adopted economics as a science that deals with human maladies. He was more concerned with human suffering than application of the mundane tools of economics to understand the issues at stake. As among the branches of economics he was at ease with almost every branch but worked more on monetary economics, public finance, macroeconomics, agricultural economics, and social economics with use of data.

Making of the personality

Dr. Babasaheb Ambedkar had severely bad experiences of the prevailing caste discrimination in his childhood. Throughout his early days he suffered the pains and pangs of the fellow members of the depressed caste group.

After the arduous childhood, he began his training at Columbia University under the influence of an outstanding American philosopher and economics professor John Dewey. The influence of Professor Goldenweiser and Professor Dewey on Dr. Ambedkar's thinking process could be seen during the formation years of his career. Among them one was an accomplished social anthropologist and another a world known philosopher. Dr. Ambedkar was always attracted towards these subject but understood these from the perspective of the pathetic situation of the depressed castes, failure of governance and the economic situation in India. He, therefore, undertook to present his renowned work on "Caste in India: Their Mechanism, Genesis and Development", in the presence of Professor Goldenweiser. He was just 25 years old when this authoritative work on Castes in India was penned.

It is in this book that Dr. Ambedkar brought forth the concept of "Infection of Imitation" and that was beginning of the idea Prof. M. N. Srinivas picked up in his work on "Sanskritisation" (1952, 1956). Actually, Dr. Ambedkar elaborated this to understand the perpetuation and hierarchy in Indian Caste System. The concept of "Infection of Imitation" was the essence of the spread Brahmanical practices among the other castes and inherently accepting the customs and culture dictated by the Brahmins. Prof. M. N. Srinivas does not refute this idea of Brahmin superiority in customs and actually he writes

> A low caste was able, in generation or two, to rise to a higher position in the hierarchy by adopting vegetarianism and teetotalism, and by Sanskritizing its ritual and pantheon. In short, it took over, as far as possible, the customs, rites and beliefs of the Brahmins, and adoption of Brahminic way of life by a low caste seems to have been frequent, though theoretically forbidden.
>
> (Srinivas 1952: 30)

Therefore, he bypassed the Infection of Imitation of groups in the non-Hindu society which Dr. Ambedkar did not evade. Besides, Dr. Ambedkar uses the word "Infection" (a sort of a negative connotation) wherein, M. N. Srinivas preferred "Sanskritisation" (a sort of superiority notation). The conditions for imitation, according to this standard authority are that the source of imitation must enjoy prestige in the group and there must be numerous and daily relations among the group. As a result, non-Hindu religions also formed castes as enclosures of class. Today, caste is not just a Hindu phenomenon and has extended to Muslims, Christian, and Sikh, etc.

The imitation and observance of the customs vary directly with the social distance of castes that separates them, depending upon the intensity and integrity of imitation. Those castes were near to the Brahmins have imitated many customs and insisted the strict observance of them and those castes that were less near had imitated a few customs. Therefore, the whole process of caste formation in India is a process of imitation of the higher by the lower. At the same time, caste in the singular number, is an unreality, it exist only in the plural number. There were other factors contributed to form a new caste as excommunicated group and these had basically deeper socio economic contexts of deprivation. The penalty and punishment was on its members and, as a result, emergence of these new groups emerged. Dr. Ambedkar emphasised this (1917) almost half a century before M. N. Srinivas wrote (1952, 1956) about that. Therefore, Dr. Ambedkar had actually picked the pulsating problems of the Indian society at a very early stage of his life. He wrote Castes in India when he was barely 25 years old and with an authority of an in-depth scholar.

We are venturing here to understand depth of the academic pursuits of Dr. Ambedkar reflected through his writings and speeches to establish the turning point ideas, he postulated. Through this writing, we are trying to reconstruct the academic personality of Dr. Ambedkar as a social scientist of different category and not as usually done. We know how dwarf are our competences to understand and review the social science thinking of this inter-disciplinary intellectual colossus, but we make a humble attempt here. Dr. Ambedkar emerged after facing insurmountable challenges right from early childhood. Before taking up his higher education, he was literally shaken by the discrimination in the Indian society as also the maladies of British rule in India. Therefore, first he argued the case of discrimination against depressed castes in India and the caste problems of the Indian society convincingly. Unfortunately, during those days not even up to 1980s, Indian social scientists took any note of his seminal contributions in sociology or social anthropology in the best universities. One may overlook this as it might have happened by chance but there is enough room to believe that this neglect was by design. This long neglect of using Dr. Ambedkar's writings as teaching material was possibly deliberate by the academic fraternity. The first facet of his personality was built under the indelible ulcerating injury inflicted on his tender mind by the evils of the prevailing Caste System. That produced the essay on Castes in India.

Administration and finance of East India Company

Dr. Ambedkar initially got into public finance, and his love for public finance emanated from, two important standpoints: one, his closeness with Professor Seligman, a giant academics working in public finance and former president of American Economic Association; and two, Dr. Ambedkar liked this discipline, as it directly dealt with the State Craft and the treasury operations that influence the welfare of the masses. Welfare of people was close to the heart of Dr. Ambedkar and attracted him to public finance. He believed that only through the State intervention he can reach to disentangle the maladies of the society. That would also give him close access to understand the mind of the Government then. He chose to write his MA dissertation on the *Administration and Finance of East India Company* (1915), possibly to understand the economic tools used by the Colonial rulers to strengthen their iron clench on the Indian subcontinent. Initially, he wrote the dissertation on "Finances of East India Company" but it seems he lost that manuscript, and he expressed his desire to work on "The Stabilisation of Indian Exchange System". He expressed his desire through a letter to Prof. Seligman. But his dissertation came through on the finances of East India Company (1915). His critical look at the East India Company financial operations must have been resented by many in England during those days. Economic apparatus was effectively being used by the East India Company to drain out the surpluses from the Indian economy. Dr. Ambedkar was quite clear about this phenomenon and right from the beginning of the dissertation, he emphasised that colonial rulers had a design to squeeze India of its wealth & resources. He wrote "Apparently the immenseness of India's contribution to England is as much astounding as the nothingness of England's contribution to India". He was quite clear about the depletion of Indian resources by the East India Company and analysed the administrative setup of the East India Company by describing the Court of Proprietors and Court of Directors as the board of control of the company. He categorised the Governor General as an autocrat with all the powers concentrated in the hands of a single person. In the initial chapters of this thesis, Dr. Ambedkar brought out the transition of the East India Company from a commercial concern to a political controlling authority with an autocrat at the helm of affairs. The economic clutches used by the East India Company are analysed in detail to bring home the way revenue was being collected. The revenue system of British India is analysed to a great depth describing the *Zemindari* and *Ryotwari* systems of land revenue. He goes further into details of the revenue through Opium Tax, Salt Tax, Customs, Tobacco Tax, Wheel Tax, Abkaree Duty, Stamps Duty and so on. All these swelled the revenue to the Company impoverishing the natives. Dr. Ambedkar for his thesis painstakingly collected huge data on the revenue earned during British India and the expenditure conducted by the East India Company under the orders of the Governor General. While quoting John Bright about the plight of infrastructure and drinking water, Dr. Ambedkar brought forth that no doubt a few useful works were only carried out in the territories of the Native Chiefs and Princess. He supports this argument by quoting Dr. Spray's work *Modern India* published in 1837 (p. 26). The Land Tax as well as other taxes levied by the British were certainly exploitative in their content. To emphasise this point, Dr. Ambedkar quotes Colonel Briggs (p. 29) that "A land tax which now exists in India professing to absorb the whole of the landlords rent was never known under any government in Europe or Asia". He further writes that the revenue officers had destroyed all the temptation of labour. Any insightful reader can see the tinge of Marxist inside Dr. Ambedkar's writing and we know that he further wrote on Marx and Buddha drawing parallels and analysing the two in detail . . . The second facet of his personality as a nationalist who could not digest the exploitation of the natives by the Colonial ruler comes out in his thesis.

It is interesting to read this thesis of Dr. Ambedkar showing his full control on a large amount of historical literature on one side and painstakingly collected data on the revenue and expenditure in British India from 1792 onwards, on the other. Very elaborate tables are presented by Dr. Ambedkar to bring out the fact that taxes collected from various sources and across time were exploitative. He brings forth the fact that colonial rulers took extreme advantage of the Indian subcontinent by collecting huge taxes in terms of revenue. On the expenditure side, he has also shown the meagreness of expenditure conducted by the British government in India on infrastructure and other components. He shows through the tables that in total 46 years starting with 1810–11 the gap in revenue and expenditure was very substantial; earning substantial sums for the Company. The revenue surpassed expenditure in 32 years out of 46 years and the surplus was extracted by the Company and repatriated to England. The deficit was visible only in 14 years in the total period and this was too thin compared to the surpluses generated during many years. The surplus was always more than £3 million over years. After presenting this revenue-expenditure account, Dr. Ambedkar writes that "The last Mohamedan ruler of Bengal, in the last year of his administration (1764) realized a land revenue of £817,553: within 30 years the British rulers realized a land revenue of £2,680,000 from the same Province" (p. 29) to bring forth the exploitative land revenue system. Similarly, showing the debt incurred by India was about £7 million in 1792 and that increased to more than £60 million by 1857–58. The Afghan War and the Sepoy Mutiny raised the figures of the Home Bond debts incurred by India to £3,894,400, besides £ 40,000,000 as the cost of the Mutiny (!). Dr. Ambedkar quotes a British officer Mr. Martin, the in-charge of Madras Province, as "When carloads of silver were going out of his Cutcherry (office), he remembered the poor in the hinterlands of the province" (p. 31). He further discusses the 1858 legislation handing over India's administration in full and final form to the British Governor General and at the time when the debts on Indian government was astronomically large, which constituted the expenditure incurred by the East India Company in India. This was to be earned by increasing the revenue and the taxes in India which the British government did subsequently. Commenting on the debts incurred by the Company, Dr. Ambedkar quotes at length from Major Wingate. He emphasises the point that in "The Indian debt has really been incurred by the Government of this country: and how then can we possibly shake ourselves free of Indian liabilities" (p. 41). Here we meet Dr. Ambedkar as a young socialist mind with the influence of Marx peeping out of his writing. We all know that later on he wrote the famous monograph on Marx and Buddha.

Through this dissertation, Dr. Ambedkar concludes that only a few benefited as against many who suffered, the seeds of perpetual poverty to take roots in India were sown. He writes that the horrific peace in India that followed the Sepoy Mutiny was rather a dreadful peace that brought India under the stronghold of British Empire. India not only became debt ridden but slipped under the strong clutches of the colonial rulers. Dr. Ambedkar then concludes "But whether mere animal peace is to be preferred to economic destitution, let everyone decide for himself" (p. 47). Here the revolutionary deep inside Dr. Ambedkar peeps out to say that it is necessary to see and speak about the horrific economic experience that India has gone through. The conclusion itself brings forth the true Indian spirit and a revolutionary economist of par excellence inside Dr. Ambedkar. The thesis overtly addressed to the problem of finances by the East India Company but actually through the tools of political economic analysis brings to the foreground the diarchy. He further shows that diarchy is not a good form of Government and it is welfare deteriorating. The personality of Dr. Ambedkar as a welfare economist with an outlook of social economist features here.

Malady of small holdings and the agricultural sector

Dr. Ambedkar always had welfare of the depressed social groups close to his heart. Seldom he wrote about the sophisticated sections of the society and never attempted to get into the high echelon areas of economics frequented by the sophisticated western economists during his times. He engaged himself with the problems of the downtrodden and have-nots, to disentangle the intricate issues. The poverty among small and marginal holdings was plaguing India. Even today, the problem continues to dominate among the agrarian issues. Cultivators of India, over centuries are being 'marginalised' in terms of their land holding as also by their economic conditions. The situation was aggravated during the Colonial rule and one must recall the heinous Deccan Riots (1875), when cultivators were deeply entrenched in distress due to the debt of money lenders. Dr. Ambedkar had deep concern about the plight of the small and marginal farmers. He pinpointed the proliferation of small and uneconomic holdings in India and further identified that as the major hurdle in stepping to higher income level for these farmers. He writes that also impacts the growth of the sector. After analysing the issue he puts forth the idea of "Joint Cultivation by the Small farmers", the idea that found takers now in the Approach Paper of the (now aborted) Twelfth plan (FPOs) of the Government of India. But more incisively, he argued about the relation between agriculture and industrial sector, an issue that became predominant in the debates after Sir Arthur Lewis published his paper on "Economic Development and Unlimited Supplies of Labour" in the *Manchester School Journal* in 1954. Following the same thinking as that of Dr. Ambedkar, Arthur Lewis combined the historical analysis in the development process to speak about the uneconomic holding and transfer of labour. Lewis also speaks of the law of inheritance as one of the glitch and goes further to find remedy in the relationship between industrial (capitalist) sector and the underdeveloped agricultural sector. He presumes transfer of capital as one change as also the shift of labour as another. Dr. Ambedkar in his 1918, article had argued that "These small and scattered holdings have given a real cause for anxiety regarding our great national industry. Comparative statistics go to swell this feeling by laying bare two very noteworthy but equally sad facts regarding economic life in India; (1) that it is largely an agricultural country and (2) that its agricultural productivity is the lowest". At the same time he did not advocate 'consolidation' as understood from the literature on Land Reforms. He seriously discounts the consolidation as a non-remedy. He instead suggests land nationalisation as a possible solution to save the vulnerable farmers. He writes:

> A more serious criticism against these projects of consolidation consists in the fact they have failed to recognize that a consolidated holding must be an enlarged holding as well. If it is said that Indian agriculture suffers from small and scattered holdings we must not only consolidate, but also enlarge them. It must be borne in mind that consolidation may obviate the evils of scattered holdings, but it will not obviate the evils of small holdings unless the consolidated holding is an economic holding, i.e. an enlarged holding.

Actually a few arguments of Dr. Ambedkar are almost similar to those furthered by Prof. Theodore Schultz, much later, in his famous book on *Transforming Traditional Agriculture*. Schultz recommends the breaking away from clutches of low productivity trap or "low-level" equilibrium, with the help of transfer of surplus labour to high wage sector for which Schultz was awarded a Nobel Prize. Schultz also writes of enhancing the capital flow that includes quality of human resources. Dr. Ambedkar had recommended far before (in 1918) increasing capital intensity in agricultural sector. Dr. Ambedkar wrote "Consequently the remedy for the ills of agriculture in India does not lie primarily in the matter of enlarging holdings but in the matter of increasing capital and capital goods. That capital arises from saving and that saving is possible where there is surplus is a commonplace of political economy". Dr. Ambedkar then moves to industrialization as an important antidote for the evils of the proliferation of small holdings: "Industrialization is a natural and powerful remedy and is to be preferred to such ill-conceived projects as we have considered above. By legislation we will get a sham economic holding at the cost of many social ills. But by industrialization a large economic holding will force itself upon us as a pure gain". Further he stated that "Consideration of another aspect of consolidation as well points to the same conclusion: That industrialization must precede consolidation." Strikingly, one witnesses the holistic approach of Dr. Ambedkar as an economist and not a compartmentalised view of the situation. That stands to the testimony of his incisive thinking about the rural agrarian issues as an accomplished rural economist and an agricultural economist who proposed the same theorem as that of Arthur Lewis almost five decades prior to the year in which Arthur Lewis got his Noble award.

Besides these arguments Dr. Ambedkar took note of the changes elsewhere in the world and points to the fact that India must move towards progressive industrialization and that will have a positive impact on the agricultural wages as also poverty in India. Idea that formed the central theme of many Dual Economy models, beginning with Arthur Lewis and going through Ranis and Fei to Dixit and Marglin. Dr. Ambedkar wrote "While other countries like the U.S.A. starting as agriculture are progressively becoming industrial, India has been gradually undergoing the woeful process of de-urbanization and swelling the volume of her rural population beyond all needs. The earlier we stem this ominous tide, the better". He wanted connecting of the industrial growth with agriculture and supporting the agricultural sector with capital as also capital goods. This was also advocated far before Theodore Schultz who got the Nobel Memorial Prize jointly with Sir Arthur Lewis for his work on Transforming Traditional Agriculture (1964), almost on the similar theme of highlighting the connection between the agricultural sector and industry, besides emphasizing the fact that human capital enhancement through education could be one of the major remedies for backwardness of agriculture. Dr. Ambedkar throughout his writings emphasized the importance of human capital enhancement through education and even started institutions to get this on the ground for the most depressed groups (Peoples' Education Society). This idea later on picked by the scholars working on Economics of Education.

The problem of the rupee

Dr. Ambedkar joined London School of Economics and worked on his Doctor of Science dissertation in economics. This work could be taken as an excellent piece in monetary economics, but with a flavour of political and institutional economics to it. *The Problem of the Rupee* stemmed out the controversy that rocked the monetary economics field debating gold and silver standards and Dr. Ambedkar had expressed with Prof. Seligman that he wanted to work on India's exchange rates. As an economist, till then Dr. Ambedkar was more concerned with issues in public finance and it is possibly the personality of Prof. Edwin Cannon that shifted Dr. Ambedkar's interest from public finance to monetary economics. One must read the earlier dissertations as also *The Problem of the Rupee* and the reflection of an expert political economist fused with monetary and institutional economics becomes visible. He traversed through the theories and the literature on monetary economics with utmost ease and wrote this dissertation in a very accomplished style. He uses data and a large mass of literature to bring forth his points. There was a noticeable rise in prices in India compared to England. Here the preposition of the actual exchange rates corresponding to the purchasing power parity came for discussion. Professor Keynes in his book on *Indian Currency and Finance* maintained that the exchange standard contained an essential element in the ideal standard of the future.

It is argued by Dr. Ambedkar that the actual exchange rates are related to the "purchasing power parities" of the two countries. The actual exchange rate is the ratio of the two purchasing power parity of the two currencies.

The Problem of the Rupee revolves around the issue of gold standard/gold exchange standard as against silver standard that was being discussed during that period under the price non-parity between India and England to the advantage of the later. He brought out a revised edition of his thesis and titled it as *History of Indian Currency and Banking* in 1947. The original thesis was published in 1923 by Butler and Tanner Ltd, London. The theme of both volumes run hand-in-hand. Before Dr. Ambedkar wrote his dissertation there was hardly any work on the gold standard, and only the work by Lord Keynes was available. Dr. Ambedkar did not support the arguments put forth by Lord Keynes but in fact he contradicted Lord Keynes vehemently. Dr. Ambedkar writes

> This difference proceeds from the fundamental fact, which seems to be quite overlooked by Professor Keynes, that nothing will stabilize the rupee unless we stabilize its general purchasing power. That the exchange standard does not do. That standard concerns itself only with symptoms and does not go to the disease: indeed, on my showing, if anything, it aggravates the disease.
>
> (Dr. Ambedkar's writings Volume 6, p. 328)

Let us look into the main arguments put forth by Dr. Ambedkar in this monumental work. Until 1893, the Indian currency was based on silver standard which means that the value of a coin of rupee was equivalent to the silver content in it. The Colonial rulers introduced gold coin in 1841 and that became legal tender equal to Rs. 15. Confronted with the huge output of gold in the mines of Australia and United States, the relative value of gold fell down and by the year 1853, Colonial rulers stopped it. Many suggestions were made to reintroduced gold standard, as its absence was having significant impact on the exchange value of rupee. As a consequence the trade between India and England benefitted the colonial rulers. During 1872 to 1893, the Indian rupee collapsed significantly and also the value of Indian exports. In 1893, the British Government stopped silver rupee and introduced a gold coin the value of which was £1.04/rupee. The continued devaluation of Indian rupee had its impact on the Indian economy. The exports increased; however, India had to commit more expenses to England which were in gold terms. In 1893, the government stopped whining silver rupees and agreed to coin rupee in exchange of gold. The government managed the exchange system. The currency committee headed by Mr. Fowler recommended opening the mints to issue gold coins along with silver rupees. By 1906, the exchange standard was well-established and silver rupee was guaranteed convertibility into sterling pounds based on its gold value at a fixed price. The system broke down in 1916, with a huge rise in the price of silver. But by then the system became silver standard. Dr. Ambedkar dealt with the issue of this entire management of exchange system in India by the colonial government. Dr. Ambedkar's main argument was against the reckless issue of the rupee currency management by the British. His commitment was the internal stability of the Indian economy and that could be possible only with gold standard and gold currency. He repeated this point in his memorandum given to the Hilton Young Commission (1925). He was afraid that the chance of mismanagement by the government was greater because of the issue of money. And any such mismanagement would explode the prices that will be extremely disastrous. He did not mince words in order to criticise the then British government and went up to saying that the coinage is manipulated by the government. Dr. Ambedkar writes

> What really concerns those who use money is not how much gold that money is worth, but how much of things in general (of which gold is an infinitesimal part) that money is worth. Everywhere, therefore the attempt is to keep money stable in terms of commodities in general, and that is but proper for what ministers to the welfare of people is not so much the precious metal as commodities and services of more direct utility.
>
> (Dr. Ambedkar's writings, Volume 6, pg. 563)

He was more concerned about the commoners confronting huge price rises because of the mismanagement of currency standards. He had argued elsewhere that managed currency is to be avoided altogether. He was more concerned about the price stability through conservative and automatic monetary management. Here we can visualise the personality as an accomplished macro-monetary economist.

Graded inequality

Caste has been discussed by many a sociologist but the genesis of caste and its perpetuation in the society was not an issue of discussion in sociology as also in economics. In fact economists have always kept away themselves from the issue of caste and it is only recently probably after the work by George A. Akerlof that the caste as an issue surfaced in the academic writings of economists. It was argued among other by authors like Deepak Lall (1988 in his book *Hindu Equilibrium* that caste is also a division of labourers and civilized society needs division of labour. It was further demonstrated with a sophisticated production function analysis that the society is in equilibrium if the castes carry out their economic activities assigned to them traditionally. But in no civilized society is the division of labour accompanied by this unnatural division of labourers into water-tight compartments. Therefore, it is a hierarchy in which the division of labour accompanied by this gradation of labourers. It does not provide scope for the development individual capacities rather it imposed the social status of parents on the children to go for hereditary occupation. Individual sentiment and preference has no place in it and it is based on the dogma of predestination (Ambedkar 1936: 47).

Most of the researchers on caste system have got into the routine description of the system that attracted attention of western scholars as many intricacies of social systems were not known to outside world. But an intriguing externality of such research is that the focus was shifted from diagnostic analysis to a symptomatic and descriptive analysis. Dr. Ambedkar, however, went further in depth of understanding the emergence and perpetuation of the system and also provided Buddhism as a solution to get rid of the inhuman practices. He writes that caste system does not demarcate racial division and is a social division of people of the same race (Ambedkar 1936: 49). Caste does not result in economic efficiency or cannot and has not improved the race. Rather it has completely disorganized and demoralized the Indians and created an economically inefficient society dropping the GDP growth abysmally (Ambedkar 1936: 50). The system actually leads to perpetuation of poverty.

According to Dr. Ambedkar the ideal society should be based on liberty, equality and fraternity. It should be mobile, full of channels for conveying a change taking place in one part to other parts. In an ideal society there should be many interest consciously communicated and shared. There should be varied and free points of contact with other modes of association. Finally, there should be social endosmosis in the society (Ambedkar 1936: 57). As a Constitutional expert he emphasised these issues throughout his writing and enshrined in the Constitution of India.

Caste has two aspects as per his analysis. First, it divides human being into separate communities. Second, it places these communities in graded order one above the other in social status. Each takes its pride and its consolation in the fact that in the scale of castes it is above some other castes. As an outward marks of this gradation, there is also a gradation of social and religious rights technically spoken of as *Ashtadhikaras* and *Sanskaras*. Therefore, the higher the grade of a caste, the greater the number of these rights, and the lower the grade, lesser their numbers. All are slaves of the caste system but all of them are nor in equal status (Ambedkar 1936: 72). Dr. Ambedkar points out to the economics of this graded system as the cause of perpetuation of poverty among the depressed castes as there is hardly any labour mobility and the rewards for work also follows the same order.

According to him, the fundamental principle of caste system is graded inequality. It vertically ordered the classes and not on horizontal plane. They are not only different but unequal in status. There is no sphere of life which is not regulated by the principle of graded inequality (Ambedkar 1987: 107, Vol. III). The process of graded inequality involves: 1. Fixity of occupations according to hierarchy; 2. Graded wage structure – Higher wages for Brahmins per unit of work and lower to Shudras; 3. Forced immobility of labour and wages; 4. Prevention on any enhancement of skills and closed knowledge hubs; 5. Graded punishments for enforcing the compliance by the lower strata of the society.

In a social system of graded inequality the possibility of a general common attack by the aggrieved parties is non-existence and they are not on common level. In this kind of social system there are highest, higher, high, lower and lowest. Therefore, all have a grievance against the highest and would like bring about their down fall but will not combine together. The high wants to over-throw the higher who is above him but does not want to join hands with the low and the lower. In the system of graded inequality there is no such class as completely unprivileged class except the one which is at the base of the social pyramid. Even the privileges are graded. And each class is privileged; every class is interested in maintaining the social system (Ambedkar 1987: 102, Vol. IV). It is here that we can make out Dr. Ambedkar as one of the accomplished social economist who could use economic tools in order to demonstrate the long-lasting impact of a social phenomenon.

Understanding Dr. Ambedkar as multi-faceted social scientist

Dr. Ambedkar was trained as an economist at the two best institutions in the world, namely Columbia University and London School of Economics. He actually began writing on social anthropology and then shifted to public finance. His personality emerged by confronting many obstacles and observing the pathetic realities in the society prevailing during his early age. He obtained his education very painstakingly and under severe economic stress. Confronting discrimination even from the much unexpected sources, he was deeply hurt. Therefore, in order to understand the personality of Dr. Ambedkar as a social scientist, one must get into his thinking about the social evils and the building of the personality on that background. Dr. Ambedkar always had his umbilical cord connected with the suffering of the depressed social groups back in India and pathetic Indian economic condition. The social structure and the melodies of the social structure there are always behind his thinking and therefore, the state and state policies was the focus of his thinking. Naturally he was inclined towards public finance initially as it touches the state policies as well as welfare of the people. It is certainly difficult to comprehend Dr. Ambedkar into a strait jacket personality and in one such attempt Ambirajan writes "Ambedkar firmly belonged to Judeo-Greek – enlightenment tradition and was an upcoming modernist. This shows in his approach to economics, politics, law, society and everything else including the matter of sartorial habits" (Ambirajan. 1999, p. 3285). One must look at this pluralistic, multifaceted personality from the viewpoint of the welfare of the masses and therefore he got involved into public finance, welfare economics, institutional settings, Colonial rule and monetary economics and at the same time had the national interest at his heart.

We are quite aware that comprehending Dr. Ambedkar's personality as colossus in social sciences is a difficult task and especially, when someone like us who are trained in economics as a basic discipline. Dr. Ambedkar began with the mission against social maladies of caste that was dear to his heart and in order to comprehend this ulcerating problem he traversed through the maze of various disciplines broadly of social sciences. He worked through a large number of dual material and a large number of books and publications that were available at London School of Economics and many higher learning institutions in India. He did not leave any stone unturned in order to get to a satisfactory level and said to his hypotheses. His arguments have been always unequivocal and clear to the last detail. He non-provided strong and solid evidence in order to support his arguments whenever, he wrote something non-palatable to the traditional thinkers during those days. As a lawyer he vehemently defended the arguments of social reformers like Dr. Karve on family planning, who was charged with printing material on family planning. His speeches were well-researched and provided exact references whenever needed. He was a giant in full right and an academician par excellence.

References

Ambedkar, B.R. (1915). *Administration and Finance of the East India Company*. New York: University of Columbia (republished in 1989) *Dr. Babasaheb Ambedkar Writing and Speeches* (Vol. VI). Government of Maharashtra.

Ambedkar, B.R. (1917). *Caste in India: Their Mechanism, Genesis and Development*. New York: Indian Antiquary.

Ambedkar, B.R. (1923). *The Problem of the Rupee: Its Origin and Its Solution*. Westminster, UK: P.S. King & Son Ltd (republished in 1989) *Dr. Babasaheb Ambedkar Writing and Speeches* (Vol. VI). Government of Maharashtra.

Ambedkar, B.R. (1925). *The Evolution of Provincial Finance in British India: A Study in the Provincial Decentralization of Imperial Finance*. Westminster, UK: P.S. King & Son Ltd (republished in 1989) *Dr. Babasaheb Ambedkar Writing and Speeches* (Vol. VI). Government of Maharashtra.

Ambedkar, B.R. (1936). *Annihilation of Caste: Speech Prepared for the Annual Conference of the Jat-Pat-Todak Mandal of Lahore*. But Not Delivered, BR Kadrekar (republished in 1979) *Dr. Babasaheb Ambedkar Writing and Speeches* (Vol. I). Government of Maharashtra.

Ambedkar, B.R. (1939). *Federation versus Freedom*. R.R. Kale Memorial Lecture, Gokhale Institute of Politics and Economics, Pune.

Ambedkar, B.R. (1987). The Hindu Social Order. In B.R. Ambedkar (Ed.), *Dr. Babasaheb Ambedkar Writings and Speeches* (Vol. III, p. 107). Maharashtra, India: Government of Maharashtra.

Ambirajan, S. (1999). Ambedkar's Contribution to Indian Economics. *Economic and Political Weekly*, Vol. 34, No. 46/47 (Nov. 20–26, 1999), pp. 3280–3285.

Jadhav, N. (1991). Neglected Economic Thought of Babasaheb Ambedkar. *Economic and Political Weekly*, Vol. 26, No. 15 (Apr. 13, 1991).

Lal, D. (1988). *The Hindu Equilibrium. Volume II: "Aspects of Indian Labour"*. Oxford: Clarendon Press.

Srinivas, M.N. (1952). *Religion and Society Among the Coorgs of South India*. London: Oxford University Press.

Srinivas, M.N. (1956). A Note on Sanskritisation and Westernisation. *The Far Eastern Quarterly*, Vol. 15, No. 4 (Aug. 1956).

Thorat, S. (1996). Ambedkar and the Economics of the Hindu Social Order, Understanding Its Orthodoxy and Legacy. In W. Fernandes (Ed.), *The Emerging Dalit Identity*. New Delhi: Indian Social Institute.

Thorat, S. (2002). Oppression and Denial: Dalit Discrimination in the 1990s. *Economic and Political Weekly*, 572–578.

Thorat, S. (2006). *Ambedkar's Role in Economic Planning Water and Power Policy*. Shipra Publication.

Thorat, S. and Kumar, N. (2008). *B.R. Ambedkar: Perspectives on Social Exclusion and Inclusive Policies*. New Delhi: Oxford University Press.

4 Economics of Babasaheb Ambedkar

Anand Teltumbde

Despite a plethora of literature available on Babasaheb Ambedkar, he is scarcely described as an economist. Several reasons may be cited for it. The foremost is the reluctance of the Brahmanical establishment to acknowledge him as anything more than a Dalit leader. When he returned to India after completing his academic studies and plunged into public life, Ambedkar mainly engaged himself with battling against caste and its source ideology of Brahmanism. In process, he spoke and wrote volumes, much of which may belong to anything but economics. Nonetheless, his writings are interspersed with profound economic insights. For instance, *States and Minorities*, a treatise he wrote as a memorandum to the constituent assembly on behalf of his party, the Scheduled Caste Federation (SCF), may not be classed under economics but is replete with economics content. Though tenuous, but one more reason may also be advanced for the lack of emphasis in his writings on economics, which is his contention with the communists (Teltumbde, 2017). His writings and speeches, at times appear contemptuous of economics because it was obsessively upheld by the communists as 'base' and ignored social and religious issues, mapping caste, which had become his target as 'superstructure'.[1] He wrote, "the Communist Philosophy seems to be equally wrong for the aim of their philosophy seems to fatten pigs as though men are no better than pigs."[2]

This aspect of his contention with the communists got so much amplified both by a section of the post-Ambedkar Dalit leaders as well as the ruling classes that it completely eclipsed the fact that Ambedkar was among the most qualified economists, who was trained under the stalwarts of his times.[3] Those who view Ambedkar as an economist also take a constricted view of economics and lament that he could not contribute much to his fond discipline. This article, while reviewing his economics through familiar texts tries to argue that his entire politics is fraught with economic insights and is capable of guiding the Dalits both through its successes as well as failures.

Classification approach

While Ambedkar studied many subjects,[4] he chose economics as his major for his postgraduate and doctoral degrees both in Columbia University and

London University. After coming back to India, circumstances thwarted his pursuit of economics except for his formally working as Professor of Political Economy in Sydenham College of Commerce, Mumbai from 1918 to 1920 and publishing a brilliant essay, (Ambedkar, 1918) both during his three years' interim stay when he had not yet fully plunged into public life. After he finally returned to India in April 1923, he soon plunged into public life taking cudgels for the Dalits and just could not devote time for economics. Still, one finds, his economic scholarship spilled over his memoranda and pieces of evidence given to various government commissions, speeches in the different legislative bodies, and book reviews.

His formal economic writings are his academic theses. He submitted "Ancient Indian Commerce" (1915) and "National Dividend of India – A Historic and Analytical Study"[5] for his MA degree at Columbia University. He extended the research of his second thesis for his PhD, which was submitted in June 1916. He wrote "Provincial Decentralisation of Imperial Finance in British India" for his MSc in June 1921 to London University. And finally, submitted his thesis for his DSc, "The Problem of the Rupee: Its Origin and Its Solution" to London University in 1923. All these theses dwelt into the uncharted waters of public finance. His DSc thesis dealt with the currency problem – in the wake of replacing gold standard with gold currency by gold exchange standard, the topic that had engaged brilliant economic minds of those days. All these works were rooted in contemporary issues and were primarily meant to fulfil academic requirements. The methodology followed in them is that of historical exploration in which facts rather than principles dominated. Therefore, these theses may not appear directly relevant to us today but the underscoring concerns they reflect still touch a chord with our own situation. His other (non-academic) work, however, deal with issues that are still alive and reflect principles rather than facts. Therefore, they are directly relevant even today.

Ambedkar's economic writings reflect many strands and, therefore, may be classified variously. S Ambirajan in his seminal paper, for instance, divided them along four themes: (1) Monetary standards, (2) Public finance, (3) Cannon of public expenditure, and (4) Agrarian economy (Ambirajan, 1999). I would take a simpler and broader approach and discuss them in two categories: (1) Writings in fulfilment of his academic requirement and (2) Writings beyond academic requirement. The reason I wish to adopt this approach is to distinguish volition from compulsion and also to stress that Ambedkar's economics should be read through his entire politics. The first category of writings is somewhat constrained by academic framework and schedule and may also be influenced by his teacher's views. They may, thus, have less volitional content compared to the second category of voluntary writings. The latter, hence, can be relied on for truer views of the writer than the former.

Academic writings

Surprisingly, Ambedkar's entire academic work does not reflect a trace of his latter day engagement with the emancipation of Dalits from caste bondage.

What might be his motivation in choosing the subjects that are singularly related to the governance issue of state? The primary motivational concern in academic studies is the learning and its demonstration, which should not be missed out even in Ambedkar's case. The issues he handled had enormous contemporary relevance and, therefore, had excellent learning potential too. Next, the professors he worked under were considered world authorities in those subjects[6]. Ambedkar repeatedly chose the issues of public finance in the British East India Company. This fact, coupled with the kind of observations he came out with, reflect some purpose, which perhaps was to expose the mechanism of colonial exploitation of India. This was the dominant theme of the nationalist movement then back home, which would not have left young Ambedkar uninfluenced. Those were the turbulent times charged by the militant anti-colonial struggles that arose in the wake of 1905 partition of Bengal. A colossal patriotic fervour was unleashed in response to the partition of Bengal in 1905. It marked a shift from political moderation to political extremism, from constitutional agitation to radical struggle, and from politics of petition to direct action. It also gave birth to the anti-colonial swadeshi movement, which had colonial exploitation as its plank.

One may see a kind of patriotic streak in all his academic work. They point out how the colonial policies were detrimental to the interests of India and Indian people. As a matter of fact, this patriotic stripe made him the target of critics on his various academic interpretations which prompted him to confess, "it is my second justification, which affords me a greater excuse, it consists in the fact that I have written primarily for the benefit of the Indian public".[7] It may be interesting to note that he had previously chosen "Ancient Indian Commerce", dealing with economic history, but after a remarkable study and its submission for his MA degree,[8] he unusually took up another subject that – while still rooted in economic history – allowed a peep into colonial operations and shift towards public finance. It was submitted as the second thesis for his MA and became the nucleus of his research for his PhD degree. He made the East India Company a target of his study. By that way, he would feed Indian public with detailed information on its exploitative processes. It was not for nothing that he was suspected to be an Indian revolutionary and was checked off his luggage.[9] As a matter of fact, he was approached by Lala Lajpat Rai, one of the prominent nationalist leaders in India, who was a friend of his guide Prof Seligman to join his Home Rule League but Ambedkar politely declined citing the reason that he was on a scholarship of Baroda State and would like to abide by its terms.

Any further discussion on this may be speculative as paradoxically, one does not get any evidence to show that he was interested in the anti-colonial struggle that was going on in India during those days. He has never reflected rebellious anti-colonial sentiment or sympathies for it either before or after the Columbia period. One may discern three reasons for this. Firstly, like Jotiba Phule and unlike the nationalist leaders, he did not subscribe to the view that India was a nation. It thus invalidated the very premise of the nationalist struggle. Secondly, notwithstanding whether India was a nation or not, he contended that concern for people reflected in humanism with its values of liberty, equality and fraternity, and was above nationalism. Thirdly, he clearly saw that the colonial rule was beneficial to the Dalits and hence opposed the project of India's independence. The so called freedom that the nationalist sought entailed, according to him, the restoration of the Brahmanic rule. During the first session of the All-India Depressed Classes Congress (AIDCC), on August 8, 1930, at Nagpur, he argued that "The depressed classes welcomed the British as their deliverers from age-long tyranny and oppression by the orthodox Hindus". He had rather strategically decided to use the colonial rule to extract rights for Dalits. During his public life, he had made it a point never to be on the wrong side of the colonial state and rather became willing part of the colonial state as a minister in the government.

Public finance

Ambedkar's research in Columbia as well as in LSE dealt with the system of public finance of the British Raj. His study explored the evolution of federal structure and administrative system for public finances within it, during the colonial rule. In the economic history of India, this should have naturally constituted an important area for academics. Surprisingly, however, it did not attract much attention of scholars. With a solitary exception of M.G. Ranade, incidentally not an economist or academic in the formal sense, who presented a fragmentary sketch of 'provincial decentralisation' in 1887, the subject remained un-trodden till Ambedkar took it up. The importance of this work was highlighted by none other than his guide, Prof. Edwin R.A. Seligman, who was an authority on public finance and taxation:

> the value of Mr. Ambedkar's contribution to this discussion lies in the objective recitation of the facts and the impartial analysis of the interesting development that has taken place in his native country. The lessons are applicable to other countries as well, nowhere to my knowledge, has such a detailed study of the underlying principles been made.[10]

A progressive centralisation of fiscal power was the striking feature of the East India Company. Initially, the three presidencies, Bengal, Madras, and Bombay created by the Charter of George I in 1726 were separately possessing the powers of sovereignty: legislation, penal, and taxation, and therefore independent in their financial activities. They functioned as "separate clocks each with its own mainspring in itself", as Ambedkar metaphorically termed them. The Act of 1833 put an end to this arrangement ushering in the system of imperial finance. However, the Imperial system of government suffered from the fatal disease of financial inadequacy. The causes of financial inadequacy were identified by him as (i) Unsound fiscal policy and state economy, (ii) The heaviest land tax impost (the ratio of land revenue ranged from 31.68 to 66.17per cent, with an average of 52.48per cent), (iii) Unequitability forced in taxation and thereby impairment of the productive powers of society, (iv) Irregular custom duties on both internal and external items that blocked trade and smothered industry. Ambedkar concludes, after analysing on the basis of his data that the government's faulty revenue system was entirely responsible for this.

On the expenditure side, he observed, military devouring from 45.55 to 65.29 per cent of the total revenue since 1809 to 1857. In addition, there was the internal charge on war debts, which ranged from 7.19 to 18.00 per cent during the same period. Thus, the bulk of money raised by injurious taxes was spent in unproductive ways and nothing was left for developmental work. After the 1857 mutiny, as a result of the grave condition of the imperial finances, during the 1860s a federal plan was proposed in the interest of economy, responsibility, plenty and equity, which brought what Ambedkar would call a system of "Imperial finance without Imperial management" (Govt. of Maharashtra, 1989, Vol. 6, p. 100). A new scheme of "Budget by Assignment" was announced on December 14, 1870, in which assignment of funds from the imperial treasury was adopted as a method of balancing the provincial budgets. Subsequently, the scheme of provincial budget was introduced, which Ambedkar called "Budget by assigned revenue", which, according to him, was a great improvement over the past but still fell short of the requirements of elasticity in finance (ibid, p. 131). In addition to two distinct categories in the budget, wholly imperial and wholly provincial, a third category of joint imperial and provincial was created. Ambedkar termed this system as "budget by shared revenue". The principle to all the provinces from 1882–83, would work up to 1921.

Ambedkar considered finance as "the fuel of the whole administrative machine" and hence wanted a public fiscal system that will enable it to be "administratively workable". The main objective according to him was, "To make administrative polities independent by requiring them to finance themselves entirely out of their own respective resources without having to depend upon one another" (ibid, p. 282). Ambedkar studied some of the consequences of the Montague-Chelmsford reforms (1919) in provincial finances and argued against the provincial deficits being financed by accumulated revenue balances. He advocated that provincial governments must augment their tax revenue commensurate with the growing need of national prosperity. However, he thought the government run by a ministry recruited from the elected members of the provincial legislature would not dare to increase taxes because of the consideration of votes.

As regards public expenditure, he blamed the diarchy. He saw that the governor in council may not be interested in effecting economies in public expenditure. He faulted the diarchy for "its basic undemocratic character" and its lack of respect for "the principle of collective responsibility". He wrote, "The conclusion is unmistakable: Hybrid executives, divided responsibility, division of functions, reservation of powers, cannot make for a good system of government, and where there is no good system of government, there can be little hope for a sound system of finance" (ibid, p. 307). The main point he makes is that an alien government cannot be expected to use the funds it has to the betterment of the people because it cannot "feel the pulse of the people".

This discussion of the fiscal state, as Ambirajan observed, is quite analogous to what obtains today. Indeed, if one takes a glance at the administration of public finance today, one may be stunned to see that all criticism that Ambedkar makes 100 years ago of the colonial system appear applicable, almost in toto, to the present system of public finance. It is surprising that the post-colonial system that claims in the name of the Indian people to be their 'sovereign, socialist, secular, democratic republic' should continue with the same evils as that of the colonial system. The relevance of this work comes alive in asking this very question.

It is not the administration of public finance; the entire colonial state with its structure as well as processes continued after the transfer of power. Ambedkar's charge of colonial taxation being regressive is held out starkly, right through the post-colonial decades. Currently, our tax ration is at 16.7 per cent of GDP (Gross Domestic Product), which is too low compared to its potential estimated at 53.0 per cent. The tax structure is far from being progressive as direct taxes account for only a third of total taxes. South Africa, a country comparable in many respects to India, raises 27.4 per cent of GDP in taxes, half of which are direct taxes. The economic survey of India by the Organisation for Economic Cooperation and Development (OECD) published in March 2017 showed India's poor standing among its peers in tax-GDP ratio. India's dependence on indirect taxes is much higher than the OECD average or that of other emerging economies. OECD shows that India's income tax slabs are also not progressive. India's top tax rate becomes applicable only at very high levels of income, i.e., at around 1,200 per cent of the average wage in the organised sector, which is much higher than the level in its peer countries. While income tax slabs are not as progressive as they are thought to be in India, corporate taxation structure is regressive; bigger companies paying relatively lower effective tax rates than smaller ones.

As regards expenditure of the state that Ambedkar was most critical about, the wasteful spend on military, police, and paramilitary interest has been glaring in face of persisting contraction on education, healthcare, and other essential social services. The total non-developmental expenditure of the government has been jumping consistently year by year. As per government statistics, non-developmental expenditure of the state in 1990–91 was Rs. 69,195 crore, which has risen to Rs. 18,15,763 crore in 2015–16. As against this, developmental expenditure between these years rose from Rs 74,000 crore to Rs. 19,38,737 crore, but remained approximately at the same level of 50 per cent. The expenditure on education and healthcare which are basic ingredients for peoples' empowerment has been one of the lowest in the world. While expenditure on education languished between

3–4 per cent, as against 6 per cent desired in the 1960s by the Kothari Commission, the expenditure on healthcare has been as low as 1 to 1.2 per cent. India's healthcare remains one of the most neglected and, therefore, most privatised systems in the world. Ambedkar's exposé of the colonial rule vis-à-vis public interest in this and other of his economic theses are equally, if not more starkly, applicable to the current regime of India.

The problem of the rupee

After completing his studies in Columbia, Ambedkar enrolled himself at LSE for postgraduate studies and graduated to do his second doctoral degree. In his much-acclaimed thesis for D Sc, *The Problem of the Rupee*, he zealously argued in favour of the gold standard that automatically limited money supply in an economy by the amount of gold reserves it possessed. As against that, the gold exchange standard did away with this limitation and allowed the government the reckless issues of currency. His advocacy of the gold standard against the dominant opinion was perhaps influenced by the foundation of the US Federal Reserve, which had gold standard in 1914 and the history of successful operation of the active monetary policy by the Bank of England under a gold standard for two and a half centuries. Ambedkar's main criticism was that the gold exchange standard gave enormous power to the government to expand money supply without commensurate expansion in production of goods and services, leading to an unstable currency value within the economy. The gold exchange standard ensured external stability of exchange but sacrificed internal stability of the value of currency. He contended that an unstable currency could lead to uncontrolled inflation since a "managed currency system" allowed the government to indulge in fiscal extravagance and wasteful government expenditure. He was mainly concerned with disproportionately heavy burden of inflation imposed on the poor than on the rich. He was, thus, arguing for price stability through conservative and automatic monetary management. This argument has great relevance in these days of burgeoning budget deficit and its automatic monetisation.

Ambedkar's key advocacy for gold standard as the means of price stability, however, is not held out by history. The history of the gold standard is also fraught with crises, devaluations, suspensions of convertibility, and defaults on sovereign debt. It also did not eliminate debt crises or debt-induced inflation. The success of a gold standard in achieving stable prices depended heavily on governments' rules and commitments against devaluation. Insofar a gold standard is a commitment to exchange currency for something real and hence protection of real purchasing power, an inflation-indexed instrument also could perform the same function in the event of inflation. In place of gold, the central bank could freely buy and sell such inflation-linked securities at fixed prices. This scheme would protect against deflation as well as inflation, automatically providing more money when there is a true demand for it, as in a financial crisis. The critique argued that it is not the gold standard but the government as a credible steward of money supply that ensures stability. The gold standard, rather, is criticised for imposing a limitation on government's ability to respond to fiscal crises, the necessity of defending against speculative attacks in times of crises, and the possibility of independent changes in the relative price of gold, which could make the economy more unstable.

Contrary to Ambedkar's view, Keynes did not see the gold standard as a self-regulating system. If trade became heavily unbalanced, as it did in the late 1920s, deficit countries were forced to adjust, by raising interest rates to curb demand for imports and cutting wages to restore export competitiveness. Wages did not fall naturally when gold (and thus money) was in short supply; they fell in response to higher unemployment. Keynes proposed a scheme for a "clearing union" that would benefit trade of a fixed exchange-rate system but without the gold standard's shortcomings. At its heart was an International Clearing Bank (ICB) that would settle the balance of transactions that gave rise to trade surpluses or deficits. This scheme formed the basis of Britain's position in the negotiations in 1944 at Bretton Woods, which created the post-war system of exchange rates. While various countries viewed the collapse of the gold standard from their own perspective, they cohered to adopt this new scheme. America associated its earlier prosperity with the standard's stability and the Depression with the system's breakdown. Britain linked the misery of the 1920s to "the gold straitjacket and its subsequent recovery to being freed from it".[11].

Ambedkar directly challenged the Keynesian view advocating delinking of money supply from gold reserves. Keynes had argued that due to the development of the monetary-exchange mechanism in advanced capitalist economies such as the UK, there was no need to limit the supply of money by linking it with the gold reserves. Ambedkar's main point was that delinking money supply from gold reserve would lead to excessive money supply and, thereby, inflation which may be staved off by the rich in many ways but would certainly hit the poor hard. In his memorandum given to the Hilton Young Commission in 1925, he pointed out: "a managed currency is to be altogether avoided when the management is to be in the hands of the government". While there is less risk with monetary management by a private bank because "the penalty for imprudent issue or mismanagement is visited by disaster directly upon the property of the issuer". In the case of the government "the chance of mismanagement is greater" because the issue of money "is authorised and conducted by men who are never under any present responsibility for private loss in case of bad judgment or mismanagement", he argued. (ibid, p. 627).

Extra-academic writings on small holdings

Besides the above noted economic theses, which were written in fulfilment of the requirements of his academic degrees, Ambedkar had published a brilliant paper in 1918 during the interlude in his studentship, which was on the problem of small agricultural land holdings. The dominant opinion among the experts was that the small holdings were the main problem of Indian agriculture. Ambedkar considered the opinions of Prof. H. S. Jevons of Allahabad University, Harold Mann and G. F. Keatinge of Bombay, and the committee appointed to make proposals on the consolidation of small and scattered holdings in the Baroda State. All of them had offered solutions in terms of consolidation or preservation or both. Criticising their obsession for large holdings, Ambedkar scathingly observed that there was no such thing as an ideal size of economic holding. He wrote:

> *The mere size of land is empty of all economic connotations. Consequently, it cannot possibly be the language of economic science to say that a large holding is economic while a smallholding is uneconomic. It is the right or wrong proportion of other factors of production to a unit of land that renders the latter economic or uneconomic. Thus a small farm may be economic as well as a large farm; for, economic or uneconomic does not depend upon the size of land but upon the due proportion among all the factors including land.*
>
> (Govt. of Maharashtra, 1979, Vol. 1, p. 468)

Ambedkar actually brought in the concept of operations research that to see optimisation of inputs for maximising the productivity of land. He discussed, on the basis of data, how draught animals used for agriculture and other implement point towards sub-optimality. In his own word:

> *Given this state of affairs can we not say with more propriety that not only the existing equipment is inadequate for the enlarged holdings but that the existing holdings, small as they are, are too big for the available instruments of production other than land? Facts such as these interpreted in the light of our theory force upon us the conclusion that the existing holdings are uneconomic, not, however, in the sense that they are too small but that they are too large.*
>
> (ibid, p. 471)

He makes another economic observation differentiating capital and labour to put a finger at what ailed Indian economy. After observing that there was huge idle labour in Indian agriculture, he explained how it was eating into the vitals of Indian economy. He wrote,

> *Idle labour and idle capital differ in a very important particular. Capital exists, but labour lives. That is to say, capital when idle does not earn but does not also consume much to keep itself. But labour, earning or not, consumes in order to live. Idle . . . labour is, therefore, a calamity; for if it cannot live by production as it should, it will live by predation as it must. This idle labour has been the canker of India gnawing at its*

> *vitals. Instead of contributing to our national dividend it is eating up what little there is of it.*
>
> (ibid, p. 474)

He noted that while there was a massive population engaged with small plots of land as there were no alternate vocations in villages, there was an acute shortage of capital. He called them "superfluous and idle" employment, anticipating the concept of disguised unemployment introduced into the theory of underdevelopment by Rosenstein-Rodan in his famous 1943 article "Problems of Industrialisation in Eastern and Southern Europe". As a matter of fact, the term was first coined by Joan Robinson in 1936, who defined it as, "the adoption of inferior jobs by the workers laid off from their normal jobs due to lack of effective demand during the depression." Even then it was clearly 18 years before Robinson that Ambedkar pointed out that to be the bane of Indian economy. His propositions had striking similarities with the key insights of Nobel Prize-winning economist Arthur Lewis who formulated his famous two-sector model of the economy. Lewis presumed that developing economies had surplus and idle labour in the farm sector, and showed how transferring labour from farms to factories would raise savings and productivity levels in both sectors, leading to overall growth. No doubt, the model Lewis formulated in 1954 was far more elaborate than what Ambedkar outlined in his essay, but none can miss the essential similarities in them.

He proposes the remedy in the form of industrialisation, which would not only sponge off the surplus labour in villages but also provide much-needed capital. He writes:

> *If we succeed in sponging off this labour in non-agricultural channels of production, we will at one stroke lessen the pressure and destroy the premium that at present weighs heavily on land in India. Besides, this labour when productively employed will cease to live by predations it does to-day, and will not only earn its keep but will give us surplus: and more surplus is more capital. In short, strange though it may seem, industrialisation of India is the soundest remedy for the agricultural problems of India.*
>
> (ibid, p. 474)

Industrialisation, he envisaged would even "foster the enlargement of holdings and that it will be the most effective barrier against sub-division and fragmentation". He lamented the trend of de-industrialisation in India when other countries had made huge progress graduating from agriculture to manufacturing. He wrote:

> *"Figures for India, however, run counter to this dictum illustrating a universal tendency observed by an expert. While other countries like the*

> *U.S.A. starting as agricultural are progressively becoming industrial, India has been gradually undergoing the woeful process of de-urbanisation and swelling the volume of her rural population beyond all needs. The earlier we stem this ominous tide, the better. For notwithstanding what interested persons might say no truer and more wholesome words of caution were ever uttered regarding our national economy than those by Sir Henry Cotton when he said, "There is danger of too much agriculture in India."*
>
> (ibid, p. 479)

The relevance of this essay can never be overemphasised. Over the years, while the problem of small holdings continued and rather aggravated, Indian agriculture suffered many more problems during the post-colonial period. The government brought in a capitalist strategy of the green revolution to increase agricultural productivity but did not strategize to stave off its ill-impact in the long run. Although rich farmers benefitted from it hugely, even they could not manage the long run optimisation problem. The capitalist thrust entailed intensive cultivation of cash crops to the neglect of soil degradation. India's adoption of neoliberal policies which meant subjection of farmers to vagaries of global prices of agricultural inputs as well as output, coupled with persistent neglect of investment in agriculture created an endemic debt crisis for farmers that has been manifesting into a horrific phenomenon of farmers suicides in hundreds of thousands. Ambedkar's solution of industrialisation of labour-intensive industrialisation assumes far more importance in this context. "In short, strange though it may seem, industrialization of India is the soundest remedy for the agricultural problems of India," Ambedkar concluded. "The cumulative effects of industrialization, namely a lessening pressure (on land) and an increasing amount of capital and capital goods will forcibly create the economic necessity of enlarging the holding. Not only this, industrialization by destroying the premium on land will give rise to few occasions for its sub-division and fragmentation." He argued that the enlargement of landholdings by controlling the partition of immovable property and sale of consolidated holdings would create a small crust of wealthy landowners and a large mass of landless "paupers". Ambedkar would return to this theme in a 1927 speech made on the floor of the Bombay legislative assembly, which was debating a proposal for regulating landholdings.

States and minorities

The next prominent text under this category is the memorandum he wrote on behalf of his party, Scheduled Caste Federation, to the CA when there were no prospects for him to enter the latter. Unlike "Small Holdings", *States and Minorities* does not enunciate any economic principle and, in fact, is informed more by politics. Nonetheless, insofar as it proposed economic structure of the society, it deserves to be seen as the distillate of his economic philosophy. In it, Ambedkar proposed nationalisation of all agricultural lands and leasing them out to agricultural cooperatives of villagers. While the state would take over lands from landowners by compensating them with the equivalent value of debentures, redeemable in future, it would undertake responsibility of providing all necessary inputs for cultivation to the agriculture cooperatives against the charge that would be recovered from their produce. Besides land, the scheme contained state owning and operating all key and basic industries as also life insurance, which would be made compulsory for all citizens. The overall scheme he proposed vide Clause 4 of Article II of *States and Minorities* contained the following points:

- Agriculture shall be a state industry,
- Key and basic industries shall be owned and run by the state,
- Insurance policy shall be compulsory for every citizen and a monopoly of the state,
- The state shall acquire the subsisting rights in such industries, insurance and agricultural land held by private individuals,
- The state shall divide the land acquired into farms of standard size,
- The farm shall be cultivated as collective farms,
- The farms shall be cultivated in accordance with rules and directions issued by government,
- The tenants shall share among themselves the produce of the farm left after the payment of charges properly leviable on the farm, in the manner prescribed,
- The land shall be let out to villagers without distinction of caste or creed,
- There will be no landlord, no tenant and no landless labourer,
- The collective farms shall be distributed the water, draft animals, implements, manure, seeds etc.,
- The state shall be entitled to levy the following charges on the produce of the farms:
    - A portion for land revenue,
    - A portion to pay the debenture-holders,
    - Portion to pay for the use of capital goods supplied.

He urged the implementation of the above provisions as early as possible, so that the economic development of people and national development as a whole can be possible. It was a proposal of state socialism that he wanted the constituent assembly to incorporate into the Constitution.

This memorandum was prepared when he did not expect to get elected to the constituent assembly (CA). But when he actually did, he realised the impracticability of it. With the CA, being dominated by the propertied interests, he would not even propose it for discussion. As a matter of fact, he did refer to it while speaking on the Objective Resolution proposed by Jawaharlal Nehru, saying that the justice social, economic, and political could not be achieved without society's structure being socialist. However, in the very next sentence he gave it up. It was an impossible proposition in any society to change the economic structure through such dictum as it negates the existence of conflict of interests in the society. As the chairman of the drafting committee of the CA, he had an awkward responsibility of defending the decisions of such a majority. In one of the notable discussions in CA, Prof. K. T. Shah, (an alumnus of LSE, like him), proposed that the Indian constitution should adopt secularism and socialism, paradoxically, it was Ambedkar who repudiated saying that the directive principles, which would not even be justiciable were nothing but socialism. He said, "If these directive principles . . . are not socialistic in their direction and in their content, I fail to understand what more socialism can be".

Ideological anchors

The above provides a customary review of Ambedkar's economics. His views on economics, however, are not classifiable in customary silos and they seamlessly spill into his politics and vice versa. They cohere into a broad underlying concern for the poor and downtrodden people reflected in all his work. In his academic writings, there is a focus on administration of public finances by the state and recommendation of the currency system with which many apologists of free market economics project him as a monetarist and place him in the company of neoliberals like Rosa and Milton Friedman. Later, he proposed collectivisation and co-operatisation of agriculture which is still rooted in public policy domain but with entirely different focus. He saw agriculture as the sector that would generate surplus with which appropriate model of industrialisation could be promoted to sponge off surplus labour in the former and progressively optimise entire operations of the economy. And still later, he graduated to advocate state socialism as a logical extension of his thinking through democracy, which he conceived in terms of actualization of liberty, equality, and fraternity. He, however, would not accept Marxism because of his methodological infirmities, viz., reliance on violence and dictatorship, as he himself explicated (Buddha or Karl Marx) and would have no truck with the communists. Of course, he had converted to Buddhism, which act again was perhaps not devoid of economic considerations. He imagined that the Buddhist countries may rush in solidarity with their new coreligionists in the birthplace of their faith and lend them helping hand. Can this all be fitted into an ideological frame? The importance of this exercise is in creating a possibility of extrapolation of his thinking beyond his times as a future direction to the posterity. Otherwise, it would stay confined to its space and time, which may be of interest to historians but not to the followers. In the case of Ambedkar, this ideological frame can be easily discerned through the influences he imbibed during his intellectually formative days in Columbia. The biggest influencer, the debt of whom he would acknowledge as late as 1952, when he was himself counted among the living greats, was his professor John Dewey (Zelliot, 2013, p. 69). When Ambedkar visited Columbia University to receive an honorary doctorate conferred on him for writing India's constitution, he wrote to his wife, Dr. Savita Ambedkar,

> *there are many old friends who have gathered around me and [are] helping me in all sorts of ways. I was looking forward to meet[ing] Prof Dewey. But he died on the 2nd when our plane was in Rome . . . I am so sorry. I owe all my intellectual life to him. He was a wonderful man.*
>
> (Rattu, 1997, p. 35)

K.N. Kadam tells us that

> *"Dr. Ambedkar took down every word uttered by his great teacher [Dewey] in the course of his lectures; and it seems that Ambedkar used to tell his friends that, if unfortunately Dewey died all of a sudden, "I could reproduce every lecture verbatim".*
>
> (Kadam, 1997, p. 1)

Kadam further argues that "unless we understand something of John Dewey, one of Dr. Ambedkar's teachers at Columbia University, it would be impossible to understand Dr. Ambedkar" (ibid, 1997). This influence of pragmatism on Ambedkar from Dewey was so deep that Arun Mukherjee warns us against examining Ambedkar's thought "in isolation, without paying attention to his dialogue with Dewey." Also, Scott R. Stroud tells us that Ambedkar's pragmatism drew heavily on the 1908 'Ethics' written by Dewey and Tufts. [www.forwardpress.in/2018/01/ambedkars-pragmatism-drew-heavily-on-the-1908-ethics/]

Dewey was one of the progenitors of pragmatism.[12] "Pragmatism is a philosophical movement that includes those who claim that an ideology or proposition is true if it works satisfactorily, that the meaning of a proposition is to be found in the practical consequences of accepting it, and that unpractical ideas are to be rejected."[13] In a reductionist and somewhat simplistic way, it may mean, what works is right or still stretched, sans ideology. A pragmatist may back-justify their ideology when things worked. Dewey also was one of the earliest converts to American Fabianism[14] Among the early converts to Fabian socialism was Prof. John Dewey. He remained associated with Fabian institutions formed thereafter, such as, Rand School of Social Sciences, (1905) which was considered as Fabian equivalent of LSE, Intercollegiate Socialist Society (1907) and lastly, the League of Industrial Democracy, founded as America's Fabian Society, of which Dewey was president for life.

Fabian socialism was based on beliefs which were quite in variance with scientific socialism propounded by Marx. Fundamentally, it did not believe in the Marxian premise that history follows certain laws. Fabians believed that socialism could be achieved gradually (and not through revolution) by the enlightened classes (and not by the working class) by infiltration into colleges, the news media, religious groups, labour unions, business organizations, and other political parties (and not by smashing the state apparatus), as emancipation of land and industrial capital (and not by eliminating exploitation of labour). In the Fabian scheme, the 'infiltrated' state brought about socialism.[15] Through the influence of Dewey, Ambedkar also reflected pragmatic streaks and Fabian beliefs but with his "creative additions and communicative flavour" (Stroud, 2017). As Stroud observed, Ambedkar's pragmatism drew heavily on the 1908 'Ethics' by John Dewey and James Hayden Tufts (Stroud, 2018).

Ambedkar was not convinced about many a postulation of Marxism like its viewing human history as manifestation of matter. Although he himself spoke of material (economic) interests of man dominating other interests, he had reservation in accepting it as a theorem. While he accepted Marxism's goal of socialism, he was sceptical about achieving it through a 'violent' revolution. He thought that both the political and economic structure should be hard-coded into the constitution to translate the rule of 'one man, one vote' to the doctrine of 'one man, one value'. It was a creative departure from Fabian intervention but more impracticable than the latter as he himself experienced it. He had to be content with much of his radical provisions relegated to the Directive Principles of State Policy. His strategy of reservation for the Dalits and relatively high emphasis on higher education echoes the 'talented ten' proposition of WEB Dubois, another Fabien who championed the rights of African American in the US. It basically reflected the Fabian outlook that few people entering the state bureaucracy could change the character of the state vis-à-vis Dalits.

Conclusion

The conventional way to consider Babasaheb Ambedkar's economics is to identify such of his writings (and speeches) that has economic content in familiar terms. This approach however is utterly inadequate in the case of Ambedkar and of many others whose life was fraught with struggle. For instance, is Gandhi's politics or writings like Hind Swaraj devoid of economic content? One may lament that Ambedkar who had best academic credentials in economics could not devote his time to his academic pursuit. But I would argue that what he did contains far more economics than if he had focused on academic aspects. It is, therefore, I classified Ambedkar's work into academic and non-academic and reviewed it in somewhat familiar manner. But I contend that many of his thoughts and accomplishment are strewn with economic insights. For instance, none would class *Annihilation of Caste* as an economics treatise. But if one views caste as a distorter of market transactions, it may appear to hold forth profound economic sense. So also is the case of his conversion to Buddhism, that envisages ethical foundation to a sustainable society may be seen to possess particular economic vision. Future researchers on this topic may take this approach and read Ambedkar in new light.

The most unfortunate thing about Ambedkar is his misprojection, most times by his self-appointed followers. They are basically guilty of either completely sapping him of his economist identity or projecting him as a pro-capital, pro-market, pro-globalization economist. Ambedkar had elaborately argued against capitalism and saw unfettered capitalism turning into a force of oppression and exploitation. He argued that an economy based purely on the profit motive violated two tenets of political democracy: one, it allowed private employers, rather than the state, to govern the lives of individuals, and two, it may force an individual to give up his constitutional rights to gain a living. It was in this dilemma that he saw the state as an impartial arbiter between classes and not a coercive machine of the ruling classes. Moreover, it also prevented him from imagining equal treatment of mankind proposed by Marx. As he saw the state as a controller of the exploitative instincts of the powerful classes and protector of the interests of the powerless ones, he saw the utility of religion too as the ethical controller of inner instincts of humans. Both of them may be seen as based on absolutist but negative assumption about human nature. Human nature, after all, may be seen as the product of circumstances created by humans themselves.

Notes

1 B. R. Ambedkar and V. Moon (1979). *Dr. Babasaheb Ambedkar: Writings and Speeches*. "Ambedkar argued, against communists' belittling social and religious struggle, "Political revolutions have always been preceded by social and religious revolutions". See Govt. of Maharashtra. (1979). *Dr. Babasaheb Ambedkar: Writings and Speeches*, Vol. 1. Bombay.
2 B. R. Ambedkar, Buddha or Karl Marx in Vasant Moon (Comp.) (1987). *Babasaheb Ambedkar Writings and Speeches [BAWS]*, Vol. 3. Mumbai: Govt. of Maharashtra, p. 462.
3 S. Ambirajan (1999). Ambedkar's Contributions to Indian Economics. *Economic and Political Weekly*, 34(46/47), pp. 3280–3285.
4 His coursework during his three years (including summers) at Columbia consisted of: 29 courses in economics, 11 in history, 6 in sociology, 5 in philosophy, 4 in anthropology, 3 in politics, and 1 each in elementary French and German. Source: Office of the Registrar, Columbia University. www.columbia.edu/itc/mealac/pritchett/00ambedkar/timeline/1910s.html.
5 B. R. Ambedkar (1925). *Evolution of Provincial Finance in British India: A Study in the Provincial Decentralization of Imperial Finance*. London: PS King and Sons. This was the title of his thesis as submitted to Columbia University. It was later on published in the book form as per rules of the university with the title.
6 In Columbia University his guide was Edwin R. A. Seligman, McVickar Professor of Political Economy, and firmly placed as an authority in public finance and history of economic thought at that time. Later, he edited the monumental Encyclopaedia of Social Sciences published in the 1930s. In London School of Economics, he worked under the supervision of Prof. Edwin Cannon who was also an acknowledged authority on the history of economic thought. He was a critic of classical economics and an ally of interventionists, but moved sharply to

the side of classical liberalism in the early 20th century. He had emphasized the institutional foundation of economic systems.

7 B. R. Ambedkar (1989). *Writings and Speeches*. Education Department Government of Maharashtra, p. 329.

8 For his outstanding achievement, he was honoured by students and professors of the Faculty of Arts at a special dinner. www.columbia.edu/itc/mealac/pritchett/00ambedkar/timeline/1910s.html

9 J. C. H. Lobo (1983). *Dr. B.R. Ambedkar: The Champion of Social Democracy in India*. Bangalore: Hilerina Publications, p. 14.

10 Indian Public Finance Statistics 2015–2016, Ministry of Finance Department of Economic Affairs Economic Division. http://dea.gov.in/sites/default/files/IPFSper cent20Englishper cent202015–16.pdf.

11 A Keynesian Prototype Standard Solution. www.economist.com/briefing/2010/09/23/standard-solution.

12 John Dewey (1859–1952) was the third major figure in the classical pragmatist pantheon, whose wide-ranging writings had considerable impact on American intellectual life for a half-century.

13 Douglas McDermid, Internet Encyclopaedia of Philosophy, Internet Encyclopedia of Philosophy and its Authors, ISSN 2161-0002 (www.iep.utm.edu/pragmati/)

14 When Sidney Webb, one of the founders of the Fabian Society of England, visited the USA in 1988 on a lecture tour, he circulated his book "Socialism in England" among leading universities.

15 George Bernard Shaw unmasked this mind set of the Fabian movement in "The Intelligent Woman's Guide to Socialism and Capitalism": "under socialism, you would not be allowed to be poor. You would be forcibly fed, clothed, lodged, taught, and employed whether you liked it or not. If it were discovered that you had not character and industry enough to worth all this, you might possibly be executed in a kindly manner, but whilst you were permitted to live, you would have to live well."

References

Ambedkar, B. R. (1918). Small Holdings in India and their Remedies. *Journal of Indian Economic Society*, Vol. 1.

Ambedkar, B. R. (1925). *Evolution of Provincial Finance in British India: A Study in the Provincial Decentralization of Imperial Finance*. London: PS King and Sons. This was the title of his thesis as submitted to Columbia University. It was later on published in the book form as per rules of the university with the title.

Ambedkar, B. R. (1989). *Writings and Speeches*. Education Department Government of Maharashtra, p. 329.

Ambirajan, S. (1999). Ambedkar's Contributions to Indian Economics. *Economic and Political Weekly*, 34(46/47), pp. 3280–3285.

Govt. of Maharashtra. (1979). *Dr. Babasaheb Ambedkar: Writings and Speeches*, Vol. 1. Bombay.

Govt. of Maharashtra. (1987). *Dr. Babasaheb Ambedkar: Writings and Speeches*, Vol. 3. Bombay.

Govt. of Maharashtra. (1989). *Dr. Babasaheb Ambedkar: Writings and Speeches*, Vol. 6. Bombay.

Indian Public Finance Statistics 2015–2016, Ministry of Finance Department of Economic Affairs Economic Division. http://dea.gov.in/sites/default/files/IPFSper cent20Englishper cent202015–16.pdf.

Kadam, K. N. (1997). *The Meaning of the Ambedkarite Conversion to Buddhism and Other Essays*. Popular Prakashan.

Lobo, J. C. H. (1983). *Dr. B.R. Ambedkar: The Champion of Social Democracy in India*. Bangalore: Hilerina Publications, p. 14.

Rattu, N. C. (1997). *Last Few Years of Dr. Ambedkar*. Amrit Publishing House.

Stroud, S. R. (2017). The Like-Mindedness of Dewey and Ambedkar. *Forward Press*, by and for India's Aspiring Millions, The Marginalised Prakashan, New Delhi. https://www.forwardpress.in/2017/05/john-dewey-pragmatism-communication-and-bhimrao-ambedkar/

Stroud, S. R. (2018). Ambedkar's Pragmatism Drew Heavily on the 1908 'Ethics'. *Forward Press*, by and for India's Aspiring Millions, The Marginalised Prakashan, New Delhi. https://www.forwardpress.in/2018/01/ambedkars-pragmatism-drew-heavily-on-the-1908-ethics/

Teltumbde, A. (2017). *B. R. Ambedkar, India and Communism*. Introduction by Anand Teltumbde. New Delhi: LeftWord Books.

Zelliot, E. (2013). *Ambedkar's World: The Making of Babasaheb and the Dalit Movement*. Navayana Publishing.

5 Ambedkar's anti-caste ideology and the making of a nation

R. Thirunavukkarasu

Colonial rule and caste in India

> Indeed if the British rule has achieved anything in India, it is to strengthen and reinvigorate Brahmanism.[1]

Understanding India indeed requires a thorough understanding of caste and it is also equally true of the vice versa. When the Portuguese traveller Vasco de Gama finally had triumphed landing on the west coast of the Indian subcontinent through sea route, a new era began. That was not just an arrival of a European traveller to India. It was an opening up of a closed continent to the European colonizers. No doubt, it laid the foundation for a new phase in global trade and eventually to colonialism. It was a new era not only for the native Indians, but also for the European rulers. What the Europeans had constructed of Indian subcontinent based on their own social imaginaries, began to shape later to alter natives' opinion about themselves.[2]

European colonizer ushered in a paradigm shift in the Indian subcontinent. It was certainly not an exaggeration to declare that European colonizers brought along with them certain basic institutional values of European modernity as well. Indian subcontinent slowly but steadily began to embrace modernity. This process however was not a simple one. Colonial rule was not merely a sign of shame or servitude for the Indians. It had actually provided avenue for the natives to interact and embrace and adapt themselves to institutional modernity and its values. While recognizing that there was no uniformity in natives' response to and adapting the values of colonial modernity, it is a pertinent fact that natives in their own peculiar and unique ways did respond to this new era.

Conventional sociological analysis on social change would depict the events during colonialism as mere transition from tradition to modernity. While concurring with the fact that there was a transition from tradition to modernity, the transition however was not uniform across the subcontinent; oversimplified, ahistorical approach is quite insensitive to 'regional' variations which are extremely vital to understand the issues. Similarly, the classical Marxist approach delineates the changes through different conceptual category: that the Indian subcontinent underwent a change from feudalism to the incipient stages of capitalism.

Perhaps even in highly differentiated not hierarchized social structure where cultural practices remain subservient to economic dominance, classical Marxist class-determinism is often identified as inadequate theoretical proposition. In fact, what Karl Marx has elaborated in his journalistic writings on Indian society during the colonial period, would give us a clear picture. He says, 'England has to fulfill a double mission in India: One destructive and the other regenerating – annihilation of old Asiatic society and the laying of the material foundations of western society in Asia.'[3] The resonance of this proposition is found in Indian Marxist scholars who have accomplished remarkable works though, but could not move beyond the restricted framework of class analysis or mode of production.[4]

The metamorphosis of caste and the dawn of new ideology

It is pertinent to historicize the trajectory of caste over the years as it would help us comprehend the changing nature of caste especially under colonialism. The relationship between caste and the political establishment or the state in the pre-colonial old regime had been one of the highly contested terrains. It was now conclusively established that until the emergence of British colonial rule especially in southern India, the political establishment namely the crown was not as hollow as it has been made out to be in Indian history in general and comparative sociology in particular. Kings were not inferior to Brahmins; the political domain was not encompassed by a religious domain. State or the political establishments were powerful elements in Indian civilization. Indian society and caste were indeed shaped by political struggles and processes.

While stressing on a conceptual category-political, it is necessary to remind ourselves of the intriguing relation between ritual and political forms in Indian context. The rationale for such a caveat arises out of the fact that ritual and political forms were often fundamentally same. However, it is not inappropriate to stress the 'political' for both to redress the previous emphasis on 'religion' and to underscore the social fact that caste structure, ritual form and political process were all dependent on relations of power. These relations were constituted in and through history; and these relations were culturally constructed. But this cultural construction took place in the context of the British colonial, in which caste constructed as the religious basis of Indian society, a cultural form that became viewed as a specifically Indian form of civil society.[5] It is therefore not an exaggeration to state that colonialism purposefully altered many of the forms of old regimes and yet preserved some of them. But certain forms were frozen and only the appearances of the old regime – without its vitality connected political and social processes – were saved. What has come to be known as modern Indian tradition is indeed the construction of colonialism itself, including an autonomous caste structure with the brahmin clearly and unambiguously occupying the top in the hierarchy, village based systems of exchange, isolated ceremonial residues of the old regime state and fetishistic competition for ritual goods that no longer played a vital role in the political system, asserts Nicholas Dirks.[6] It is quite evident now that a new socio-cultural landscape was meticulously constructed to serve the colonial regime. The privileging of Brahmanical supremacy in the new religio-ritual structure precipitated to a great extent the strengthening of the imperial rule in Indian subcontinent. Colonial intervention had paid enthusiastic attention in removing politics from colonial societies; it was not merely convenient for the British to detach caste from politics. It was necessary for them to do so in order to rule an immensely complex society by a variety of indirect means; but caste lived on without its political context. In this disembodied form, caste was appropriated and reconstructed by the British.

The 1857 uprising against the Company Raj left profound restlessness among the British and that had led them to take further stringent punitive action against the agitating locals. The British became highly determined to subdue all remaining low-status caste groups including wandering groups. It apparently became a matter of great urgency and vital importance for the British. By the mid-19th century, the colonial regime preferred to ensure peaceful, settled village society under the strict supervision of conservative landed elite as the 'order' and 'peace' became their paramount concern if regime had to continue. This administrative compulsion led to the dawn of structural adjustment with the landed elites; initially a tacit approval for their locally endowed status and honour and later a full-fledged administrative patronage for their localized power centre became the hallmark of the colonial regime. However, one of an enduring impact of the colonial policies was the differentiation of 'martial races' from 'criminal tribes'. All those agitating communities who were first purged and subsequently neutralized of their social honour were effectively declared criminal tribes with strict punitive measures taken against them.[7]

During the incipient stages of the colonial rule, like many other parts of the subcontinent, South Indian in general and Madras presidency in particular also had advanced feudalism and complex economic activities. This would obviously result in the emergence of highly unequal and strictly hierarchical distribution of power within the social structure. In other words, ascriptive status had effectively dictated norms and rules for both inter personal and inter community interactions. Ascriptive hierarchy and unequal distribution of power in India is best known as caste system. The caste system is a unique organizing principle in the subcontinent and had been surviving majorly with the patronage from religious dogma and endogamous marriage system and by strictly adhering to segmented occupation based on birth. This broader parameter about caste system has been truly a pan-Indian phenomenon. However, its spread, internal structure and its methods of maintaining framework had been uneven and varied from one region to the other.

The Indian subcontinent began to slowly capitulate to a new wave of social, cultural, economic and political upheaval from the time the British traders turned rulers brought in formidable changes in every aspect of Indian life. This change was in unambiguous term could well be described as the beginning of modernity in the subcontinent. A new world view quite antithetical to the hitherto existing native perception of self and community evolved. The birth of a modern mind would be the most significant corollary of colonialism in India. A word of caution and perhaps a caveat is needed right here – modern mind does not certainly presuppose colonialism for its genesis nor that the end of colonialism in anyway ensured the completion of this process at least in India. Colonial rule precipitated the birth of a modern mind and with its own peculiarities the subcontinent reshaped it according to its convenience.

What is a modern mind and what makes him/her what he/she is? This question obviously would lead us to certain inevitable controversies and almost no one enters on a discussion without arousing a good deal of emotion. Transcending the traditional values either in part or in total could well mean that something new has evolved – this could mean that someone has given up his own unique and particular way of thinking and feeling that could go back decades sometimes even centuries; and to abandon these ways often seems to be abandoning principle itself. The characteristic mark of the modern mind has two parts – one internal, the other external; one dealing with his/her environment, the other with his/her attitudes, values and feelings.[8] The external characters have already been well documented in terms of urbanization, industrialization, education and mass communication. The focus here is about the internal character. The emergence of the Individual over the collective; the invention of individual self as a self-conscious political being and his/her location in the new cultural and social landscape as a rational being endowed with all natural rights to be an active agent of new social order is the indicator. Individual as 'empirical agent' exists in India as everywhere, yet because of Hindu culture stresses collective identities over those of individual and individual achievement, which is a measure of individuality, has been overlooked and sometimes out rightly rejected as a cause of history and social order.[9]

It is true that Dumont was not the first one to hold this view that in Indian social structure, individual remains subservient to the collective; long ago, Max Weber described Indian social structure as epitome of collective identities.[10] However, it was Dumont's description about Indian social structure that paved way for a long debate over the location of individual in Indian social structure.[11] For Dumont what distinguishes Indian from the West is that its organization and continuity is founded on a principle of religious hierarchy that order the society as a whole, submerging the individual within the collectivity. The orientation of Indian society is towards the collective whole. Each 'particular man in his place must contribute to the global order.[12] Reflecting this, the values of equality and liberty, which support Western style individualism are absent from traditional thinking and individuality is submerged in holistic/collectivist identities.[13]

Therefore, for Dumont it is inappropriate to analyze Indian society from the point of Individualism. The absence of 'Individual/Individualism' symbolizes the character of non-modern or traditional social character of Indian society. The traditional India, says Dumont, lacks the economic market instead Indian society is integrated by a distributive economy which is a sort of cooperative economy, where the main aim is *to ensure the subsistence of everyone in accordance with his social function*. In the final analysis traditional Indian society is a *hierarchical collectivity integrated by interdependence derived from a caste based division of labour that is itself derived from religion*.[14]

This hierarchical character of the non-modern Indian social structure arguably should have been transformed into a liberal-democratic social fabric; in other words a modern society must have emerged wherein individualism remains the nucleus and equality becomes non-negotiable ethos of its everyday life. On the contrary, as it was delineated above, the hierarchical character of the Indian society reconfigured during the British regime to be more rigid in its character.

David Washbrook in his unerring observation notes that the simultaneity of peasantization of economy and Brahminization of culture was the hallmark of colonial regime. Peasantization of economy was the primary focus and greed of the British for its exorbitant revenue, the same also constituted the nurturing environment for the growth of social relational Brahmanism.[15] In other words, in concert with the Brahminization of caste ideology, taking place during colonial regime, had created a context in which vast majority of subaltern masses became culturally as well as socially the Shudras or unclean humans denigrated to sub human location in the changing social order; this caste society in the later 19th and early 20th centuries became the tradition and cultural epithet of modern India. The instruments of 'capitalist' modernization and of Indian 'tradition' had combined perfectly to produce for the property holding castes particularly to the Brahmins of colonial India the much needed supremacy and dominance.[16]

While concurring with the fact that the subcontinent in general and South India in particular underwent radical changes at social, cultural and economic realm, the nature of change in caste system as a social order encountered was enormous. It is highly naïve to argue that caste never existed before colonial era; but what we have today as a social system and an instrument of organizing social order caste is indeed a product of colonialism. The British regime with its administrative initiatives, legal instruments reshaped caste system into a modern phenomenon. In addition to the efforts of the colonial regime, Orientalist scholars, Christian missionaries had rendered adequate conceptual insights to shape caste system to assume the character of a modern phenomenon. In other words, caste became a single term capable of expressing, organizing and above all systematizing India's diverse forms of social identity, community and organization during the British regime.[17]

Quite similar to the changes which altered the character of pre-colonial social structure, the new pedagogical enterprise introduced by the British to a great extent replicated a highly hierarchical social structure in the modern era also. There is a grand consensus among almost all scholars of Indian nationalism that the biggest and highest beneficiaries of the modern education were the upper castes particularly the Brahmins in almost all parts of the subcontinent. Anil Seal has noted this fact persuasively; he describes how in Bengal 'it was the brahmins, kayasthas and baidyas, in Bombay the brahmins in solitary, perilous pre-eminence and so too in Madras held the near monopoly of education and that they were not any new class but just the same old wine in new bottles' for 'yesterday's scholars of Persian now became enthusiasts for English'.[18]

Thomas Macaulay – the chief architect and the principal protagonist of modern education system in the subcontinent stated his actual intention while proposing his education policy – to create 'a class who may be interpreters between us and the millions whom we govern'; it was intended to be applicable in administrative arena also. Colonial regime's well established obsession to maximize revenue to a great extent converged with the interests of not only caste elites but also with the newly emerged literary groups in terms of secular interests.[19] In the newly established state administrative set up, the products of the new education system jelled and crystallized well. By the end of 19th century, what the modern education had created was no different from the pre-colonial monopoly of literary knowledge by ritually high-ranking castes of course suitably altered by the collaborators. In fact, the colonial rulers were at one point under intense pressure not to vernacularize education from beneficiaries of modern English education.[20] Contrary to the popular wisdom that 'modern-English' education would annihilate irrational, ascriptive identities and would help the subcontinent masses to emerge as locale of equality turned out to be a charade. On the other hand, the new education system was utilized to remodel miniscule elite into 'imitation Englishmen' with the same notions of ascriptive and hierarchical character.[21]

Elusive equality: the newly etched landscape

The most striking feature in spite of its inter-regional variations is that those who are atop in the hierarchy across the India remain the brahmins. M. N. Srinivas has summed up quite categorically,

> caste is undoubtedly an all-India phenomenon in the sense that there are everywhere hereditary, endogamous groups which form a hierarchy . . . everywhere there are Brahmins, untouchables and peasants, artisan, trading and service castes. Relations between castes are invariably expressed in terms of pollution and purity. Certain Hindu theological ideas such as *samskara, karma and dharma* are woven into the caste

> system . . . as the ordering of different varnas is clearly intended to support the theory of brahminical supremacy.[22]

Therefore, it would be correct and appropriate to arrive at a conclusive statement that caste system particularly the ideological manifestation had pervaded the entire subcontinent in varying degrees. It is equally appropriate to declare that a near organic and symbiotic relationship between religious order and its symbolism, mythologies especially temples as vital power centres cum institutions had indeed sustained the caste system to remain active and alive. This effectively means the dynamic functions of ascriptive hierarchy where one caste – Brahmins remains atop with other upper castes collaborating with them had created what is called a social cohesion.[23]

Expectedly the much adored social cohesion was deemed to be the essential ingredient for any ruler to establish his/her political/power supremacy. The subcontinent displays interesting picture of cultural/social structure remains reasonably independent when the political establishment retains its autonomy. Yet, the sanctions and mutual patronage between socio-cultural structure and political establishment had been highlighted as one of the salient features of the subcontinent's history.[24] Several political uncertainties – inherent character of oriental despotic context, to a great extent maintained cautious distance from the basic tenants of caste system. However, recently published nuanced studies point out that political agency did play a vital role subsuming the power of caste elites.[25] However, several studies undertaken by several scholars in different disciplinary realm have unambiguously proved the nature and character of the political establishment in a highly hierarchical social order like that of the Indian society. The kingly system of political structure in the pre-colonial era had several limitations and restrictions for the kings in terms of specific ways.[26]

While recognizing variations from the dominant caste ideology at micro level at many parts of the subcontinent, one can strongly afford to believe that by and large caste system as an ideology and a single most powerful organizing principle had knitted Indian socio-cultural rubric. Hence, if it is caste system that unites and offers a pan-Indian picture, there are innumerable anti-caste movements in different forms and content had emerged from various parts of the subcontinent at different times. Starting from Buddhism and Jainism both at the pan-Indian level and at localized levels, there were several anti-caste movements in general and anti-Brahmanical movement in particular. Therefore, while accepting caste system as a pan-Indian phenomenon, it is absolutely necessary to recognize the powerful anti-caste, anti-hierarchical character of many parts.

It has become abundantly comprehensible that colonial regime had crafted new modes of cultural interaction and economic activities by effectively freezing the flexibilities available within caste hierarchy in the pre-colonial era. A near perfect enmeshing of British greed for revenue and Brahmanical supremacy had resulted in a milieu which has ironically been characterized as modern. In the process of India becoming 'modern,' caste had effectively become an instrument of governance and singular identity. The depiction of M. N. Srinivas is quite self-evident of the changing character,[27]

> the brahmin writers on law propounded a model caste system which placed them on the top and gave them the privilege of declaring the duties of the other castes; the institution which prevailed till 1864, of attaching brahmin pundits to the British established law courts, the presence in every town of a body of western educated lawyers who tried to apply Brahmanical law to all Hindus. The translation of a vast mass of sacred literature from Sanskrit into English, the rise everywhere of 'caste sabhas' which tried to introduce reforms by Sanskritizing the way of life of their respective castes and the *growth of a vigorous anti-brahmin movement which attempted to displace brahmins from the position of power and influence.*

Anti-caste movements: the beginning of a new political discourse

The forcefully muted rebellion in 1857 against the East India Company rule and the subsequent direct rule of the British imperial government was indeed a turning point in the subcontinent's history. While maximizing revenue remained common to both, the direct British rule reshaped administrative character of the Indian society. The British found it very important to reach out to the interior parts especially into the vast rural areas to have total grip over India. One of the powerful and highly nuanced modes operandi adopted by the British to accomplish their drive to reach out to the rural masses was the very effectively and highly successfully method of vivisecting the organic association between local political patronage and caste. For the sustenance of caste as a system, the hitherto existing political patronage was effectively neutralized and Brahmanical oligarchy had been patronized to be the sanctioning authority. By virtue of this transformation the well-known agrarian economy was turned into caste feudalism with Brahminic ideology.[28] The resentment was quite profound and palpable across the subcontinent. If 19th century was to be considered the age of Brahminization of culture, rise of agitation politics and invention of new anti-Brahminic tradition became the hallmark of later 19th and early 20th century. If conventional wisdom and historiography depicts the last half a century of colonial rule as 'Indian awakening against the British rule', a critical sociological probing would help us declare this period as the 'era of anti-caste and anti-Brahmanism'.

What is more important to assess here would be the relentless struggle for justice and equality against caste oppression by the subjugated masses. The modes operandi had been perhaps unique and acquired its own peculiar style and structure. Nevertheless, the striking feature is the anti-caste or anti-Brahmin character intrinsically embedded in all these movements.

In general, three major dimensions emerge as social facts during the last six decades of colonial regime in India: an agitational politics and mass mobilization against caste system or/and Brahmanical social order; attempts were made sporadically to escape and flee from the Brahminism based caste hierarchy; virulent struggle against caste based land relations.

A comprehensive mapping exercise would help us grasp the overall picture of the subcontinent – it would be unambiguously an era of revolts, protests and desperation for change against caste feudalism and Brahmanical ideology. Plethora of protests and struggles against the old social order with varying degree, intensity and spread has swept across the subcontinent in different types and nomenclatures. In fact, M. N. Srinivas in his unusual aphoristic style exclaimed that 'it was as though they suddenly woke up to the fact that they did no longer inhabit a prison'.[29]

Similarly, one would find a relentless quest to reinvent one's own tradition and cultural past as a common feature of almost every social movement. A strikingly unique feature in these movements is the urgency to redefine each cultural community's identity; it is usually as superior status with mythological origin followed by concerted action to get the new identity officially and socially recognized. Furthermore, a search for an egalitarian, non-hierarchical cultural-religious framework either through a rediscovery of the different forms of non-Brahmanical Hinduism or by forsaking the whole of Hinduism itself or rarely by taking to atheistic rationalist ideologies would have been the hallmark of these movements.[30]

Another important feature of these movements remains their appeal and urge to establish a new form of camaraderie whose membership extended to the broadest possible understanding and definition of caste – maximizing the space and scope for horizontal solidarity. This is undoubtedly antagonistic both in content and structure vis-à-vis the old social order of the pre modern era which was exclusivist, endogamous and vertical social structure. It is certainly not a misnomer to state that the seeds for a nascent form of progressive civility were sown during this tumultuous moment in history.

A closer look at the history of the subcontinent during the turn of 20th century, one would come across several strong resistances emerging from several communities; similarly, several scholars/leaders played seminal role in determining the nature and dynamics of the anti-caste/anti-Brahmanical hegemony. Dr. Ambedkar has been designated rightfully so as the chief architect of India's constitution. His vital contributions in the making of India as a nation remain to be explored. India as a political entity eternally owes to Ambedkar for his extraordinary contribution as the father of its constitution; but his thoughts and insights for India-to-be-a-nation process requires a thorough delineation.

Ambedkar and anti-caste ideology

Quite akin to the recent refreshing debates initiated by several leading scholars like Benedict Anderson (1983) and Ernest Gellner (1983) on nation and nationalism, well over half a century ago Ambedkar proposed the contours of the same. Careful reading of Ambedkar's writings would help us understand the intensity of his arguments which defy many conventional wisdom and popular opinion on nation and nationalism. When almost all his contemporaries in the political realm virtually endorsed the 'external' dimension of nation/nationalism, Ambedkar delineated the limits of privileging the 'external' dimension in defining nation. More so, he unambiguously cautioned the ever enlarging dangers of simply designating a territory as mother land; and deeply apprehensive of the Eurocentric understanding of one nation-one language and one religion to be emulated as a viable model for India.

Ambedkar insisted that a nation indeed requires certain fundamental changes in social and relational orientation and he squarely latched his faith that the dawn of this new orientation must lead to the genesis of new consciousness among the members of the new community. Ambedkar totally rejected the idea that the old social order cannot be refurnished and offered as nation; instead, he declared if a community is to be designated as 'national', there must be some fundamental structural changes must have been initiated and institutionalized. Similarly, he has also cautioned us the likely consequences of conflating citizenship with membership of a national community. Well before the arrival of advance theorizations on issues such as citizenship, Ambedkar had unambiguously declared that why it is necessary to unravel the organic relationship among citizenship, nationality and social justice. In other words, it is not being rather 'becoming a nation' as a socio-cultural-political category occupies a vital position in Ambedkar's arguments.

> without social union, political unity is difficult to be achieved. If achieved, it would be as precarious as a summer sapling, liable to be uprooted by the gust of a hostile wind. With mere political unity India may be a State. *But to be a state is not to be a nation and a State which is not a nation.*[31]

The unerring observation and a profound assessment by Ambedkar elucidates that any attempt to conflate state with nation is not only a historical fallacy but would effectively prevent all of us inventing a nation itself. This sanity in terms of conceptual understanding had actually emboldened him to probe what *ought* to be a nation.

Nation as like-mindedness – Ambedkar's assessment

The birth of a nation would not simply be the result of an encounter between two monoliths – insiders and outsiders. In the case of India, it was not merely the encounter between the colonial rule and the local protests would effortlessly result in the advent of nation. As it has been mentioned earlier here, the natives' response has been a complex one. A dispassionate scrutiny would clearly prove that the natives' resistance wasn't a homogenous one and more so its contours were quite complex. Resorting to a highly reductionist perspective that the 'natives' were a homogenous community was not only a historical fallacy but deeply a flawed framework too. In a heightened hierarchical social order, it would be unwise and premature to expect a uniformity of resistance from the natives'. Ambedkar's assessment of the necessary and highly pertinent structural modifications as a non-negotiable prerequisite keeps him apart from many of his contemporaries.

Ambedkar was acutely aware of the dichotomy as well as the imminent danger of being accused as stooge of the colonial raj. The anti-colonial stand he took revolves around his fathomless commitment to both social and political democracy.

> an ideal society should be mobile, should be full of channels for conveying a change taking place in one part to other parts. In an ideal society, there should be many interests consciously communicated and shared. There should be varied and free points of contact with other modes of association. In other words, there should be social endosmosis. This is fraternity which is only another name for democracy. Democracy is not merely a form of government. It is primarily a mode of associated living of conjoint communicated experience. It is an essentially an attitude of respect and reverence towards fellowmen.[32]

One would perhaps unwittingly end up attributing a highly ecclesiastical notion while having a cursory look at Ambedkar's words like respect and reverence towards fellowmen; however, these are moral statements to begin with and subsequently quintessentially political declarations. The purpose and mandate of both social and political democracy is to invent a self-conscious political being which in turn forms the nucleus of a nation asserts Ambedkar. A much nuanced declaration of his ideas in this regard would help us comprehend his vision towards the idea of a nation itself.

> a democratic form of government presupposes a democratic form of society. The formal framework of democracy is of no value and indeed be a misfit if there was no social democracy. It may not be necessary for a democratic society to be marked by unity by community of purpose by loyalty to public ends and by mutuality of sympathy. But it does unmistakably involve two things – the first is an attitude of mind, an attitude of respect and equality towards their fellows. The second is a social organization free from rigid social barriers. Democracy is incompatible and inconsistent with isolation and exclusiveness resulting in the distinction between the privileged and the unprivileged.[33]

Thus, the 'social' is as important as the 'political'; in other words, the social indeed determines the nature of the political itself. For him, it is quite naïve to say that a nation becomes/adopts a democratic polity. A nation itself is a democratic community hence inevitably ends up in democratic polity; one cannot conclusively or authentically confirm the vice versa. A conglomeration people must necessarily undergo a metamorphosis at the socio-cultural realm. The paradigm shift towards inventing a nation begins here declares Ambedkar. In order to achieve this transition, a sense of togetherness or culturally sanctioned/socially approved similarity must be evolved. Here Ambedkar is quite forthright in both identifying and analyzing the lacuna.

> The significant fact about the Hindus is that before they are Hindus they are members of some caste. The castes are so exclusive and isolated that the consciousness of being a Hindu would be the chief guide of a Hindu's activity towards non-Hindu. But as against a Hindu of a different caste his caste consciousness would be the chief guide of activity. From this, it is plain that as between two Hindus, caste like-mindedness is more powerful than the like-mindedness due to their both being Hindus.[34]

Thus, the vertical social order – caste hierarchy requires to be dismantled in order to achieve the transition which subsequently ensures the birth of a nation asserts Ambedkar. While identifying major obstacles towards realizing the like-mindedness, Ambedkar has been quite categorical in his assessment about Indian village structures. Contrary to what Mahatma Gandhi insisted in one of his letters to Jawaharlal Nehru that 'for me India begins and ends in the villages,'[35] Ambedkar resolutely rejected any romantic ideas about villages in India.

Villages in the Indian subcontinent had been a perennial social-cultural-economic and political category. However, reinventing the villages as no less than 'republics' was indeed the construction of the colonial administrators. Ronald Inden was quite forthright in saying that many civilizations especially Asia and Africa have villages as a vital unit of their socio-economic and political structure it was in India that villages have been constructed as essential aspect.[36] While Mahatma Gandhi remained all along in his life an ardent admirer and an advocate of village, Ambedkar found no reason to celebrate village-based world view. His contempt for villages is deeply stemmed from his foundational philosophy of establishing a modern-rational-nation. As he has in his unerring observation said, 'I hold that these village republics have been the ruination of India; what is the village but a sink of localism, a den of ignorance, narrow-mindedness and communalism'.[37]

A highly localized and parochial affiliation coupled with formidable caste loyalties, Ambedkar believed would be quite detrimental in achieving the 'nation' in India.

> If India has not succeeded in producing nationalism, if India has not succeeded in building up a national spirit, the chief reason for that in my opinion is the existence of the village system. It made all people saturated with local patriotism. It left no room for larger civic spirit none whatever.[38]

Therefore, it is more of a civic union among members of a supra-community that would ensure the birth of a nation, advocates Ambedkar. He further asserts that nationality is a social feeling. It is feelings of a corporate sentiment of oneness which makes those who are charged with it feel that they are kith and kin. It was not only a comradeship in terms of political rights or citizenship. It must be, for him, more of a socio-cultural entity. That's why he very strongly advocated nation as a 'feeling of conscious-of-a-kind' which on the other hand binds together those who have it.[39] Therefore, for him fighting against caste especially Brahmanical supremacy is an imperative to establish a nation.

Dismantling Brahminism as prerequisite for nation: Ambedkar's analysis

Thus, a highly hierarchical social order becomes antithetical to the very realization of national feeling, according to Ambedkar. Therefore, anti-caste/anti-brahmin movements precipitated the birth of caste based mobilization subsequently upward social mobility within the newly evolved social order. Hereditary based occupation which was the quintessential feature of the old era began to crumble with the dawn of modernity. And with the birth of new social order wherein the hitherto existing subjugated masses revolted against the ascriptive ideology and heredity based occupation. Strong rebuttal to ascriptive ideology and caste based occupation had indeed paved the way for a new social context wherein for the first time social mobility and anonymity became the key characteristic features. Here it is pertinent to draw inspiration from Ernest Gellner who strongly endorses profound social change, anonymity and social mobility as important social ingredients for a nation to emerge.[40] In fact, caste based mobilization was found to be prudent and sustainable method of attaining upward social mobility during the new era. In the newly emerged system caste identity became the metaphorical currency to negotiate with the state apparatus for distribution of resources.

With the advent of colonialism and its intellectual companion Orientalism, the Brahmanical ascendency became unified, adopted to modern ways of ruling and eventually constituted the structure as well as culture of the entire politically unified subcontinent through the emergence medium of tradition and custom particularly political Hinduism.[41] The Indian Empire had already become a *de facto* Hindu/brahmin Raj by the time the East India Company rule ended; it became increasingly so under the British crown.[42] The transformational cusp is delineated with more nuances by Susan Bayly; to quote her,

> there were still in the 18th century powerful ideologies working against hierarchy and rigid caste boundaries. In the early 19th century however, the spirit of hierarchy and ritual distinction became more pervasive. The British peace speeded the rise of high Hindu kingship, brahminism and the advance of principles of purity and pollution in the country

> side. The brahmin interpretation of Hindu society which was theoretical rather than actual over much of India as late as 1750 was firmly ensconced a century later.[43]

By the end of 19th century and the beginning of 20th century, the revitalization and aggrandizement of the Brahmin and Brahmanical supremacy within practically all spheres of the new political economy; the ascendency of Brahmanical imaginary concerning the unity, organic nature, religiosity of the subcontinent through the new and renewed social discourse on 'Hinduism'; as Chris Fuller pointedly states that the dream of *Manu*, the author of *Manusmriti* became a reality for the first time in the 19th century.[44] With the taking over of subcontinent's administration, the Royal pledge to bring in equality of opportunity seemed to be a paradigm shift from the colonial regime's time tested policy of non-interference. The fact that the reinvigorated Brahmanical middle class refused to be party to the 1857 upsurge, the British Royal administration became sensitive to the dangers of unconditional modesty and dependency over the Brahmanical collaborators.[45] The colonial masters increasingly became receptive to the restlessness among vast majority of subaltern, non-Brahmin masses over Brahmanical supremacy. In this context, it is pertinent scrutinize the character of what came to be known as 'Indian Nationalism'.

The Imperialists' attempts to include non-Brahmin, subaltern masses into a sphere of power sharing had indeed triggered petulant and knee-jerk reaction from the upper echelon of the new social order. It was quite unlikely that the British intensions were highly driven by their commitment to liberty and equality. It could be even be charade to subdue the subaltern masses from organizing themselves against the Raj. Anil Seal's observation is quite sharp, 'for all their (British Raj and the brahmins) squabbles among themselves, they still had a common interest in preventing these *arrivistes* from arriving'.[46] The fact remains quite vivid that anti-colonialism *per se* does not constitute nationalism.[47] Therefore, not only the British administration's scheming efforts to 'contain' any agitational mobilization by the subaltern masses, the Brahmanical elites also with the same impulse regrouped to neutralize similar efforts from non-Brahmin masses. This is resulted in the conflation of Brahminism with Hinduism in colonial regime; this version of Hinduism became resurgent and politically salient.[48] It was truly a tumultuous moment in the history of the Indian subcontinent – a new unequal power structure in cultural terms had successfully been established. The power elites of the new social and political organization – upper echelon of the caste system, however, began to face innumerable revolts and protests. Any sensitive mind can effortlessly gauge how the caste elites had succeeded in quelling those protests for good. If socio-religious reform movements on the one hand attempted to ease the revolt and agitational character of the subaltern masses against the Brahmanical social structure, on the other hand, a highly nuanced political discourse began to sweep across the subcontinent. It was through a highly sophisticated process of accommodation, unification and empowerment through imperial patronage, brahmins along with few other upper castes knitted pan-Indian political national Hinduism. Caste ideology was adequately reshaped to suit the modern requirements of the state. The new political Hinduism was at once Brahmanical as well as national. Nationalism and nationalist consciousness was the context in which the ideology of sacred and secular hierarchy transformed itself into the new political Hinduism. In fact, Hans Kohn has persuasively elaborated this point, 'religious renaissance in India became a source of renewed strength of Hindu orthodoxy. All these movements finally merged in India's new consciousness of her unity and her mission in Indian nationalism'.[49]

A new discourse of 'Hinduism' emerged and 'Indian Nationalists' voluntarily became its patrons and protagonists. An aggressive campaign in defense of 'Hinduism' thus enunciated as part of 'Nationalism'. Any individual or group disagreed or sought to deviate from the above mentioned version of Hinduism – Indian Nationalism found themselves to be in precarious position as either being branded as anti-national or as a British stooge. It is equally true that anti-colonial struggle passively facilitated this trajectory rather than ensuring the arrival of rational, secular public sphere at the end of colonialism.[50] In other words, nationalism in the Indian subcontinent both as an ideology and as a movement sought to preserve status-quo and pleaded for exclusive privileges for the upper echelon of the caste hierarchy in the modern era.

Ambedkar's nationalism: concluding remarks

As an unconventional crusader, Ambedkar was quite conscious of the xenophobic character of nationalism. For him, nationalism has to be an inclusive phenomenon; it cannot be an exclusive ideology. Thus, a nation is a power-homogenized fraternity and a social democratic unit. In other words, homogenization of cultural/social values, the total destruction of ascriptive ideology and discarding Brahmanical supremacy are absolutely necessary conditions for a community to be 'nationals'. For him, those who believe in the pre-modern primordial loyalties and ascriptive ideologies cannot ensure the transformation of a society into a nation. The Brahmanical supremacists have always displayed their exclusivist politics and aimed to declare such politics as 'nationalistic' in its content and orientation. Ambedkar's determination in dismantling this particular ideology cannot be reduced to mere anti-brahmin tirade. It must be seen as the fiercest battle towards establishing a nation.

Ambedkar's argument here is that the anti-Brahmanical, egalitarian and anti-caste-feudal movements of the colonial era were fundamentally aiming at creating a national community. Anti-Brahmanical political discourse of Ambedkar did attempt to envisage the birth of a distinct form of new society which is qualitatively different from the colonized society, above all from the hierarchical, ascriptive identity based, discriminatory society. One of the important axiomatic principles of anti-Brahmin movements especially of Ambedkar was unambiguously their relentless quest to create a new form of social order wherein equality in opportunities and in distribution of resources ought to prevail. In other words, his appeal and struggle was to ensure homogenization of power – social, political, economic, within its cultural boundary. A sense of culturally patronized equality, emphasis on mass and universal education, denial of fixation in one location in the cultural landscape based on birth or ensuring hurdle-free social mobility would be the essential ingredients of a new society, these movements were hope to actualize.

What did anti-Brahmin movements especially Ambedkar's assertions attempt to achieve – the answer to this question is not merely socio-cultural and economic equality among the members of its cultural community. While conventional scholarship may seek to designate the consequences of these movements as mere social reforms, some of the recent sociological enquiry unearths another dimension. Rudolph and Rudolph found a more progressive content in these movements, to quote them, 'by imitating, managing and encouraging the efforts of the lower castes to become twice born, to don the sacred thread symbolizing high ritual rank and culture it, in effect if not in intention drains the caste hierarchy of meaning by homogenizing and democratizing'.[51] One might find the concept homogenization little problematic as the idea of hegemony is well camouflaged in it. It is true one would find the hidden layers of power embedded into the idea homogenization; however, what assumes the role of hegemonic presence in the new social reality is equality, mass literacy, social mobility, democratization and fraternity. In fact, Gellner takes this formulation to higher pedestal as he states, 'in an age of universal clerisy and mamlukdom, the relationship of culture and polity changes radically. A high culture pervades the whole society, defines it and needs to be sustained by polity. That is the secret of nationalism'.[52]

This seems to be the moment of departure. Indian subcontinent during the last half a century witnessed to the rise of plethora of 'reform' movements with their anchorage mainly in religious and social realm. However, it is inappropriate to designate all such 'reform' movements as movements having national aspirations; perhaps one can cautiously say these 'reform' movements *were* contributing to the emergence of national consciousness in a particular social context. Colonialism by establishing a powerful unitary State in the subcontinent had conferred national status to India. This conflation caused myriad of conceptual haemorrhage.

Notes

1 Dhananjay Keer (1962) *Dr. Ambedkar: Life and Mission*. Bombay: Popular Prakashan, pp. 72–80.
2 Ronald Inden (1990) *Imagining India*. Oxford: Blackwell; for more details, see Edward Said (1978) *Orientalism*. New York: Vintage Books.

3 Karl Marx and Frederick Engels (1977) *Selected Works*, Vol. I. Moscow: Progress Publishers, pp. 494–499.
4 See for details, Manabendra Nath Roy (1971) *The Future of Indian Politics*. Calcutta: Minerva Associates; Palme R. Dutt (1948) 'Right Wing Social Democracy in the Service of Imperialism (Der rechte Flügel der Sozialdemokratie im Dienst des Imperialismus)', *For a Lasting Peace, for a People's Democracy*, #21; A. R. Desai (1948) *Social Background of Indian Nationalism*. London: Oxford University Press.
5 Nicholas Dirks (1987) *The Hollow Crown: Ethnohistory of an Indian Kingdom*. Cambridge: Cambridge University Press, pp. 19–54; for an elaboration of this argument see also Arjun Appadurai and Carol Brekenridge (1976) 'The South Indian Temple: Authority, Honour and Redistribution', *Contributions to Indian Sociology*, 10(2), pp. 187–211.
6 Nicholas Dirks (2003) *Castes of Mind: Colonialism and the Making of Modern India*. New Delhi: Permanent Black, pp. 3–19.
7 Sandria Freitag (1991) 'Crime in the Social Order of Colonial North India', *Modern Asian Studies*, 25, pp. 227–241.
8 Alex Inkeles (1966) 'Modernization of Man', in Myron Weiner (ed.), *Modernization*. New York: Basic Books, pp. 152–155.
9 Louis Dumont (1970a) *Homo Hierarchicus: The Caste System and Its Implications*. Chicago: The University Press, p. 107.
10 Max Weber (1958) *The Religion of India*. Glencoe: The Free Press, pp. 48–51.
11 Andre Beteille (1986) 'Individualism and Equality', *Current Anthropology*, 27(2), pp. 212–234; and also Donald E. Brown (1988) *Hierarchy, History, and Human Nature: The Social Origins of Historical Consciousness*. The University of Arizona Press; Nicholas Dirks (1987) op. cit.; Stephan A. Barnett (1976) 'Approaches to Changes in Caste Ideology in South India', in Burton Stein (ed.), *Essays on South India*. New Delhi: Vikas Publishing House, pp. 149–155.
12 Louis Dumont (1970a) op. cit., p. 9.
13 Louis Dumont (ed.) (1970b) *Religion, Politics and History in India: Collected Papers in Indian Sociology*. The Hague: Mouton Publishers, p. 133.
14 Ibid., p. 108 (emphasis mine).
15 David Washbrook (1993) 'Economic Depression and the Making of "Traditional" Society in Colonial India 1820–1855', *Transactions of the Royal Historical Society*, 3, pp. 237–263, p. 85.
16 Stephan A. Barnett (1976) op. cit., pp. 149–155.
17 Nicholas Dirks (2003) op. cit., p. 5.
18 Anil Seal (1968) *The Emergence of Indian Nationalism*. Cambridge: Cambridge University Press, pp. 38–97; see also Judith Brown (1984) *Modern India: The Origins of an Asian Democracy*. New Delhi: Oxford University Press.
19 This point was noted in detail by Judith Brown (1984) op. cit., chapter II, Ashok Rudra (1989) 'The Emergence of the Intellegentia as a Ruling Class in India', *Economic and Political Weekly*, XXIV(3), pp. 142–150.
20 Sri Ram Mehrotra (1971) *The Emergence of Indian National Congress*. New Delhi: Vikas Publications, p. 248.
21 Angus Maddison (1974) *Education, Inequality and Life Chances: The Major Policy Issues*. Paris, France: Organisation for Economic Cooperation and Development, p. 43.
22 Mysore Narasimhachar Srinivas (1966) *Social Change in Modern India*. Hyderabad: Orient Longman Ltd., p. 3.
23 David Shulman (1985) 'Reconsidering Hinduism', in G.D. Sontheimer and Herman Kulke (eds.), *Hinduism Reconsidered*. New Delhi: Manohar, pp. 7–10.
24 Eric Stokes (1978) *The Peasants and the Raj: Studies in Agrarian Society and Peasant Rebellion in Colonial India*. New Delhi: Vikas Publishers, pp. 19–23.

25 Nicholas Dirks (1987) op. cit., pp. 1–5, 126–129. See also Arjun Appadurai (1981) *Worship and Conflict Under Colonial Rule*. Cambridge: Cambridge University Press.
26 Romila Thapar (1966) *A History of Indian*, Vol. I. Middlesex: Penguin Books, p. 19; for more details see Andre Wink (1986) *Land and Sovereignty in India*. Cambridge: Cambridge University Press, pp. 214–220.
27 Mysore Narasimhachar Srinivas (1970) *Social Change in Modern India and Other Essays*. Bombay: Asia Publishing House, pp. 5–6 (italics mine).
28 Ashok Rudra (1981) 'Against Feudalism', *Economic and Political Weekly*, XVI(52), pp. 2133–2146; see also Omvedt, Gail (1982). *Caste, agrarian relations and agrarian conflicts in Sociological perspectives of land reforms*, edited by Sheo Kumar Lal, In All-India Seminar on Sociological Perspectives of Land Reforms (1980: University of Jodhpur). Agricole Publishing Academy.
29 Mysore Narasimhachar Srinivas (1966) op. cit., p. 91.
30 G. Aloysius (1997) *Nationalism Without a Nation in India*. Oxford: Oxford University Press, p. 77.
31 Dr. Babasaheb Ambedkar Writings and Speeches, Vol. VIII, pp. 193–194 (italics mine).
32 Dr. Babsaheb Ambedkar Writings and Speeches, Vol. I, *Annihilation of Caste*, pp. 57–58.
33 Ibid., Vol. I. *Ranade, Gandhi and Jinnah*, pp. 222–223.
34 Ibid., Vol. I, *Evidence before the Southborough Committee*, pp. 249–250.
35 The Collected Works of Mahatma Gandhi, Vol. LXXVII, p. 45.
36 Ronald Inden (1990) op. cit., p. 30.
37 Dr. Babasaheb Ambedkar Speeches and Writings, Vol. XIII, p. 62.
38 Ibid., Vol. II, *On Village Panchayats Bill*, p. 106.
39 Ibid., Vol. VIII, *Pakistan or Partition of India*, pp. 30–33 (italics mine).
40 Ernest Gellner (1983) *Nations and Nationalism*. Oxford: Basic Blackwell, Chapter I.
41 Robert Frykenberg (2009) *Construction of Hinduism at the Nexus of History and Religion*. New Delhi: Critical Quest, pp. 3–12.
42 Robert Frykenberg (2005) 'The Emergence of Modern Hinduism as a Concept and as an Institution', in Gunther-Diez Sontheimer and Herman Kulke (eds.), *Hinduism Reconsidered*. New Delhi: Manohar.
43 Susan Bayly (1988) *Indian Society and the Making of the British Empire*. Cambridge: Cambridge University Press, pp. 156–158.
44 Christopher John Fuller (1977) 'British India or Traditional India? An Anthropological Problem', *Ethnos*, 42(3–4), pp. 95–121.
45 Anil Seal (1968) op. cit., p. 8.
46 Ibid., p. 39 (italics original).
47 Eric Hobsbawm (1990) *Nations and Nationalism Since 1780*. Cambridge: Cambridge University Press, pp. 102–130.
48 Romila Thapar (1998) 'Imagined Religious Communities: Ancient History and the Modern Search for a Hindu Identity', *Modern Asian Studies*, 23(2), pp. 203–223.
49 Hans Kohn (1924) *A History of Nationalism in the East*. London: George Routledge and Sons Ltd., p. 56.
50 Suniti Ghosh (1989) *India and the Raj 1919–1947: Glory, Shame and Bondage*, Vol. 2. Calcutta: Prachi Publications, Chapters II and III.
51 Lloyd Rudolph and Susanne Rudolph (1967) *The Modernity of Tradition*. Chicago: University of Chicago Press, p. 36.
52 Ernest Gellner (1983) op. cit., p. 18.

References

Aloysius, G. (1997) *Nationalism Without a Nation in India*. Oxford: Oxford University Press, p. 77.

Anderson Benedict (1983). *Imagined Communities. Reflection on the origin and spread of nationalism*, London: Verso. pp. 427–449.

Appadurai, Arjun (1981) *Worship and Conflict Under Colonial Rule*. Cambridge: Cambridge University Press.

Appadurai, Arjun and Brekenridge, Carol (1976) 'The South Indian Temple: Authority, Honour and Redistribution', *Contributions to Indian Sociology*, 10(2), pp. 187–211.

Barnett, Stephan A. (1976) 'Approaches to Changes in Caste Ideology in South India', in Burton Stein (ed.), *Essays on South India*. New Delhi: Vikas Publishing House, pp. 149–155.

Bayly, Susan (1988) *Indian Society and the Making of the British Empire*. Cambridge: Cambridge University Press, pp. 156–158.

Beteille, Andre (1986) 'Individualism and Equality', *Current Anthropology*, 27(2), pp. 212–234.

Brown, Donald E. (1988) *Hierarchy, History, and Human Nature: The Social Origins of Historical Consciousness*. The University of Arizona Press.

Brown, Judith (1984) *Modern India: The Origins of an Asian Democracy*. New Delhi: Oxford University Press.

Desai, A. R. (1948) *Social Background of Indian Nationalism*. London: Oxford University Press.

Dirks, Nicholas (1987) *The Hollow Crown: Ethnohistory of an Indian Kingdom*. Cambridge: Cambridge University Press.

Dirks, Nicholas (2003) *Castes of Mind: Colonialism and the Making of Modern India*. New Delhi: Permanent Black.

Dumont, Louis (1970a) *Homo Hierarchicus: The Caste System and its Implications*. Chicago: The University Press, p. 107.

Dumont, Louis (ed.) (1970b) *Religion, Politics and History in India: Collected Papers in Indian Sociology*. The Hague: Mouton Publishers, p. 108.

Dutt, Palme R. (1948). 'Right Wing Social Democracy in the Service of Imperialism (Der rechte Flügel der Sozialdemokratie im Dienst des Imperialismus)', *For a Lasting Peace, for a People's Democracy*, #21.

Freitag, Sandria (1991) 'Crime in the Social Order of Colonial North India', *Modern Asian Studies*, 25, pp. 227–241.

Frykenberg, Robert (2005) 'The Emergence of Modern "Hinduism" as a Concept and as an Institution: A Reappraisal with Special Reference to South India', in G. Sontheimer and H. Kulke (eds.), *Hinduism Reconsidered*. New Delhi: Manohar.

Frykenberg, Robert (2009) *Construction of Hinduism at the nexus of History and Religion*. New Delhi: Critical Quest, pp. 3–12.

Fuller, Christopher John (1977) 'British India or Traditional India? An Anthropological Problem', *Ethnos*, 42(3–4), pp. 95–121.

Gandhi, Mohandas Karamchand (2015). *The Collected Works of Mahatma Gandhi*. Publications Division, Ministry of Information and Broadcasting, Government of India, p. 45.

Gellner, Ernest (1983) *Nations and Nationalism*. Oxford: Basic Blackwell, Chapter I.

Ghosh, Suniti (1989) *India and the Raj 1919–1947: Glory, Shame and Bondage*, Vol. 2. Calcutta: Prachi Publications.

Govt. of Maharashtra (1979) *Dr. Babasaheb Ambedkar: Writings and Speeches*, Vol. 1. Bombay.

Govt. of Maharashtra (1987) *Dr. Babasaheb Ambedkar: Writings and Speeches*, Vol. 3. Bombay.

Govt. of Maharashtra (1990) *Dr. Babasaheb Ambedkar: Writings and Speeches*, Vol. 8. Bombay.
Hobsbawm, Eric (1990) *Nations and Nationalism Since 1780*. Cambridge: Cambridge University Press, pp. 102–130.
Inden, Ronald (1990) *Imagining India*. Oxford: Basil Blackwell.
Inkeles, Alex (1966) 'Modernization of Man', in Myron Weiner (ed.), *Modernization*. New York: Basic Books, pp. 152–155.
Keer, Dhananjay (1962) *Dr. Ambedkar: Life and Mission*. Bombay: Popular Prakashan, pp. 72–80.
Kohn, Hans (1924) *A History of Nationalism in the East*. London: George Routledge and Sons Ltd., p. 56.
Maddison, Angus (1974) *Education, Inequality and Life Chances: The Major Policy Issues*. Paris, France: Organisation for Economic Cooperation and Development, p. 43.
Marx, Karl and Engels, Frederick (1977) *Selected Works*, Vol. I. Moscow: Progress Publishers, pp. 494–499.
Mehrotra, Sri Ram (1971) *The Emergence of Indian National Congress*. New Delhi: Vikas Publications.
Omvedt, Gail (1982). *Caste, agrarian relations and agrarian conflicts in Sociological perspectives of land reforms*, edited by Sheo Kumar Lal, In All-India Seminar on Sociological Perspectives of Land Reforms (1980: University of Jodhpur). Agricole Publishing Academy.
Roy, Manabendra Nath (1971) *The Future of Indian Politics*. Calcutta: Minerva Associates.
Rudolph, Lloyd and Rudolph, Susanne (1967) *The Modernity of Tradition*. Chicago: University of Chicago Press, p. 36.
Rudra, Ashok (1981) 'Against Feudalism', *Economic and Political Weekly*, XVI(52), pp. 2133–2146.
Rudra, Ashok (1989) 'The Emergence of the Intellegentia as a Ruling Class in India', *Economic and Political Weekly*, XXIV(3), pp. 142–150.
Said, Edward (1978) *Orientalism*. New York: Vintage Books.
Seal, Anil (1968) *The Emergence of Indian Nationalism*. Cambridge: Cambridge University Press, pp. 8, 38–97.
Shulman, David (1985) 'Reconsidering Hinduism', in G. D. Sontheimer and Herman Kulke (eds.), *Hinduism Reconsidered*. New Delhi: Manohar, pp. 7–10.
Srinivas, Mysore Narasimhachar (1966) *Social Change in Modern India*. Hyderabad: Orient Longman Ltd.
Srinivas, Mysore Narasimhachar (1970) *Social Change in Modern India and Other Essays*. Bombay: Asia Publishing House, pp. 5–6.
Stokes, Eric (1978) *The Peasants and the Raj: Studies in Agrarian Society and Peasant Rebellion in Colonial India*. New Delhi: Vikas Publishers, pp. 19–23.
Thapar, Romila (1966) *A History of Indian*, Vol. I. Middlesex: Penguin Books, p. 19.
Thapar, Romila (1998) 'Imagined Religious Communities: Ancient History and the Modern Search for a Hindu Identity', *Modern Asian Studies*, 23(2), pp. 203–223.
Washbrook, David (1993), 'Economic Depression and the Making of "Traditional" Society in Colonial India 1820–1855', *Transactions of the Royal Historical Society*, 3, pp. 237–263.
Weber, Max (1958) *The Religion of India*. Glencoe: The Free Press, pp. 48–51.
Wink, Andre (1986) *Land and Sovereignty in India*. Cambridge: Cambridge University Press, pp. 214–220.

Part II

Economic development and marginalised groups

6 Performance of Indian economy in the post-reform period

Growth, inequality and well-being*

R. Radhakrishna

Growth performance

The Indian economy had been virtually stagnant for several decades' prior to independence whereas the income of the developed countries had grown several-fold due to the industrial and technological revolution. The growth rate in India lagged far behind that of the developed world. The annual per capita income declined by 0.22 per cent during 1913–50 (Table 6.1). Per capita agricultural output declined by 0.72 per cent per annum during 1911–41 and food grain output, a major source of food security, declined by 1.14 per cent per annum (Blyn, 1966). India was also saddled with a large population living in abysmal conditions. The national government formed after independence accorded high priority to 'economic growth with social justice' and opted for a mixed economy model by emphasising on industrialization and import substitution as a development strategy. The growth of national income became the primary goal and other objectives such as the creation of greater employment opportunities and poverty eradication were assumed to follow from growth. The state was the prime mover of growth with public enterprises having the commanding height. This state-led growth laid the foundation for industrialization, technological change and created a pool of technical and scientific manpower. It succeeded in breaking the prolonged structural stagnation. However, national income growth remained moderate at about 3.7 per cent per annum till the 1970s and the performance in the eradication of poverty and reduction of income inequality left much to be desired. The incidence of poverty fluctuated with no significant trend during 1960–61 to 1977–78 and the rural-urban disparity in per capita expenditure widened (Radhakrishna and Ray, 2005). During this period, outward-oriented Asian countries grew much faster by taking advantage of the post-war expansion in international trade and investment flows. India responded to these developments and moderately relaxed controls on industry in the 1980s. As a consequence, the private corporate sector began to contribute to industrialisation and the contribution of public enterprises to capital formation levelled off. The annual growth rate of GDP accelerated to 5.2 per cent in the 1980s from 3.5 per cent in the

Table 6.1 Annual Growth Rates of GDP and Per Capita GDP at Constant Prices: India, 1913–2014

	1913–50	*1950–70*	*1970–80*	*1980–90*	*1990–2000*	*1993–2005*	*2005–14*
GDP	0.23	3.69	3.45	5.17	6.14	6.11	7.48
Per capita GDP	-0.22	1.58	1.14	2.94	4. 06	4.14	6.53

Note: Source for 1913–50 is Madison (2001). Growth rates of other periods are estimated from semi-log trend equation.

Source: Planning Commission (GDP data for the period 1950–2014)

1970s (Table 6.1). However, India experienced unsustainable levels of fiscal and current account deficits towards the end of the 1980s since the government had resorted to deficit financing. The fiscal deficit stood at about 9 per cent of GDP and the country had foreign exchange reserves equivalent to just two weeks' worth of imports. The international credit agencies placed India low in their ranking of countries. In the wake of high inflation, very low foreign exchange reserves and the balance of payments crisis in 1991, the Indian government initiated wide-ranging economic reforms to facilitate a shift from the state-led to market-driven growth. These reforms provided enough space for the development of the private sector by removing controls on industry and privatising public enterprises. India also shifted to floating exchange rate management, removed trade barriers and substantially reduced tariff rates. Banking sector reforms were undertaken so that Indian banks conformed to International Prudential Standards (IPS). These reforms were meant to foster greater competition in the economy.

Economic reforms placed India on a higher growth trajectory. The annual GDP growth rate increased from 4.36 per cent during 1970–90 to 7.05 per cent in the post-reform period (1993–2014) and further accelerate to 7.48 per cent during 2005–06 and 2013–14. The breakthrough in growth could be attributed to the modernisation of domestic industry as well as supply side factors accompanied by continuous strong domestic demand. A surge in savings and high investment supported by easy liquidity put the Indian economy on a high growth trajectory.[1] The major contributors to growth, other than savings and investment, were the spurt in exports and substantial flow of Foreign Direct Investment (FDI) that had complemented domestic investment. The high growth had raised collections from direct taxes, especially from the corporate sector. This enabled both the central and state governments to step up public investments in infrastructure and expenditure on agriculture and social sectors.

In three years viz., 2005–06, 2006–07 and 2007–08, India witnessed an impressive average growth rate of 9.5 per cent. This high growth could be attributed to the high rate of investment which averaged at 35 per cent and was mainly financed by domestic savings. However, the Indian economy has been experiencing a cyclical downturn since October 2008. Its growth rate has slipped to a low level and it has been affected by high inflation.

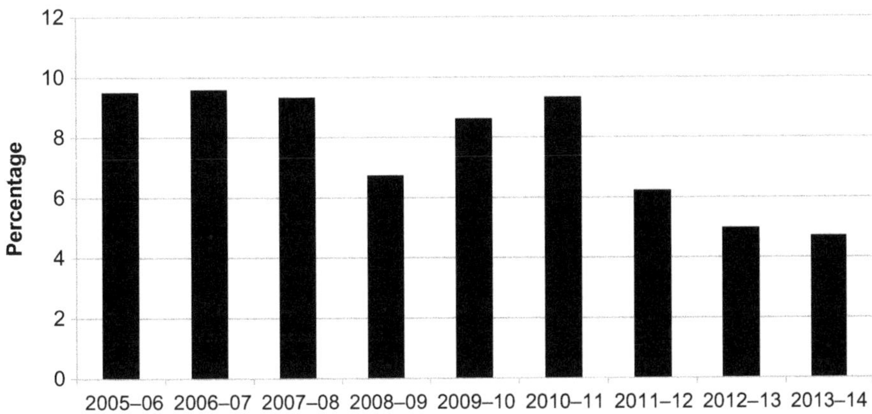

Figure 6.1 GDP Growth Rates in India at Constant Prices
Source: computed from Planning Commission data

The global economic melt-down peaked in 2008 and its aftershock had hit India's exports, remittances and foreign inflow of capital. In 2008–09 the growth rate had slipped to 6.7 per cent. To cope with the crisis, the government had implemented stimulus packages and the RBI reduced periodical interest rates as well as the CRR. The government also increased budgetary support to the large safety net programme, e.g. MGNREGA, for protecting the poor. As a result, the economy witnessed a strong recovery in effective demand and the growth rate revived to 8.6 per cent in 2009–10 and further increased to 8.9 per cent in 2010–11. However, due to the crisis in the Eurozone, the growth rate declined to 6.7 per cent in 2011–12 and remained about 4.5 per cent in 2012–13 and 2013–14 (Figure 6.1). India has also been facing high food inflation which hurts the poor the most. Further, India was hit by a weak domestic investment climate and limited fiscal space. The adversities are manifested in a slowdown in investment, low dollar inflows, depreciating rupee and high inflationary pressures, particularly in the food sector. Nevertheless, it is a challenge for fiscal and monetary policies to revive growth and reduce inflation to its comfort zone. There are some signs of recovery; the GDP at constant market prices registered a growth rate of 7.2 per cent in 2014–15 and is projected to increase to 7.6 per cent in 2015–16, which is lower than the potential growth rate of 8–10 per cent per annum (Economic Survey, 2015–16).[2]

Nature of growth

Corporate-led growth and rise of inequality

It needs to be recognized that this growth was led by the private corporate sector. Incentives provided to the private corporate sector-led to its increasing

Table 6.2 Share of Private Corporate Sector and Public Sector in NDP and Share of Private Corporate Sector in Gross Capital Formation

Sector	*1981–82*	*1991–92*	*2001–02*	*2007–08*
Share (%) of Private Corporate Sector, Public Sector and Household Sector in NDP				
Private Corporate Sector	14.4	12.3	18.0	23.4
Public Sector	18.0	23.7	23.5	19.5
Household Sector	67.6	64.0	58.5	57.1
Share (%) of Private Corporate Sector, Public Sector and Household Sector in Gross Capital Formation				
Private Corporate Sector	25.8	28.1	22.4	41.0
Public Sector	47.7	43.1	28.4	23.5
Household Sector	26.5	28.8	46.6	32.6

Note: In 2007–08, Investment in valuables accounted for 2.9 per cent of Gross Capital Formation.

Source: Ramesh Kolli (2009)

dominance. The share of the private corporate sector in investment increased from 28 per cent in 1991–92 to 41 per cent in 2007–08, while the share of the public sector declined from 43 to 24 per cent and the share of the household sector increased from 29 to 33 per cent during the same period (Table 6.2) indicating the emergence of the private corporate sector as the driver of investment, replacing the public sector. A few empirical studies have suggested that corporate dominance contributed to widening income inequality in the post-reform period.[3] However, data are not available for the income of the private corporate sector and its distribution across factors of production. But the data available for the registered manufacturing sector, which can serve as a proxy for the private corporate sector, shows that the share of profits in net value added in the industries covered by the Annual Survey of Industries increased from about 22.1 per cent in 1990–91 to 55.5 per cent in 2009–10, while the share of wages in value added declined from 25.6 per cent to 11.8 per cent (Figure 6.2). The disparity between blue and white collar workers increased sharply in the post-reform period (Figure 6.3).[4]

Walton study reveals that private corporate sector-led growth was associated with rent-seeking and under-pricing of public sector assets in the process of the privatization of the public sector and the transfer of public and private lands to the corporate sector (Walton, 2012).

It is claimed by the *Credit Suisse Global Wealth* that the top one per cent rich held 37 per cent of the wealth in 2000, which increased to 53 per cent by 2006 (cited by Bhaduri, 2016). The *Forbes dollar billionaire list* reveals that while there were only two persons in the category of "extremely high net worth individuals" in 1995, the number of such persons in this category rose to 55 in 2014 (ibid).

Bhaduri (2016) argued that incentivizing the corporate sector by successive governments, irrespective of their ideology, by giving land and other

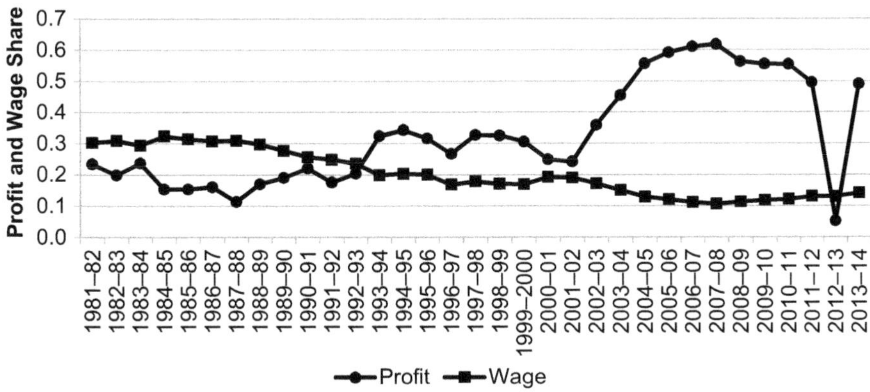

Figure 6.2 Profit and Wage Share in NVA in Organized Manufacturing Sector

Note: Wages and profits do not add up to 100. The remaining comprises rent, interest and remuneration to non-workers.

Source: computed from data provided by Institute of Human Development

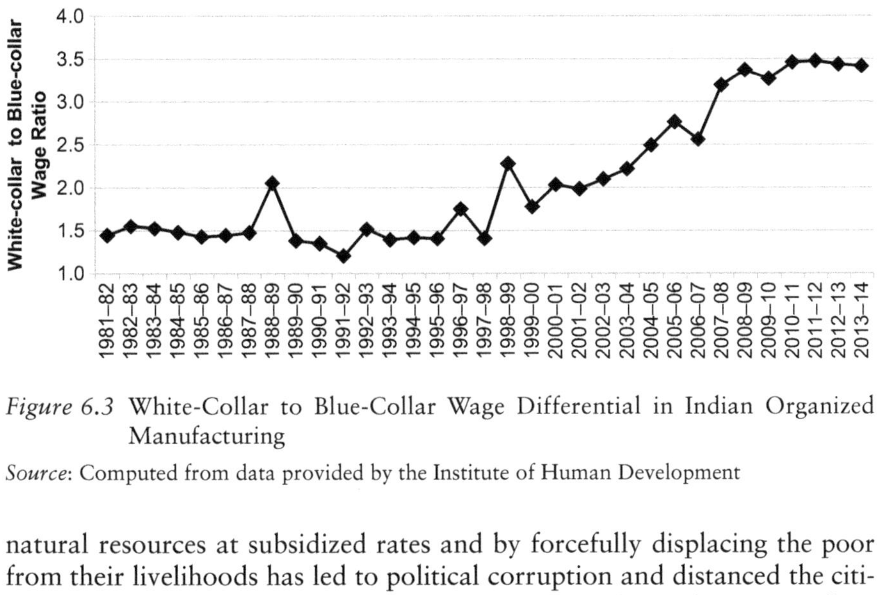

Figure 6.3 White-Collar to Blue-Collar Wage Differential in Indian Organized Manufacturing

Source: Computed from data provided by the Institute of Human Development

natural resources at subsidized rates and by forcefully displacing the poor from their livelihoods has led to political corruption and distanced the citizens from the elected representatives. According to him, about 25 million hectares of land was acquired between 2000 and 2016. He estimated that the "revenue foregone on various heads by the government to help the corporations is estimated about 2.1 trillion rupees (lakh crore), while the subsidies to the poor only amount to 2.2 billion during the first one and a half decades of the 21st century" (ibid). Besides, wilful default by corporations and large firms contributed to non-performing assets on the balance sheets of nationalized banks.

Bhaduri (2016) has also argued that the present pattern of development, which is contributing to higher growth while at the same time worsening inequality, would constrain long-term growth by adversely affecting the expansion of effective demand and thereby slow down the domestic market expansion. Hence, effective demand may emerge as a binding constraint in sustaining higher growth. Worsening of inequality leads to an economy of exclusion and to a wasteland of human potential.

The corporate sector may search for external markets for their products. But their efforts may not succeed in counteracting the deficits in effective demand since Indian exports are not competitive in the world market. It may be noted that in 2015, the share of high technology exports in manufacturing exports was low at 7.5 per cent whereas it was 25.4 per cent in China. Moreover, the dependency on external markets rather than the domestic market would expose the Indian economy to the volatilities in the world market caused by periodic cycles. Fluctuations in the domestic market affect the poor the most since they are not protected by safety-nets. Further, the concessions given in the past to the corporate sector will not be that easily forthcoming, in view of public awareness and mass-protests. This may affect growth.

Inter-state growth disparities

There are substantial inter-state variations in GSDP per capita as well as in growth rates. In 2013–14, the GSDP per capita of Gujarat was 4.3 times that of Bihar and the GSDP per capita of Kerala was 3.7 times that of Bihar. A disquieting characteristic of the growth process in the post-reform period is widening of regional inequality. The coefficient of variation in GSDP per capita across states showed an increasing trend during 1991–92 and 2013–14 (Figure 6.4). It is worth noting that in the three high growth years there had been a marked increase in interstate income disparities as revealed by the coefficient of variation. In general, high growth is associated with

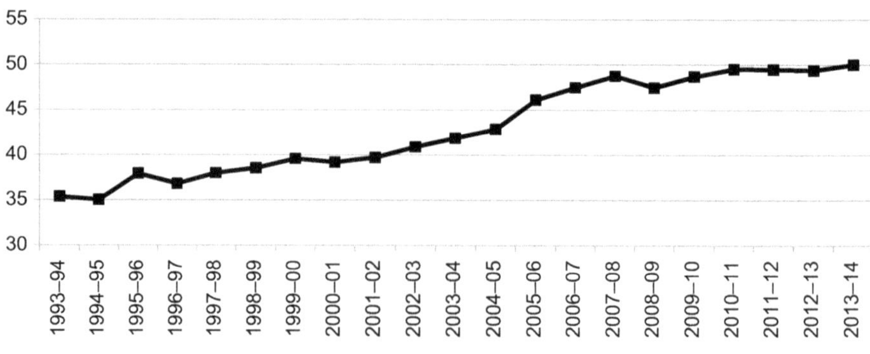

Figure 6.4 Trends in Weighted Coefficient of Variation (%) in GSDP per capita across Indian States (2004–05 prices)

Source: Computed by Author from NSS Data

worsening interstate disparities in GSDP per capita. This may act as a barrier to inclusive growth.

An analysis of the ranking of major states on GSDP per capita and on growth in GSDP during the post-reform period (Table 6.3) reveals: i) among the major states, Assam, Uttar Pradesh, Jammu & Kashmir, Jharkhand and Madhya Pradesh lagged far behind on both counts; ii) though Odisha, Bihar and Chhattisgarh had a somewhat better growth performance, their GSDP per capita levels were still low; iii) the growth performance of Punjab was sluggish, consequently its ranking among major states slipped from 1 in 1993–94 to 5 in 2011–12; iv) Kerala, Andhra Pradesh, Uttarakhand, Delhi, Gujarat, Haryana and Himachal Pradesh, in that order witnessed impressive growth and among them Kerala, Maharashtra, Gujarat and Haryana ranked higher on GSDP per capita (Table 6.3). On the whole, the poorer states gained less from economic reforms and continued to remain poor till 2011–12 while the developed states other than Punjab gained the most.

Table 6.3 GSDP Per Capita at 2004–05 Prices and its Annual Growth Rates across Major Indian States

	GSDP per capita (Rs)			*Growth Rate (%)*		
	1993–94	*2004–05*	*2014–15*	*1993–94/ 2004–05*	*1993–94/ 2014–15*	*2004–05/ 2014–15*
Andhra Pradesh	17631	29117	53666	4.31	5.73	6.20
Assam	15629	19154	29161	1.63	3.05	4.43
Bihar	6248	8864	18685	3.34	5.25	8.45
Chhattisgarh	17121	21851	39958	1.79	4.62	6.36
Gujarat	20694	38163	74729*	4.34	6.40^	7.53^
Haryana	24849	42670	80626	4.92	6.10	6.58
Himachal Pradesh	21126	38162	68307*	5.21	6.00^	6.78^
Jammu & Kashmir	19014	25706	37120	2.67	3.49	4.17
Jharkhand	15493	21050	36236	1.92	3.91	6.36
Karnataka	17799	30359	56201	4.86	5.66	5.96
Kerala	20941	36464	64568*	4.81	6.01^	6.47^
Madhya Pradesh	13797	17643	33519	2.15	3.98	6.72
Maharashtra	26110	40884	80828	3.77	5.82	6.76
Odisha	12968	20409	35541	3.34	5.47	5.60
Punjab	27213	38149	64135	3.13	4.29	5.36
Rajasthan	13202	21297	38340	3.67	4.79	6.42
Tamil Nadu	19852	34168	75063	4.34	6.55	7.94
Uttar Pradesh	11575	14789	23304	1.96	3.36	4.72
Uttarakhand	17218	27765	74814	3.89	7.98	10.58
West Bengal	14204	25044	43335	5.21	5.32	5.55
All India	16688	27536	47777*	4.50	5.50^	6.35^

Note: Annual growth rates are computed from estimated semi-log trend equation. *Data for 2013–14, ^Growth rates are up to the year 2013–14. Andhra Pradesh refers to the composite state.

Source: Radhakrishna (2016).

The state-level experiences demonstrate lack of inclusiveness in the growth process.

Labour market trends and concerns

In the post-reform period, the growth rate of GSDP accelerated to 7.1 per cent per annum (during 1993–04 and 2013–14) whereas employment increased at a low rate of 1.3 per cent per annum and decelerated in recent years. While total employment (UPSS) increased by 59 million between 1999–00 to 2004–05, it increased by a mere 14.7 million between 2004–05 and 2011–12 (Thomas, 2015) registering a growth rate of 0.45 per cent per annum in contrast to the annual GDP growth rate of 7.7 per cent. The implicit employment elasticity during the period tends to zero.[5] The slowdown in employment in the later period is mainly due a fall in agricultural employment by 33.3 million. Employment in the organized sector, which is considered to be qualitatively better, increased very slowly from 2.65 million in 2005 to 2.96 million in 2012 and accounted for about six per cent of the total workforce (UPSS). The contribution of the public sector to the growth of organized employment has been very low.

There has been a marked imbalance in the sectoral shares of employment and GDP. The dependency of labour force on agriculture was high among several developing countries (Dev, 2016). Though agriculture accounted for 14 per cent of GDP, its share in the workforce was high at 49 per cent (ibid). On the other hand, though the service sector accounted for 49 per cent of GDP, its share in employment was low at 27 per cent. In the case of the manufacturing sector, there was some balance between its share in employment (13 per cent) and in GDP (16 per cent). The declining share of agriculture in GDP is on the expected line, but the sluggish decline of employment is a cause of concern. Needless to say, the growth of the manufacturing sector which is more labour intensive has been slow and has been lagging behind the service sector,[6] which is also a cause for concern.

There has been a marked decline in the growth rate of the labour force; the annual growth rate declined to 0.58 per cent between 2004–05 and 2011–12 from three per cent between 1990–00 and 2004–05. The deceleration is explained by the substantial increase in enrolment in educational institutions and withdrawal of women from the labour market. There has been a sharp fall in labour force in the 15–24 age groups. Students accounted for 72 per cent of India's incremental population (133 million) between 2004–05 and 2011–12.

Employment in agriculture has declined not only in relative but also in absolute terms. Out of the 472.5 million workers in 2011–12, 224 million (47.5 %) were employed in agriculture and allied sectors which showed a decline from 258 million in 2004–05 (Thomas, 2015). Of the other 33 million who were no longer in agricultural work during 2004–2012, 19 million were self-employed and 14 million were wage/salary workers. This has contributed to a moderate increase in the share of casual workers in the total agricultural workforce. The proportion of female workforce in agriculture has also declined. The rate of decline of female workers has been higher in Bihar, Haryana, Assam, Karnataka, Gujarat and Kerala. It is claimed that women withdrew from agriculture and were attending to domestic duties in their own households due to an improvement in the availability of income-earning opportunities for male members of the family (ibid) and perhaps to avoid heavy manual work in agriculture. There is a degree of segmentation of agricultural labour with female workers mostly engaged in agricultural operations which are repetitive and strenuous. Even with the progressive withdrawal of female workers, there has been a feminisation of agriculture due to the shift of male labour from farm to non-farm work.

The non-farm sector is becoming an important source of livelihood in rural areas. Between 1999–2000 and 2011–12, there has been a considerable increase in rural non-farm employment; whereas, in 1983, only 19 per cent of rural workers were engaged in non-agricultural activities, this had increased to about 36 per cent in 2011–12. Overall, rural non-farm employment has increased by 12 percentage points in the past 12 years. Since agriculture is overcrowded, such a shift of workers from agriculture to the non-farm sector is a welcome trend. This shift has taken place among the economically weaker sections (Saha and Verick, 2016b). There has been an increase in the demand for specific skills in non-farm activities as well as in commercial agriculture and allied agriculture. These are positive trends. It should be noted that the non-farm sector has better scope for regional spread than agriculture.

These changes have brought about perceptible changes in the employment patterns in rural areas. While the percentage of self-employed in agriculture has risen, in contrast, increasing casualisation of the workforce has taken place in the non-farm sector. On the whole, self-employed workers still account for 60 per cent of the rural workforce. The proportion of households among the agricultural households having non-agriculture as a principal source of income, particularly from wage employment has increased considerably between 2002–03 and 2012–13 (NSSO's Situation Assessment Agricultural Households Surveys). This has been more prominent among poorer agricultural households (Saha and Verick, 2016b *op. cit.*). It is claimed that the farm households were shifting to rural non-farm self-employment as a part of better livelihood security (Binswanger-Mkhize, 2012).

The average wage-earning rates of casual workers accelerated to 3.9 per cent per annum between 1993–94 and 2011–12 as compared to 2.5 per cent between 1983 and 1993–04 (Papola, 2014). The rate of increase in wage earnings was much higher between 2004–05 and 2011–12 as compared to the period between 1999–00 and 2004–05. Rural wages have risen faster than urban wages and agricultural wages have grown at a higher rate than non-agricultural wages in the post-reform period (ibid). In rural areas, wages in non-agricultural activities have been consistently higher than in agricultural activities throughout the period; however, the gap has narrowed down.

Despite the higher growth rate of rural wages, urban wages were higher in 2011–12. The improvements in agricultural wages have contributed to the reduction in poverty among agricultural labour households as well as a rise in their real per capita expenditure (Radhakrishna and Raju, 2015).

The on-going trends in agricultural and allied sector employment signify that structural changes have been occurring in the rural labour market. Supply and demand factors are both responsible for these changes. On the supply side, the following three factors might be responsible: i) decline in the rate of population, ii) decline in labour force participation due to increasing enrolment in educational institutions and iii) rural to urban migration. On the demand side, there has been an overall decline in demand for labour due to i) mechanization on account of increased wages and labour scarcity in peak season due to the implementation of MGNREGA, ii) crop diversification from traditional labour intensive to commercial crops and horticulture crops, and iii) significant and rapid expansion of the rural non-farm sector.

Despite some positive employment trends, informal workers still constitute more than 90 per cent of the total workforce and the share of the informal sector accounted for about half of GVA. It is a fact that in India, high growth in the post-liberalization period has been accompanied by increased informalisation and de-unionization. A sizeable portion of the workforce is engaged in subsistence production. This segment is at the bottom of the production ladder, providing cheap labour without any social security. Economically and socially deprived sections of society are mostly employed as casual labour. These are some of the worrisome features of the labour market.

It is claimed that India has the advantage of the 'demographic dividend', meaning that a relatively large percentage of the population is in the working age group. If adequate employment opportunities are created; and if the working age group becomes healthy and well equipped with knowledge and skills, India can then reap the benefits of the demographic dividend. However, low levels of education and high levels of chronic energy deficiency are the basic factors underlying their low productivity. These are the obstacles for deriving benefits from the demographic dividend.

Quality education and research

The Nobel laureate Tinbergen, based on an analysis of the factors underlying inequalities, observed that human capital is a key instrument for reducing inequalities in the process of development. Another Nobel laureate, Sir Arthur Lewis, pointed out that "Education is not invented in order to enable men to produce more goods and services. The purpose of education is to enable them to understand better the world in which they live, so that they may more fully experience their potential capacities".

Are these objectives being fulfilled by the educational institutions in India? There is a substantial quantitative expansion of school education in both the public and private sectors. Now there is a school in every village, near universal enrolment of children of school going age has been achieved and the rural-urban difference and gender gap have narrowed down (NUEPA, 2015). *Sarva Siksha Abhiyan* has covered the whole of India, making access to elementary education easier. Schemes such as 'mid-day meal' and the Right to Education Act aiming at eight years of compulsory education helped in increasing enrolment and reducing the drop-out rate.

However, the lack of access to quality education is a basic malady that persists. The Annual Survey of Education Report shows that majority of students in primary classes do not have an adequate ability to read, write and solve simple numerical problems (ASER, 2014). Only 40 per cent of class-3 children can read the class-1 text, and 26 per cent can do subtraction. Absenteeism of teachers is quite significant. The infrastructure of schools in rural areas is grossly inadequate.

Seventy-first round NSSO survey found that about four-fifth of rural students and one-third of urban students at primary level were attending government institutions in 2014. As per the survey, per person expenditure at primary level incurred during a session in private unaided institutions was about 10 times the expenditure in government institutions. Admittedly, these better private educational institutions were not accessible to the children of the marginalized group. This contributes to inequality in opportunity when they enter the job market as adults and thereby fail to be included in the gains of the growth process.

According to NSSO data, in 2011–12, only 2.4 per cent of the persons aged 15 years and above (1.1 per cent in rural areas and 5.5 per cent in urban areas) had technical degrees, diplomas or certificates in fields like medicine, engineering or agriculture. The rate of vocational training barely increased between 2004–05 and 2011–12.

There has been a significant expansion of higher education over the past 60 years: the number of universities and deemed universities increased from 30 to 777, colleges from 750 to 35,500. However, the gross enrolment ratio in higher education is very low, that is half of the world average. Both India and China had gross enrolment ratio of six per cent until 1999, while China achieved 39 per cent in 2014, India lagged behind at 24 per cent (Table 6.4).

The quality of higher education imparted to the students leaves much to be desired. For instance, some years ago out of six lakh engineering graduates produced by the engineering colleges, a mere one lakh obtained employment through on-campus interviews, another 2.5 lakh graduates managed to get jobs after some waiting period and the rest were considered unemployable and ended up in odd jobs (Radhakrishna and Chandrasekhar, 2008). Many IT companies were compelled to recruit diploma holders and graduates and subject them to rigorous training by incurring huge costs. There is also an associated problem of lack of quality teachers as the market has been driving out some of the best talents from academic pursuits to IT industry and in search of greener pastures abroad.[7] This will accentuate the problem for the next generation.

Table 6.4 Social Sector Development Indicators in BRICS

Country	*Brazil*	*Russia*	*India*	*China*	*South Africa*
Adult Literacy Rate, 15 year+ (%) 2005–13	91.3	99.7	62.8	95.1	93.7
Mean Years of Schooling, 2014	7.7	12	5.4	7.5	9.9
Population with at least Secondary Education (% ages 25 and older) (2005–13)	53.6	90.9	42.1	65.3	39.8
Gross Tertiary Enrolment Ratio, 2014	46	79	24	39	20
Pupil-Teacher Ratio, 2008–14	21	20	35	18	29
Public Expenditure on Education as a % of GDP, 2014	5.9	4.2	3.8	–	6.1
Researchers in R&D per million people, 2005–15	698	3102	157	1113	405
Expenditure for R&D as a % of GDP, 2005–15	1.24	1.19	0.82	2.05	0.73
High-technology Exports as a % of Manufactured Exports, 2015	12.3	11.5	7.5	25.4	5.9

Source: World Development Indicators, World Bank (2016); UNDP (Human Development Report (2015)

The Kothari Commission, way back in 1966, recommended that 6 per cent of GDP should be set aside for public expenditure on education, but the public expenditure (centre and state governments combined) was 3.8 per cent of GDP in 2014 (Table 6.4). India paid inadequate attention to Research and Development (R&D) in terms of the number of researchers engaged in R&D per million persons as well as in expenditure on R&D among the BRICS countries (Table 6.4). In 2005–12, the number of researchers engaged in R&D in China was nearly seven times more than in India, and R&D expenditure as a percentage of GDP in China was 1.9 times the percentage in India. It is reported that India's share in the world scientific output was three per cent while that of China was 10 per cent. The contribution of Indian Industry to R&D was abysmal.[8]

Welfare implications

Growth in consumer expenditure and inequality

Real Monthly Per Capita Expenditure (MPCE) during 1983 to 1997 (broadly pre-reform period) increased at an annual rate of 1.02 per cent in rural areas and 1.73 per cent in urban areas (Table 6.5). During 1993–94

Table 6.5 Annual Growth Rates (%) of Per Capita Monthly Expenditure by Broad Expenditure Groups

Period	*Bottom 30 %*	*Middle 40 %*	*Top 30 %*	*All classes*
Rural				
1983–97(URP)	1.29***	1.01***	0.96***	1.02***
1993/94–20011/12 (MRP)	1.72***	1.81***	2.49***	2.13***
Urban				
1983–97(URP)	1.35***	1.43***	1.99***	1.73***
1993/94–2011/12 (MRP)	2.10***	2.70***	3.82***	3.25***

Note: The growth rates are derived from weighted regression estimated with the square root of the number of households canvassed in NSS rounds as weights. While estimating the trend equation, an intercept dummy has been included to distinguish between annual and quinquennial NSS rounds. URP: Uniform Reference Period; MRP: Mixed Reference Period.

*** Significant at 1% level.

Source: Radhakrishna et al. (2013).

to 2011–12 (post-reform period) the growth rate accelerated to 2.13 per cent in rural areas and 3.25 per cent in urban areas. It is evident that the growth rate picked up in the post-reform period and that urban areas gained the most from the higher growth. All expenditure classes gained from the accelerated growth of MPCE and the growth rate of MPCE was higher in the second period for all expenditure groups (Table 6.5). However, the difference between the two periods was modest for the bottom expenditure group and comparatively very striking for the top expenditure group. While the improvement in the growth rate was 0.10 percentage point per annum for the rural bottom expenditure group and 0.35 for urban bottom expenditure group, it was as high as 0.96 for rural top expenditure group and 1.32 for urban top expenditure group. It is evident that the growth in the post-reform period was pro-rich and urban groups had higher growth in both the periods.

Trends in social welfare

The Social Welfare Function (SWF)[9] shows an improvement in economic welfare over the past three decades. It has been observed that MPCE and SWF moved closely during 1983/84–2009/10 (Radhakrishna et al., 2013). This is due to the fact that the real per capita consumption expenditure was the main contributor to the changes in economic welfare as it compensated the loss in welfare due to growing rural and urban inequality. The gap between MPCE and SWF had been progressively widened in both rural and urban areas, more prominently, in urban areas during the post-reform period due to rising inequality. The rural-urban disparity widened over the period (ibid). Hence worsening of intra-rural and urban inequalities and widening of rural-urban disparity acted as barriers for achieving potential welfare gains from the growth.

Table 6.6 Annual Growth Rates of Social Welfare

	ε					
	0.5	*1.5*	*2.0*	*2.5*	*3.0*	*3.5*
Rural						
1983–97 (URP)	1.01***	1.06***	1.10***	1.15***	1.20***	1.24***
1993/94–2011–12 (MRP)	2.04***	1.89***	1.85***	1.81***	1.79***	1.78***
Urban						
1983–97 (URP)	1.57***	1.45***	1.41***	1.38***	1.35***	1.34***
1993/94–2011–12 (MRP)	2.95***	2.55***	2.41***	2.30***	2.22***	2.15***

*** Significant at 1% level.

Source: Radhakrishna et al. (2013).

During 1983–97, SW in rural areas increased at an annual rate of 1.01–1.24 per cent and in urban areas at an annual rate of 1.34–1.57 per cent, depending on the value given to the inequality aversion parameter (Table 6.6). The growth rate tended to increase, though marginally, with an increase in the value of the inequality aversion parameter in rural areas suggesting a decline in rural inequality during 1983–97. In contrast, it tended to decrease with an increase in the inequality aversion parameter in urban areas suggesting the worsening of urban inequality in the later period.

During 1993/94–2011/12, SW grew at a rate between 1.78 and 2.04 per cent per annum in rural areas and between 2.15 and 2.95 per cent per annum in urban areas. Clearly, the growth rate of SW was higher in the post-reform period. As expected, in this period, since the inequality trend was positive in both rural and urban areas, the SW growth rate was lower particularly at higher values of the inequality aversion parameter. It is worth observing that at a very high value of the inequality aversion parameter, i.e. as the SW approaches the Rawlsian Social Welfare Function, the growth rate of SW would be closer to that of the MPCE of the bottom classes. On the whole, if more weight is given to the welfare of the poor in the evaluation of social welfare, the progress made by India in welfare improvement was undoubtedly modest and as will be seen later, it could have been better had inequality not become worse.

The Atkinson Social Welfare Function is observed to move closely with real per capita expenditure. This is due to the fact that the real per capita expenditure was the main contributor to the changes in economic welfare as it compensated for the loss of welfare due to growing rural as well as urban inequality. The gap between MPCE and SW widened prominently over time in the urban areas and could be attributed to the worsening of inequality over time.

On the whole, rising inequality in both the periods, particularly in the post-reform period, reduced the potential growth in economic welfare.[10] Radhakrishna et al. (2013) have shown that had inequality remained constant during the post-reform period (1993/94–2009/10), SW would have increased at an annual rate of 1.6 per cent instead of 1.4 per cent in rural areas and 2.8 per cent instead of 2.3 per cent in urban areas. It should also be recognized that the growth of MPCE compensated for the adverse effect on welfare caused by rising inequality in MPCE. There are two possibilities for enhancing overall welfare. It can be easily shown that a uniform MPCE growth rate across the states would have a positive effect on welfare. It should be noted that the MPCE growth rate lagged behind the per capita GDP growth rate, which lowered the growth effect on welfare. It could be argued that it would have affected the growth of the rate of saving and hence the growth rate. This is a valid argument if there is no inefficiency in capital use and higher MPCE does not improve the total factor productivity of the economy.

Trends in expenditure inequality

Atkinson inequality coefficient (Table 6.7) confirms the pattern of inequality seen in Table 6.5. The rural inequality trend during 1983–97 was negative but statistically not significant; during 1993/94–2011/12, it was positive and statistically significant. Urban inequality registered a significant positive trend in both the periods and its growth rate was markedly higher during 1993/94–2011/12. It is also worth noting that the rural-urban gap in MPCE progressively widened during 1993/94–2011/12. Urban MPCE which was about 40 per cent higher than rural MPCE in 1993–94 was 60 per cent higher in 2011–12. Quite clearly, the worsening of intra-rural/ urban inequality and widening rural-urban disparity should be a cause of concern for India from the perspective of enhancing overall economic welfare.

Table 6.7 Annual Growth Rates of Atkinson Inequality Coefficient (Aε)

	ε					
	0.5	*1.5*	*2*	*2.5*	*3*	*3.5*
Rural						
1983–97 (URP)	-0.17	-0.19	-0.39	-0.44	-0.50	-0.51
1993/94–2011-12 (MRP)	1.64***	1.34***	1.20***	1.08***	0.97***	0.88***
Urban						
1983–97 (URP)	1.07*	0.84**	0.75**	0.67**	0.60**	0.55**
1993/94–2011-12 (MRP)	2.21***	1.89***	1.74***	1.61***	1.49***	1.39***

***Significant at 1% level, **significant at 5% level, *significant at 10% level.

Source: Radhakrishna et al. (2013).

Atkinson rural-urban inequality computed from unit level data of quinquennial surveys showed an increase in inequality between 1993–94 and 2004–05 and no change between 2004–05 and 2009–10. However, it showed an increase between 1993–94 and 2011–12 (Table 6.7).

The Gini coefficient confirms that inequality worsened in the post-reform period, particularly between 2004–05 and 2011–12. In rural areas, the Gini coefficient declined from 0.282 in 1994–94 to 0.266 in 2004–05 and then increased to 0.280 in 2011–12. In urban areas, it increased in both the periods – from 0.340 in 1993–04 to 0.348 in 2004–05 and further to 0.367 in 2011–12. The changes in the Gini coefficient indicate that inequality has worsened considerably in the latter period.

Definite changes have occurred in expenditure inequality from 2004–05 to 2011–12. During this period, India witnessed a higher growth of per capita monthly expenditure at constant prices, but this was accompanied by worsening rural-urban inequality and intra-urban inequality. It is most likely that had income data been available, it would have shown much greater worsening of inequality.

Reduction of poverty

The incidence of poverty fluctuated and declined at a slow rate between 1993–94 and 2004–05. It declined by 0.75 percentage points per annum in rural areas and 0.55 percentage points per annum in urban areas. The rate of decline was higher after 2005–06 till 2011–12 and was 1.46 percentage points per annum in rural areas and 2.33 percentage points per annum in urban areas. For rural and urban areas put together, these figures were 0.74 percentage points in the pre-reform period and 2.18 percentage points per annum in the post-reform period. The absolute number of poor in All India declined by a meagre one million in the first period and by 38 million (10 million in rural and 28 million in urban) in the second period, still leaving an unacceptably high number of 270 million (217 million in rural and 53 million in urban) poor in 2011–2012. It is important to recognize that there is a concentration of poor in rural areas. Throughout the period, 80 per cent of the poor continued to be in rural India. Clearly, the performance of India in the reduction of poverty essentially depends on the performance of rural areas in poverty alleviation, which in turn depends on total factor productivity in agriculture, expansion of the rural non-farm sector and improvement of rural wages.

Inter-state variations in poverty reduction

There are substantial inter-state variations in the performance on poverty reduction. States such as Goa, Kerala, Himachal Pradesh, Andhra Pradesh, Sikkim, Tamil Nadu, Punjab, Haryana, Meghalaya and Uttarakhand performed better (Table 6.8). They also had a lower incidence of poverty in 2011–12. At the other extreme, Mizoram, Nagaland, Chhattisgarh, Madhya

Table 6.8 Incidence and Performance of States in Poverty Reduction between 1993–94 and 2011–12

Best Performing States			*Moderate Performing States*			*Worst Performing States*		
State	*1993–94*	*2011–12*	*State*	*1993–94*	*2011–12*	*State*	*1993–94*	*2011–12*
Goa	20.7	5.1	Pondicherry	24.7	9.7	Bihar	60.4	33.7
Kerala	31.3	7.1	Jammu & Kashmir	26.3	10.4	Manipur	65.2	36.9
Himachal Pradesh	34.7	8.1	Maharashtra	47.7	17.4	Uttar Pradesh	48.4	29.4
Andhra Pradesh	44.6	9.2	Rajasthan	38.3	14.7	Jharkhand	60.7	37.0
Sikkim	31.8	8.2	Tripura	32.9	14.1	Assam	51.8	32.0
Tamil Nadu	44.5	11.3	Gujarat	37.8	16.6	Ar. Pradesh	54.5	34.7
Punjab	22.4	8.3	Karnataka	49.5	20.9	Madhya Pradesh	44.0	31.7
Haryana	35.9	11.2	West Bengal	39.4	20.0	Chhattisgarh	50.9	39.9
Meghalaya	35.2	11.9	Delhi	15.7	9.9	Nagaland	20.4	18.9
Uttarakhand	32.1	11.3	Odisha	59.1	32.6	Mizoram	11.8	20.4
All India	45.1	21.9						

Note: Performance of the States in poverty reduction is arranged from the best to the lowest. Figures are the percentage of poor in respective states/UTs; Performance, as suggested by Kiwanis (1993), is measured by computing Performance Index: {Ln ($P_{1993–94}$ – $P_{2011–12)}$ – Ln ($P_{2011–12}$– P_{min}))}/ Ln (P_{max} – P_{min})). The maximum and minimum values of poverty considered are 66 and five per cent respectively.

Source: Radhakrishna (2015)

Pradesh, Arunachal Pradesh, Assam, Jharkhand, Uttar Pradesh, Manipur and Bihar had the worst performance in poverty reduction. These states, except Nagaland and Mizoram, also had a high incidence of poverty in 2011–12. It is worth noting that the incidence of poverty in Mizoram worsened during 1993–94 and 2011–12 and remained at the same level in Nagaland. States with the highest incidence of poverty viz., Bihar, Chhattisgarh, Madhya Pradesh, Jharkhand, Uttar Pradesh and Assam had witnessed the slowest reduction of poverty in the post-reform period. It is evident that poverty was increasingly becoming concentrated in Jharkhand, Bihar, Odisha, Chhattisgarh, Madhya Pradesh and Uttar Pradesh. While 41 per cent of India's poor (rural and urban) lived in these poorer states in 1993–94, this proportion increased to 57 per cent in 2011–12. Their share among the poor was more than their share in the population (39 per cent in 2011–12).

Growth and poverty reduction

Figure 6.5 demonstrates that growth would tend to reduce poverty. It shows that the rate of poverty reduction is positively associated with the rate of growth of GSDP per capita. The cross-classification of major states on the basis of their ranking on growth and poverty reduction shows that 11 of the 20 states fall on the diagonal cells (Table 6.9). The positive outliers on poverty reduction viz., Punjab, Himachal Pradesh, Kerala, Rajasthan and Jammu & Kashmir performed better in poverty reduction compared to their growth. The negative outliers namely Gujarat, Karnataka and Chhattisgarh had worse performance in poverty reduction compared to their growth. They also had a high incidence of poverty in 2011–12. In Gujarat, though the growth was very high during 1993–94 to 2011–12, its performance in

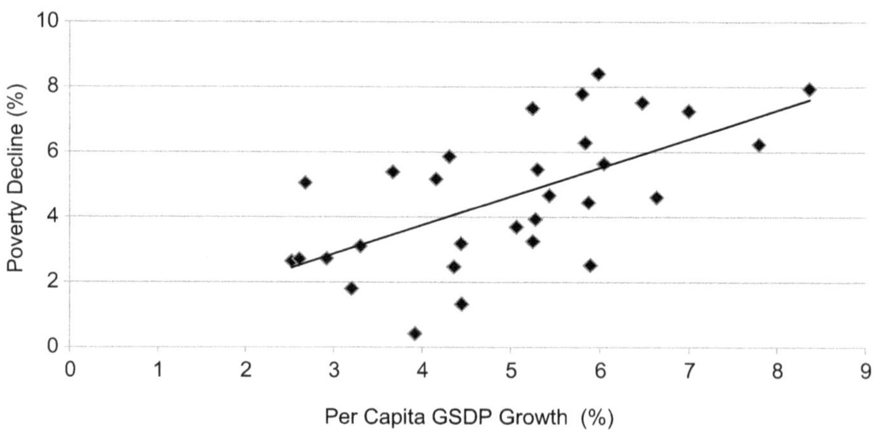

Figure 6.5 Scatter Diagram of States by GSDP Per Capita Growth and Poverty Reduction during 1993–94 and 2011–12

Source: by Author

Table 6.9 Classification of States by Growth and Performance of Poverty Reduction (1993/94–2011/12)

GSDP Per Capita Growth Rate (1993/94–2011/12)	*Performance in Poverty Reduction (1993/94–2011/12)*			
	Best	*Better*	*Moderate*	*Worst*
Best	Tamil Nadu	Haryana, Uttarakhand	Gujarat	
Better	Andhra Pradesh, Himachal Pradesh, Kerala	Maharashtra	Karnataka	
Moderate		Rajasthan	Bihar, West Bengal, Odisha	Chhattisgarh
Worst	Punjab	Jammu & Kashmir		Assam, Uttar Pradesh, Jharkhand, Madhya Pradesh

Source: by Author

poverty reduction was worse and the level of poverty remained high. Clearly, in this state, growth did not trickle down to the poor. Though Chhattisgarh has experienced moderate growth, its performance in poverty reduction was the worst and its poverty level remained high during the period. The poorer states of Assam, Uttar Pradesh, Jharkhand and Madhya Pradesh in future have to confront low growth and low reduction of poverty.

Radhakrishna et al 2013 have shown that had there been uniform growth of MPCE at the observed All India MPCE growth rate across all states and between rural and urban areas, and inequalities in population distribution remained at 1993–94 levels, the head-count ratio would have declined by 18.9 percentage points between 1993–94 and 2009–10 instead of the realised rate of decline of 14.3 percentage points. Hence the gain in poverty reduction under uniform growth would have been 4.6 percentage points. They have also shown that poverty reduction in All India would have been higher by about two percentage points if inequalities among the states had remained at 1993–94 levels. It has been observed that the pathway out of poverty also lies in the high growth of MPCE in less developed states such as Assam, Bihar, Chhattisgarh, Madhya Pradesh, Rajasthan and Uttar Pradesh.

Poverty among social groups

Scheduled Tribe (ST) households accounted for 17.4 per cent of the poor whereas they constituted 8.9 per cent of the population; Schedule Caste (SC) households accounted for 25.4 per cent of the poor as compared to

19 per cent of their share in population, and Other Backward Caste (OBC) households accounted 41.4 per cent of the poor against 44.1 of their share in population (Radhakrishna, 2015). The share of STs among the poor was higher than that of SCs and other social groups in Jharkhand, Chhattisgarh, Odisha, Madhya Pradesh, Gujarat and Rajasthan. SC households accounted for a bulk of the poor in some states. In 2011–12, they accounted for 73 per cent of the poor in Punjab, about 50 per cent in Haryana, and more than 45 per cent in Himachal Pradesh – much higher than their share in the population.

Figure 6.6 shows the relative poverty ratio defined as the ratio of poverty incidence of the social group (SCs and STs together) to the incidence of poverty of the total population. It can be seen that the relative poverty ratio at the All India level was more than one (norm) for SC and ST households together, and one for OBCs. The relative poverty ratio for SC and ST households together in 2011–12 was the highest in Gujarat (2.4), closely followed by Kerala (2.3) and close to 2.0 in Himachal Pradesh, Punjab, Rajasthan, and Maharashtra. These are the most developed states in India. It is also evident from Figure 6.6 that the relative poverty ratio increased between 1993–94 and 2011–12 in several states, particularly the developed states.

Non-income deprivations

Studies suggest that even if income poverty is eliminated in India, other forms of poverty (e.g. malnutrition) may persist. It has to be recognized that the high incidence of malnutrition among half of the children and a third of the adults should be a matter of concern. It is worth mentioning that malnutrition was higher than that of Sub-Saharan Africa. According to a recent

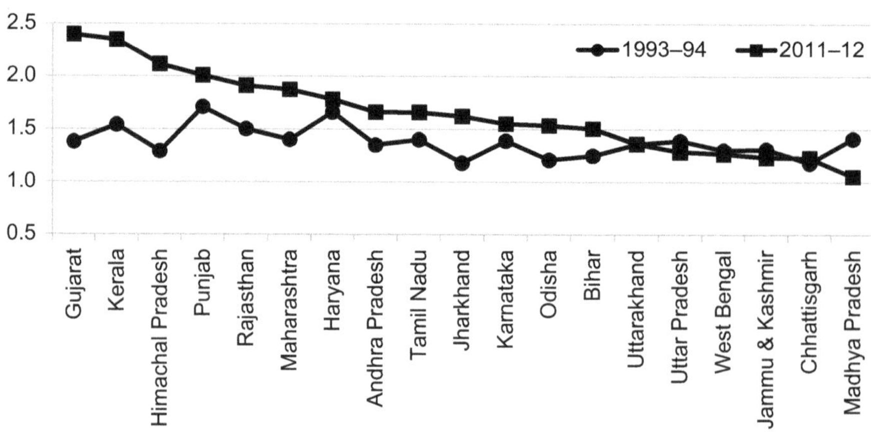

Figure 6.6 Relative Poverty of SC/ST to All (1993–94 and 2011–12)

Source: by author

UNICEF report, one-fifth of the children under five dying in the world were from India. India also contributed to a quarter of the global maternal deaths.

Most of the health and education indicators in India were worse than those in some of the Asian developing countries (UNDP, 2015; World Bank, 2016). For instance, the infant mortality rate (under five) in India was three times higher than that of China and four times more than that of Sri Lanka; the maternal mortality rate was about four times more than that of China and Sri Lanka; life expectancy at birth was about eight years less than that of China and six years less than that of Sri Lanka; mean years of schooling of adults was about three years less than that of China and about six years less than that of Sri Lanka. What is worse, India fared badly on health and education indicators even compared to some of the less developed countries. For instance, Bangladesh with less than half the per capita income improved its position on some of the development indicators and had reported better outcomes than India. It had a higher life expectancy at birth, higher mean years of schooling and lower gender inequality.

Multidimensional poverty

Radhakrishna et al. (2010) have suggested an approach to measure multi-dimensional poverty among households with a woman aged 15–49 years and a child below five years[11] by matching unit level data of the 61st Round (2004–05) NSS Consumer Expenditure Survey and 3rd National Family Health Survey (NFHS-3) 2005–06.[12] Both union and intersection approaches to multi-dimensional poverty have been adopted for estimating the incidence of multi-dimensional poverty for All India and States by considering three deprivation indicators viz., income poverty, child malnutrition and female malnutrition (see Table 6.10 for uni-dimensional and Table 6.11 for multi-dimensional poverty estimates for India).

The estimates show that multi-dimensional poverty, when measured as the proportion of households either poor or with a stunted child among the households with a woman and child below five years was 70 per cent for All India which was higher than income poverty at 49 per cent as well as child

Table 6.10 Incidence of Poverty, Malnutrition and CED of Woman in India (per cent)

	Percentage of persons below Poverty Line, 2004–05	*Percentage of Poor HH among the HH with a Women and a child below 5 years of age, 2004–05*	*Percentage of HH with a Stunted child below 5 years of age, 2005–06*	*Chronic Energy Deficiency (CED) of Female, 2005–06*
Rural	41.8	53.4	53.3	43.7
Urban	25.7	33.8	38.1	27.6
All India	38.2	49.1	49.9	40.1

Source: by author

malnutrition at 50 per cent. The incidence of multi-dimensional poverty was 75 per cent in rural and 54 per cent in urban areas (Table 6.11). If female malnutrition is also taken into account, the level of multi-dimensional poverty would be still higher at 79 per cent for All India (83 per cent for rural and 64 for urban areas). As expected, multi-dimensional poverty levels were higher than those of unit-dimensional poverty.

The distribution of multi-dimensional poverty by various levels shows that 14 per cent of the households (16 per cent in rural and 7 per cent in urban) were hardcore multi-dimensional poor, i.e. deprived in all three dimensions; 31 per cent (35 per cent in rural and 21 per cent in urban) were severely poor, i.e. deprived in any two out of the three dimensions; 33 per cent (32 per cent in rural and 34 per cent in urban) were moderately poor, i.e. deprived in one of the three dimensions; and 22 per cent (17 per cent in rural and 38 per cent in urban) were not deprived in any dimension (Table 6.12).

Whereas 51 per cent of households with a woman and a child below 5 years were not income poor, only 23 per cent were not multi-dimensionally poor. Hence, intervention to eliminate only income poverty would miss some of those deprived in other dimensions. It is a fact that growth reduces

Table 6.11 Incidence of Multi-dimensional Poverty in the Households with a Woman and a Child Below 5 years (per cent)

	Income poverty and child malnutrition	*Income poverty and CED of female*	*Child malnutrition and CED of Female*	*Income poverty, child malnutrition and CED of female*
Union of Households				
Rural	75.1	71.7	70.3	83.3
Urban	54.0	47.5	51.2	64.2
All India	70.4	64.5	65.2	79.1
Intersection of Households				
Rural	31.6	25.1	25.4	16.3
Urban	17.9	12.1	12.8	7.7
All India	28.6	21.6	22.0	14.4

Source: by author

Table 6.12 Distribution of Households with a Child Below 5 Years and a Woman by Multidimensional Poverty in India *(per cent)*

	Not Poor	*Moderately Poor*	*Severely Poor*	*Hardcore Poor*
Rural	17.18	32.37	34.62	15.83
Urban	37.86	33.67	21.28	7.18
All India	22.69	32.72	31.06	13.53

Source: by author

income poverty. However, it may not be very effective in reducing deprivation in other dimensions, particularly those which depend on the provision of public goods.

The multi-dimensional poverty estimates show substantial differences across the states in three dimensional spaces (income poverty, child malnutrition, female malnutrition); the estimates varied from 48 per cent (rural and urban) in Kerala and 63 per cent in Punjab to 92 per cent in Chhattisgarh; about 90 per cent in Jharkhand, Bihar and Madhya Pradesh; and around 85 per cent in Uttar Pradesh and Odisha.[13]

Ranking of states by multiple deprivations

The states were ranked on child deprivation index, household amenities deprivation index and a combined index of the two (Table 6.13). The indicators considered for child deprivation were: i) malnutrition (underweight) of children below 3 years, ii) infant mortality, iii) live births not attended by trained functionaries, iv) children not attending school in the age group of 7–18 years, v) prevalence of child labour (6–14 years), vi) girls married below 18 years; indicators considered for household amenities deprivation were households without: i) electricity, ii) safe drinking water, iii) accesses to toilet facility, and iv) living in a pucca house. States have been ranked on the basis of monthly per capita expenditure and per capita gross state domestic product. As expected, the inverse of the combined index of deprivation was positively associated with (i) per capita MPCE and (ii) GSDP per capita and (iii) inverse of poverty. On the whole, monthly per capita expenditure explains income poverty and deprivation better than per capita state domestic product.

The following observations can be made on the basis of the inverse of the Aggregate Deprivation Index: i) Goa, Kerala, Sikkim, Delhi, Punjab, Himachal Pradesh and Tamil Nadu, in that order, fared better in terms of low incidence of deprivation as well as poverty. On the other hand, Jharkhand, Bihar, Odisha, Chhattisgarh, Madhya Pradesh, Assam and Uttar Pradesh fared worse. ii) Gujarat, Haryana and Maharashtra though they were ranked high on GSDP per capita, had a middle position in ranking on the inverse of aggregate deprivation index perhaps due to the disconnect between their domestic product and purchasing power. Jammu and Kashmir, with a very low ranking of GSDP per capita, was in the middle of the ranking on the inverse of aggregate deprivation index perhaps because of lower inequality.

Ranking of states by progress in reduction of multiple deprivations

The progress in the reduction of multiple deprivations has been assessed on the basis of three indicators viz., i) incidence of income poverty, ii) child malnutrition and CED of women together and iii) educational deprivation.[14] Table 6.14 provides the ranking of the states on the progress made in

Table 6.13 Ranking of States Based on Inverse of Deprivations, Inverse of Poverty, Average Real MPCE and Real GSDP Per Capita

State	*Inverse of Deprivations of*			*Inverse of Poverty (2011/12)*	*Inverse Aggregate Deprivation Index**	*MPCE (2011/12) at Const. Prices*	*Per capita Real GSDP (2011–14)*
	Children	*Households*	*Combined*				
1	*2*	*3*	*4*	*5*	*6*	*7*	*8*
Andhra Pradesh	16	12	14	6	11	10	12
Arunachal Pradesh	17	8	13	24	18	16	16
Assam	19	25	20	21	22	23	25
Bihar	25	22	26	23	25	27	27
Chhattisgarh	20	22	20	27	24	25	19
Delhi	6	1	2	7	4	1	2
Goa	2	6	3	1	1	2	1
Gujarat	18	13	17	15	14	11	6
Haryana	15	3	9	9	8	5	5
Himachal Pradesh	7	5	7	3	5	8	9
Jammu & Kashmir	10	10	10	8	9	13	18
Jharkhand	23	27	27	26	27	24	22
Karnataka	13	15	16	18	14	9	13
Kerala	1	7	1	2	2	3	10
Madhya Pradesh	25	21	25	20	23	22	23
Maharashtra	9	15	12	16	12	6	4
Manipur	3	18	8	25	14	19	24
Meghalaya	14	22	18	12	17	18	15
Odisha	22	26	24	22	25	26	21
Punjab	8	2	5	5	5	4	11
Rajasthan	24	20	22	14	20	15	20
Sikkim	5	4	4	4	3	14	3
Tamil Nadu	4	9	6	10	7	7	7
Tripura	11	18	15	13	13	20	14
Uttar Pradesh	27	17	23	19	21	21	26
Uttarakhand	12	10	11	10	10	12	8
West Bengal	21	14	19	17	19	17	17

Note: *Ranking in Aggregate Deprivation Index (col. 6) is based on combination of rankings in deprivation of children (col. 2), deprivation of household amenities (col. 3) and incidence of poverty (col. 5) by using the Borda Aggregation Rule. Ranking of States in all deprivation indicators (col. 2 to col. 6) and MPCE (col. 7) and GSDP per capita (col. 8) are from least deprived condition to most deprived condition.

Source: Radhakrishna et al. (2013).

Table 6.14 Ranking of States on Performance in Reduction in Income Poverty, Decline in Malnutrition and Improvement in Education in Post-reform Period

	Reduction in Income poverty (1993–94 to 2011–12)	*Decline in Child Malnutrition*	*Decline in CED of women*	*Combined decline in child malnutrition and CED of women*	*Increase in literacy (Census 1991/ 2011)*	*Aggregate Ranking**
1	2	3	4	5	6	7
Andhra Pradesh	4	17	15	18	28	17
Ar. Pradesh	25	29	29	29	27	29
Assam	24	24	28	27	25	28
Bihar	20	20	26	25	29	27
Chhattisgarh	27	7	18	12	16	23
Delhi	18	16	3	7	10	9
Goa	1	18	8	13	6	3
Gujarat	15	19	20	22	15	19
Haryana	8	27	25	27	18	21
Himachal Pradesh	3	5	13	4	5	1
Jammu & Kashmir	11	6	10	3	30	14
Jharkhand	23	21	24	24	26	25
Karnataka	16	15	14	15	22	21
Kerala	2	22	2	11	3	2
Madhya Pradesh	26	23	27	26	21	25
Maharashtra	12	2	16	4	7	4
Manipur	21	3	5	2	13	12
Meghalaya	9	26	1	14	11	8
Mizoram	29	1	4	1	2	7
Nagaland	28	28	11	22	12	24
Odisha	19	4	17	9	19	15
Punjab	7	14	6	8	24	13
Rajasthan	13	8	21	15	23	18
Sikkim	5	25	9	19	4	5
Tamil Nadu	6	9	12	9	14	6
Tripura	14	12	23	20	1	9
Uttar Pradesh	22	11	7	4	9	9
Uttarakhand	10	13	22	20	17	15
West Bengal	17	10	19	15	20	19

Note: *Aggregate Ranking (col. 7) is based on combination of rankings in decline in income poverty (col. 2), decline in child malnutrition (col. 3), decline in CED of women (col. 4) and increase in literacy rate (col. 6) by using the Borda Aggregation Rule.

Source: by Author

reducing income poverty, child malnutrition and educational deprivation in the post-reform period and the combined ranking of the three. The following observations can be made.

Himachal Pradesh, Kerala, Goa, Maharashtra, Sikkim and Tamil Nadu with a low current level of multiple deprivations emerged as the best performing states in reducing multiple deprivations in the post-reform period. While the success stories of Kerala and Tamil Nadu are well known, the success stories of Himachal Pradesh and Sikkim are less known. At the other extreme, Arunachal Pradesh, Assam, Bihar, Jharkhand and Madhya Pradesh in that order with high current levels of multiple deprivations emerged as the worst performing states in the reduction of multiple deprivations.

It is worth mentioning that states performing better in the reduction of deprivation also had comparatively low incidence of multiple deprivations in the initial years of reform period and hence deprivation is self-perpetuating. Since the level of deprivation is likely to be self-perpetuating and some of the deprivations are related to public goods, public intervention is essential in states with high level of deprivation.

India's ranking on well-being among countries

The UN Sustainable Development Solutions Network, a Global Initiative of the United Nations, brings out the World Happiness Report[15] which enables international comparability of well-being across countries. Table 6.15 presents the ranking of selected countries based on happiness. Another index for international comparability of well-being is the Social Progress Index.[16]

It is clear from these well-being indices that social democratic countries which follow welfare policies such as Denmark, Norway, Switzerland, Netherlands and Sweden performed better than the countries under a neo-liberal regime such as US, Japan and Australia. The ranking of the above social democratic countries on the happiness index was better than their ranking on GDP per capita.

As expected, India ranked below the developed countries. As a matter of fact, none of the less developed counties fared better than the developed counties on the basis of their rankings on either the happiness index or social progress.

Among the developing countries, India fared badly compared to Indonesia, Malaysia, China and Bangladesh. Sri Lanka, though it was ranked higher than Bangladesh and India on GDP per capita and Social Progress Index, was lower on the Happiness Index. This could be due to its internal conflicts. During the period of economic crisis i.e. between 2005–07 and 2012–14, the Happiness Index showed a decline for India, Sri Lanka and Pakistan. It is worth repeating that Bangladesh with lower GDP per capita than that of India had achieved a higher level of well-being. On the whole, India ranking on international well-being indices was very low.

Table 6.15 Measures of Happiness for Selected Countries

Sl. No.	*Country*	*Happiness Index, 2013–15*			*Social Progress Index, 2016*		*Per Capita GDP, 2015*	
		Value	*Rank*	*Change Compared to 2005–07*	*Value*	*Rank*	*$*	*Rank*
1	Denmark	7.526	1	-0.401	89.39	3	45,700	31
2	Switzerland	7.509	2	+0.035	88.87	5	58,600	16
3	Norway	7.498	4	+0.082	88.70	7	68,400	11
4	Canada	7.404	6	-0.041	89.49	2	45,600	32
5	Netherlands	7.339	7	-0.119	88.65	8	49,200	25
6	Australia	7.313	9	+0.002	89.13	4	65,400	14
7	Sweden	7.291	10	-0.017	88.80	6	47,900	26
8	United States	7.104	13	-0.261	84.62	19	55,800	19
9	Singapore	6.739	22	+0.099	NA	-	85,300	6
10	United Kingdom	6.725	23	-0.161	88.58	9	41,200	39
11	Thailand	6.474	33	+0.631	67.43	61	16,100	101
12	Malaysia	6.005	47	-0.132	70.08	50	26,300	69
13	Japan	5.921	53	-0.446	86.54	14	38,100	42
14	Russia	5.856	56	+0.738	64.19	75	25,400	73
15	Indonesia	5.314	79	+0.295	62.27	82	11,100	132
16	China	5.245	83	+0.525	62.10	84	14,100	113
17	Pakistan	5.132	92	-0.374	49.13	113	5,000	170
18	Bangladesh	4.643	110	+0.17	52.73	101	3,600	179
19	Sri Lanka	4.415	117	+0.037	62.21	83	10,600	135
20	India	4.404	118	-0.75	53.92	98	6,200	158

Note:

i) The Happiness Index ranges between zero and 10 points. Denmark achieved the highest score in the happiness index with 7.526 points out of 10 and ranked first, and the country Burundi with 2.905 points ranked the lowest at 257. The figures in parentheses indicate the magnitude of increase/decline in Happiness Index when compared to 2005–07.

ii) Social Progress Index is measured in percentages and the ranks are assigned for 133 countries. For Singapore the data was not available.

iii) GDP estimates are at purchasing power parity ($), and the ranks are assigned for 229 countries, World Bank.

Source: World Happiness Report 2016, Social Progress Report 2016, CIA World Factbook 2015

Challenges for achieving inclusive growth

The preceding analysis brings out both the positive and negative features of growth as well as poverty reduction in the post-reform period. I will discuss a few major challenges involved in the rapid reduction of poverty.

First, it is a challenge to sustain higher growth and macroeconomic stability which are necessary for reducing poverty. There are several constraints in sustaining the high growth witnessed in the last decade of the reform period. The growth mainly came from raising the domestic saving rate to a very high level and from foreign capital flows and not from productivity improvement to some extent. There are limits to increasing the saving rate further, and it may be increasingly difficult to attract more foreign investment flows. Moreover, the dependence on foreign investment flows would expose India to vulnerabilities which affect the poor the most.

Second, it is a challenge to reverse the growing income inequality. The pattern of growth has been aggravating inter-state inequality, worsening rural/urban disparity and deepening intra-urban inequality. This has weakened the trickle down process. Poverty would have declined much faster if the inequality had been contained at least at the level of the pre-reform period. The recent concern of slowing economic growth should not obliterate our concern for reversing the growing inequality. For rapid poverty reduction, it is equally important to address i) worsening inequality, ii) eliminating the worst forms of deprivation in education, health and malnutrition and iii) the poor performance of public delivery systems. Public health and education should be considered as public goods and the Central and State governments should not abrogate their responsibilities to private agencies.

Third, even though much is said about India's success in reducing income poverty, there are still more than 269 million poor people in India (Planning Commission, Press Release, and 23rd July 2013). At present, the majority of the poor are concentrated in six less developed central and eastern states i.e. Bihar, Jharkhand, Assam, Chhattisgarh, Madhya Pradesh and Uttar Pradesh. These states witnessed the slowest reduction of poverty mainly attributable to the sluggish growth they experienced in the post-reform period. Even the breakthrough in growth achieved by Bihar was not inclusive enough to bring about a commensurate reduction in poverty. For sustainable poverty reduction, India has to make continuous efforts to accelerate inclusive growth in these states. What is of concern is the very low flow of private investment and foreign investment to these states due to their low levels of physical and social infrastructure. What is of more concern is the regressive nature of the flow of formal credit to these states. It is a daunting task since their agrarian systems are oppressive and public delivery systems are weak.

Fourth, the increasing concentration of the poor among the scheduled caste/tribe households who suffer from multiple deprivations is a matter of concern. In the developed states of Punjab, Haryana and Himachal Pradesh, a highly disproportionate share of the poor belong to scheduled castes. In these developed states, absolute and relative poverty are becoming more a sociological phenomenon making the economic instruments weak in the reduction of poverty. Since the governments of these states have adequate fiscal resources they can eliminate poverty provided that they overcome sociological barriers. In the states of Chhattisgarh, Rajasthan and Odisha, ST households account for more than 40 per cent of the poor. These States are facing a double burden i.e. low growth and high incidence of multidimensional poverty. Their per capita development expenditure and per capita social expenditure are also low.

Fifth, informal workers constitute more than 90 per cent of the total workforce in India. It is a fact that high growth in the post-liberalization period is accompanied by the increasing formalisation and declining influence of unions. A sizeable portion of the workforce is engaged in subsistence production. This segment is at the bottom of the production ladder providing cheap labour. Economically and socially deprived sections of the society are mostly employed as casual labour. Informality is linked to poverty. Women are particularly involved in the informal economy. However, there is some degree of dynamism in some segments of the informal sector which have an inter-linkage with the formal sector. These sunrise enterprises have positive productivity growth as well as positive employment growth. It is a moot question whether these will expand to cover rest of the informal segments. It is also a moot question whether employment in the sunrise enterprises is of an acceptable standard.

Concluding remarks

Notwithstanding the slowdown in the economy since 2008–09, India has experienced higher growth in the post-reform period. However, the present pattern of development has aggravated inter-state inequality, widened rural – urban disparity and worsened intra-rural and intra-urban inequality. Undoubtedly, growth in the post-reform period has not been inclusive. If the worsening of inequalities persists, it may thwart growth and what is worse, it may lead to social disarticulation.

For inclusive economic growth, a labour intensive process of development is vital. It can be achieved by incentivizing the small and medium-sized firms and farms, in the formal and informal sectors, and at the same time imparting education and skills to the people so that they can take advantage of the opportunities created by the small and medium enterprises. The growth of allied agriculture and rural-non-farm activities is essential for long-term poverty reduction. Producer collectives such as producer companies and a cluster-based approach for small-scale enterprises, hold promise. It would strengthen the livelihood base of small farmers and self-employed persons in non-agriculture. Good public support is essential for these initiatives.

It is imperative that efforts are made to empower the poor people so that they participate in the development process. Empowering the poor requires public investment in health, education and social protection. Healthier, educated and skilled persons can take advantage of employment and investment opportunities created by small and medium enterprises. Kerala's *Kudumbashree* and the SHG model of Andhra Pradesh are good models for empowering the poor and strengthening the livelihood base of vulnerable groups. The National Livelihood Mission's efforts to promote SHG Federations in States may yield desirable outcomes in empowering the poor. A favourable investment climate, empowerment and decent work are the *sine quibus non* for inclusive growth.

Poverty occurs in many dimensions other than income. In some dimensions, poverty depends on public provisioning. Hence even if income poverty is eliminated, poverty will remain in other dimensions. Over time, with development, poverty is getting concentrated in some less developed states which have also witnessed the slowest reduction in poverty and have not made much progress in reducing multiple deprivations. It is critical for poverty reduction in these lagging states that the structural constraints that hinder economic growth are addressed, social and physical infrastructure is upgraded with public support and the governance of delivery of services be improved, and, above all that people are empowered. Even in developed states, a large number of hard-core poor are located in remote and inaccessible areas and among specific communities. The problem of poverty alleviation in these states is going to be far more difficult than in the past, since those who were near the poverty line might have crossed it, leaving the hardcore poor much below the poverty line.

SC households account for the bulk of the poor in some of the developed north-western states and ST households' account for a sizeable proportion of the poor in the less developed states of Central and Eastern States and even in some of the developed Western States. Poverty in these states is not merely an economic phenomenon but also a social one and hence social policy should complement economic policy for the reduction of poverty. Inclusive governance is essential for making a significant dent on poverty, particularly among tribal communities. Some of the initiatives such as PESA (Panchayat extension to scheduled areas) Act and FRA (Forest Rights Act) are intended to ensure devolution and self-governance in the tribal areas. However, the implementation of PESA was partial and provisions of the Act have been diluted, and the same is the case with the implementation of FRA. Undoubtedly, their effective implementation will empower the poor and provide them with a pathway out of poverty.

Though many components of reforms such as radical land reforms, debureaucratisation and decentralised development figured in Indian Plans, they could not make much headway because of resistance from pressure groups (Rao, 1998). Had radical land reforms been implemented soon after Independence and the required investments made in human development and infrastructure, India could have achieved a sharp, sustained reduction in poverty.

Though many radical reforms are not politically feasible in India, there are some positive developments due to the electoral process such as the implementation of nationwide rights-based programmes such as MGN-REGA, Food Security, Right to Education etc. and income improvement programmes such as NRLM. If these programmes are properly implemented through social mobilisation, marginalised groups may emerge as pressure groups and this may lead to a more socially just economy. This should be complemented by a labour intensive process of development and needed institution building.

(This address draws from Radhakrishna et al., 2013; Radhakrishna, 2014, 2015).

Notes

* This paper was presented as the Presidential Address at the 99th Annual Conference of Indian Economic Association on December 27–29, 2016 and was published in *Essays on perspectives of Indian Economy*, Academic Foundation, 2018.

1 The gross saving rate increased from 21.3 per cent in 1991–92 to 36.8 per cent in 2007–08 and then declined to 31.3 per cent in 2011–12. Gross capital formation increased from 21.8 per cent in 1991–02 to 38.1 per cent in 2007–08 and then declined to 35.3 per cent in 2015–16 (Economic Survey, 2015–16). The incremental capital-output ratio fluctuated between 3.0 and 3.5 during 2005 and 2010 except in 2009 where it was very high at 6.2 (EPW Research Foundation, 2012).

2 India's growth rate was higher than the global GDP growth rate of 3.1 per cent in 2015–16 and India's share in world GDP increased from 4.8 per cent to 7 percent over 2001–16. Yet, India remains among the poorest countries of the world; its GDP per capita measured at $5214 in 2013 was lower than that of some of its neighbouring countries such as Maldives by 54 per cent, Sri Lanka by 44 per cent and Bhutan by 27 per cent (Bhaduri, 2016).

3 Banerjee and Piketty (2003), based on income tax returns, observed that inequality grew in the 1990s and the share of the top percentile in total income increased substantially. Shetty (2008), based on an analysis of company annual reports, showed a substantial increase in the remuneration of executives of top companies between 2002–03 and 2006–07.

4 The present growth is increasing the demand for skilled manpower. Due to a shortage of skilled labour, rents are accruing to the skilled workers and consequently aggravating earning differentials between the surplus unskilled workers and the scarce skilled workers. Spread of education, particularly technical and vocational, would eliminate rents which accrue to skilled labour and thereby reduce the wage differentials. Clearly, education, inter alia, is an effective instrument to moderate income inequality.

5 Some scholars characterize the employment situation as jobless growth (Bhaduri, 2016), whereas others argue that low employment elasticity should not be a matter of concern and what matters is the quality of employment and that employment elasticity is bound to decrease in the growth period since the long-term growth of employment is 1.5–2.0 per cent (Dev, 2016). While it is true that what matters is quality, jobless growth should still be a matter of concern as long as the labour force increases.

6 Ghose (2015) observes that government policies systematically discriminated in favor of skill intensive services against manufacturing by taxing services very

lightly compared to manufacturing; also, the rules for the entry of FDI have been less restrictive for services.

7 Indian students in the US increased from 31,743 in 1995 to 102,000 in 2015. They made their presence felt in the US. It is argued that they would not have achieved much success had they remained in India, the reason being an individual's inquisitiveness and creativity are affected by the excessive focus on examinations which rarely test these qualities (Prabudev Konana, 'Where the mind is without fear', Hindu, October 16, 2015).

8 In an interview to *Indian Express*, scientist CNR Rao mentioned that globally the private sector supports around 40–45 per cent of scientific research, while in India it is all by the government.

9 Social Welfare is evaluated by using the Atkinson Social Welfare Function given by

$$SW_{\varepsilon} = \left[\left[\frac{1}{n}\right]\sum_{i=1}^{n} y_i^{(1-\varepsilon)}\right]^{1/(1-\varepsilon)}$$

where, y_i (i = 1, 2, 3,.........,n) is total expenditure of the ith individual and ε is the inequality aversion parameter. In equality measure A_{ε} is given by

$$A_{\varepsilon} = 1 - {SW_{\varepsilon}}/{\mu}$$

where Atkinson inequality measure shows the proportion of total income that can be saved if each individual receives representative income (equally distributed equivalent income) in such a way that overall social welfare remains constant.

10 The social welfare function defined in (1) can also be expressed as

$$SW_{\varepsilon} = \mu(1 - A_{\varepsilon})$$

where, μ is the mean income. In (3), μA_{ε} may be considered as the welfare loss due to inequality.

11 Households with a women aged 15–49 years and child below 5 years of age constituted 1/3 of the households. Incidence of poverty among these households in 2004–05 was higher as compared to all households.

12 Details of the methodology are given in Radhakrishna et al. (2010).

13 State-wise estimates with rural and urban break up are available with the author.

14 Some of the indicators used in the preceding sub-section could not be used due to lack of comparable data between 1993–94 and 2009–10.

15 In this framework, well-being has three distinct components: i) life evaluation, i.e. the cognitive judgment by a person about their life as a whole, ii) positive effect, i.e. the experience of positive feeling and emotions by the person at a particular point of time, and iii) negative effect, i.e. the experience of negative feelings and emotions by a person at a particular point of time. Countries were ranked on the basis of happiness during 2010–12 and the World Happiness Report 2013 was put in the public domain.

16 Social Progress Index is based on three distinct dimensions of a society: i) Basic human needs (adequate nutrition, water and sanitation, shelter, personal safety), ii) foundations of well-being (basic education, access to information and communications, health care, and environmental sustainability), and iii) opportunity (personal rights, personal freedom and choice, access to higher education, and environment tolerance and inclusion) has been compiled for a number of countries. Each of the dimensions is disaggregated into four components and

each component covers three to six indicators. A large number of individual indicators have been considered for each element and simple methodologies for aggregation have been suggested.

References

ASER Centre. (2014). *Annual Status of Education Report 2014*. New Delhi.

Banerjee, A. and Piketty, T. (2003). *Top Indian Income: 1956–2000*. Photocopy. Cambridge, MA: Department of Economics, Massachusetts Institute of Technology.

Bhaduri, A. (2016). Danger zones of high economic growth. *Economic and Political Weekly*, 51(43), 14–17.

Binswanger-Mkhize, H. P. (2012, May). India 1960–2010: Structural change, the rural non-farm sector, and the prospects for agriculture. In *Center on Food Security and the Environment Stanford Symposium Series on Global Food Policy and Food Security in the 21st Century*. Stanford University.

Blyn, G. (1966). *Agricultural Trends in India 1891–1967*. Philadelphia: University of Pennsylvania Press.

Dev, S. M. (2016). Changes in labour market and rural non-farm sector in India. In *Rural Labour in India: Processes and Policy Options*. Hyderabad: S. R. Sankaran Chair (Rural Labour), National Institute of Rural Development and Panchayati Raj, 7–23.

EPW Research Foundation. (2012). *India: A Pocket Book of Data Series*. New Delhi: Academic Foundation.

Ghose, A. K. (2015). Services-led growth and employment in India. In *Labour, Employment and Economic Growth*. New Delhi: Cambridge University Press, 21–56.

Government of India. (2016). *Economic Survey 2015–16*. New Delhi: Ministry of Finance.

Institute for Human Development. (2014). *India Labour and Employment Report*. New Delhi: Academic Foundation.

Kolli, R. (2009). Corporate sector in Indian national accounts. *The Journal of Income and Wealth*, 31(2), 89–104.

Kolli, R. and Sinharay, A. (2011). Share of informal sector and informal employment in GDP and employment. In *The Association of Research in National Income and Wealth: Annual Conference*. Hyderabad: Centre for Economic and Social Studies.

Maddison, A. (2001). *The World Economy: A Millennial Perspective*. Paris: OECD.

Ministry of Human Resource Development, Government of India National University of Educational Planning and Administration (NUEPA). (2015). *Education for All: Status and Trends*. New Delhi.

Papola, T. S. (2014). Economic diversification and labour market dynamics in rural India. *Indian Journal of Agricultural Marketing*, 28(3), 18–33.

Radhakrishna, R. (2014). Performance of Indian economy in the post-reform period. *Indian Journal of Human Development*, 8(1), 5–27.

Radhakrishna, R. (2015). Well-being, inequality, poverty and pathways out of poverty in India. *Economic and Political Weekly*, 50(41), 59–71.

Radhakrishna, R. and Chandrasekhar, S. (2008). Overview: Growth, achievements and distress. In R. Radhakrisnan and I. Gandhi (eds.), *Indian Development Report*. New Delhi: Oxford University Press.

Radhakrishna, R. and Raju, D. S. R. (2015). Well-being of agricultural households in post reform India. *The Indian Economic Journal*, 63(3), 329–347.

Radhakrishna, R. and Raju, D. S. R. (2016). Well-being of agricultural households in post-reform India. In C. Ramasamy and K. R. Ashok (eds.), *Vicissitudes of Agriculture in the Fast Growing Indian Economy: Challenges, Strategies and the Way Forward*. Mumbai: Academic Foundation, 151–174.

Radhakrishna, R., Ravi, C., and Reddy, B. S. (2010). Can we really measure poverty and identify the poor when poverty encompasses multiple deprivations? *Indian Journal of Human Development*, 4(2), 281–300.

Radhakrishna, R., Ravi, C., and Reddy, B. S. (2013). Assessment of well-being in multidimensional perspective in post-reform India. *Indian Economic Review*, 48(1), 129–166.

Radhakrishna, R. and Ray, S. (eds.). (2005). *Handbook of Poverty in India: Perspectives, Policies, and Programmes*. Oxford: Oxford University Press.

Rao, C. H. (1998). Agricultural growth, sustainability and poverty alleviation: Recent trends and major issues of reform. *Economic and Political Weekly*, 33(29/30), 1943–1948.

Saha, P. and Verick, S. (2016a). State of rural labour markets in India. In *Dynamics of Rural Labour Relations in India*. Hyderabad: National Institute of Rural Development and Panchayati Raj (NIRD & PR).

Saha, P. and Verick, S. (2016b). *State of Rural Labour Markets in India*. ILO Working Paper No. 994927490402676. International Labour Organization.

Shetty, S. L. (2003). Growing inequality: A serious challenge to the Indian society and polity. In *Dr. V. K. R. V. Rao Memorial Lecture, Annual Conference of the Indian Association for Research in National Income and Wealth*. Bangalore: Institute for Social and Economic Change.

Thomas, J. J. (2012). India's labour market during the 2000s: Surveying the changes. *Economic and Political Weekly*, 39–51.

Thomas, J. J. (2015). India's labour market during the 2000s. In K. V. Ramaswamy (ed.), *Labour, Employment and Economic Growth in India*. New Delhi: Cambridge University Press, 21–56.

UNDP. (2015). *Human Development Report*. New York: United Nations Development Programme.

Walton, Michael. (2012). *Inequality, Rents and Long-Run Transformation of India*. Monograph No. 26. Bengaluru: Institute of Socio-Economic Change.

World Bank. (2016). *World Development Indicators*. Washington, DC: World Bank.

7 Economics of discrimination

Theory, evidence and the role of state

P. Duraisamy and Malathy Duraisamy

Discrimination on the basis of gender, race, ethnicity or caste can impair the efficient functioning of labour market and have adverse distributional consequences.

Lawrence Summers, Former Vice-President, Development Economics and Chief Economist, The World Bank, 1991

Introduction

Discrimination, in general, refers to the unequal treatment of equals. It can take several forms and manifest itself in social, political and economic spheres. Discrimination against individuals/ specific groups based on gender, ethnicity, caste or religion is a phenomenon that exists across the world irrespective of space and time. Economists, among other social scientists, have made significant contributions to understanding this phenomenon. There is a large volume of literature on labour market discrimination. Marshall (1974) reviewed the early theoretical and empirical works on racial discrimination while the studies on gender-based discrimination are summarised in Cain (1986), Gunderson (1989) and Terrel (1992) among others. Birdsall and Sabot (1991) contain a collection of studies on discrimination in developing countries. In the Indian context, Thorat and Newman (2010) provide an excellent collection of studies conducted at the Indian Institute of Dalit Studies, (IIDS) mainly on caste-based discrimination not only in the labour market but also in other spheres, and the consequences of discrimination on inequalities in capital assets and poverty. Rustagi (2005) also presents a comprehensive review of earlier studies on discrimination. In this chapter, we synthesise and summarise the evidence on gender and caste discrimination in India based on our works and a selection of other studies relevant to the topic.

In this chapter, we focus on labour market discrimination that is discrimination in wages and employment by gender and caste. This does not mean that other forms of discrimination are less important. In the following section, we briefly review the economic theory behind discrimination. The methodology used and the empirical evidence is presented based on our past works in section III. Section IV discusses the consequences of labour market discrimination at micro and macro levels, and section V presents the role of State and its policy options. The concluding remarks are presented in section VI.

Economic approach to discrimination

Economists' concerns about discrimination can be traced to discussions among 19th-century economists. According to Webb (1891), discrimination results from weaker demand for women workers. This is due to lower living standards, lower family situation relative to men, lower productivity, ill health, inadequate training, lack of protective power, restricted alternatives and immobility of women. Early 20th-century economists like Edgeworth (1922), and Robinson (1933) considered discrimination in wages and attributed it to occupational crowding, trade unions and market imperfections. The well-known Marxian theory of class struggle also draws attention to discrimination between two classes – capitalists and workers. The theory advocates that the difference between the price of a product and wages paid to labour would lead to capital accumulation. Improved technology and capital accumulation would lead to displacement of labour in the production process resulting in huge unemployment. This would further bring wages down and when the depressed labourers become the effective majority of the society, with nothing to lose; they will tend towards social revolution.

Modern economic theories of discrimination emanated from the seminal work of Becker (1957) who proposed the utility maximising approach to explain employer's taste for discrimination. According to Becker, discrimination arises on account of prejudice or taste factor. Employers or groups of employees may choose to recruit or work with persons who are less productive but are like themselves – males or upper caste workers – over the more productive people who are not like themselves such as women or scheduled castes. In the Indian context, culture and tradition may lead to occupational segregation based on caste or gender. Thus women may be pushed to work at home or household enterprises while men enter high productive jobs in the labour market. Therefore, the traditional practice of hiring men and not women for work outside the home hardly appears to be the borne out of deliberate taste for the majority group (males/upper caste). Under such circumstances, if two individuals with comparable characteristics seek employment, the one belonging to the weaker or marginal group will be offered the job only if he/she is ready to accept a lower wage – a wage not commensurate with productivity. Becker's model falls in the class of competitive models, which is distinct from statistical theories of discrimination.

Phelps' (1972) theory of discrimination is based on imperfect information as the cause for discrimination, that is, the information available to employers on the skill endowment of individual job aspirants are likely to be relatively sketchy while information about the average endowment of a group is, or believed to be, relatively complete. Hence in the event of lack of information on the individual job applicant, unprejudiced employers may prefer to hire or pay more for the members of privileged groups, and justify their preferences on the basis of the average characteristics of the groups, that is, rely on the probability based on the group information.

Arrow (1972) argued that the imperfect information model based on beliefs about group productivity is not very different from the Becker model. How do employers form beliefs regarding the endowment of job applicants from the privileged (upper caste) versus less privileged (lower caste) groups? Further, the job applicant may not be representative of the groups and hence may not exhibit the average skills of the group. Arrow advocates the theory of cognitive dissonance to explain why employers may come to hold beliefs regarding endowments at variance with facts, but consistent with their actions.

The classical and neo-classical theories, discussed above, are challenged by the segmented labour market theory which originated from the idea of non-competing groups in the labour market forwarded by Alfred Marshall in 1880s, dual labour market theory and radical theory.

Although several theories explain the rationale behind discrimination, it is hard to empirically test the reason behind discrimination – whether it is due to taste or prejudice, imperfect information, labour market screening, segmentation, dual or multiple labour market segmentation, imperfect competition or other reasons. The empirical studies end up testing the wage differential between two or more groups using econometric methodology. The following section elaborates the methodology widely used in the literature on labour market discrimination and also provides empirical evidence based on our previous studies.

Methodologies to test discrimination

The methodologies used to test the existence and extent of discrimination in the labour market may be classified into two types – (i) wage or earnings discrimination (at mean and over the distribution) and (ii) job discrimination. Wage discrimination is tested by examining the difference in wages that arise after controlling for observable productivity augmenting human capital characteristics and occupational differences. Job discrimination is examined using the methodology devised to examine how the discrimination is exercised at the entry point and it also indicates the extent to which the wage difference can be attributed to job discrimination. However, studies on discrimination in promotions and working conditions are yet to evolve.

Methodology to study labour market wage discrimination Mean wage differentials or Becker's method

As suggested by Becker (1957), a comparison of the wage difference between two groups will serve as an indicator of whether any wage discrimination prevails in the labour market. This can be estimated as:

$$(1)\ D = (W_p / W_q)$$

where D is a measure of discrimination, W is the annual average wage or earnings, and p and q represent the two groups that are compared – males and females or caste groups (SC vs. Others). If D < 1, then it implies that the group 'p' is discriminated against in the labour market and the converse is true if D is > 1 while D = 0 implies the absence of discrimination.

Duraisamy and Duraisamy (1996, 1998) had undertaken an extensive analysis of wage differentials in India by educational level, field of specialisation and occupation based on the Degree Holders and Technical Personnel (DHTP) survey data for the years 1961, 1971 and 1981. Although the DHTP survey was conducted along with Population Census 1991, the data quality was so poor that it was never released. Subsequently the DHTP survey was discontinued and not conducted along with the 2001 and 2011 Population Census. The researchers lost the opportunity to have valuable information about the labour market for persons with higher education in India.

The ratio of mean annual monthly earnings of females (group 'q') over males (group 'p') at the aggregate level is given in Table 7.1.

As we notice from Table 7.1, the ratio of female to male earnings is less than unity which implies that females earned less than males and the difference is marginally higher in science and technology (S&T) compared to humanities, social sciences and other related fields. Another interesting feature is that the ratio has increased over a period of time, which implies that the earnings gap between males and females has narrowed over the years. Incidentally, the study also demonstrated that the male-female earnings gap was larger in private sector than in public sector.

Table 7.1 Ratio of average monthly earnings of females over males in DHTP labour market, 1961, 1971 and 1981

Field of Specialisation	*1961*	*1971*	*1981*
Science and Technology	0.68	0.77	0.78
Humanities, Social Sciences and Others	n.a	0.78	0.84
All Fields	n.a.	0.75	0.79

Notes: n.a.: not available

Source: Duraisamy and Duraisamy (1996, 1998)

Wages and wage differentials by social group based on NSS data for the period 1983–2012

Duraisamy (2002) and Duraisamy and Duraisamy (2016) examined the inequality among social groups using the National Sample Survey's Employment and Unemployment data for the periods 1983, 1993–94, 2004–05 and 2011–12. The study found that there is considerable inequality in education and employment across social groups and it is plausible that this will pass through to wages. If one looks at the trends in overall average daily wages, over a period of three decades as depicted in Figure 7.1, it is obvious that real daily wages have increased by about three times in the period. Moving to wages by gender and social groups shown in Figures 7.1 and 7.2 respectively, the following distinctions emerge. Irrespective of gender or caste, average daily wages have increased for males and females as well as for each of the caste groups considered. Throughout the period, wages of the marginalised groups have been lower than their seemingly higher status counterparts, but interesting contrasts emerge when the trend in wage gap is examined. Male wages are substantially higher (a little less than double), compared to female wages in the recent period but the gender gap, (male wages were twice female wages) has reduced over the years. On the other hand, the wage gap has widened over the time period in the case of caste groups. The difference, which was about two times between SC/ST and Others, has nearly tripled in the recent period taken for study.

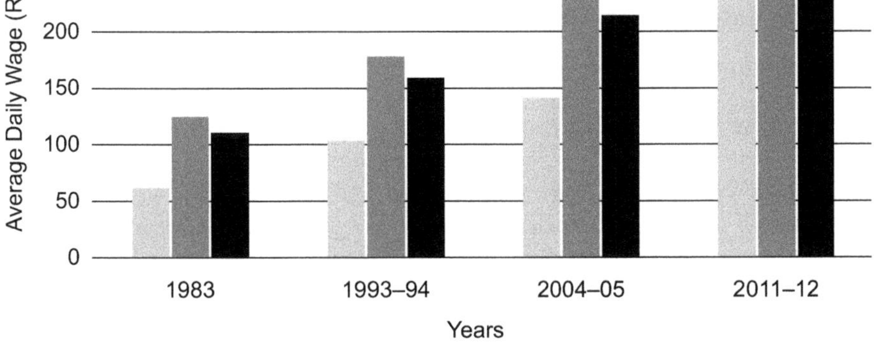

Figure 7.1 Trends in Real Wages by Gender, 1983–2012

Source: Duraisamy and Duraisamy (2016)

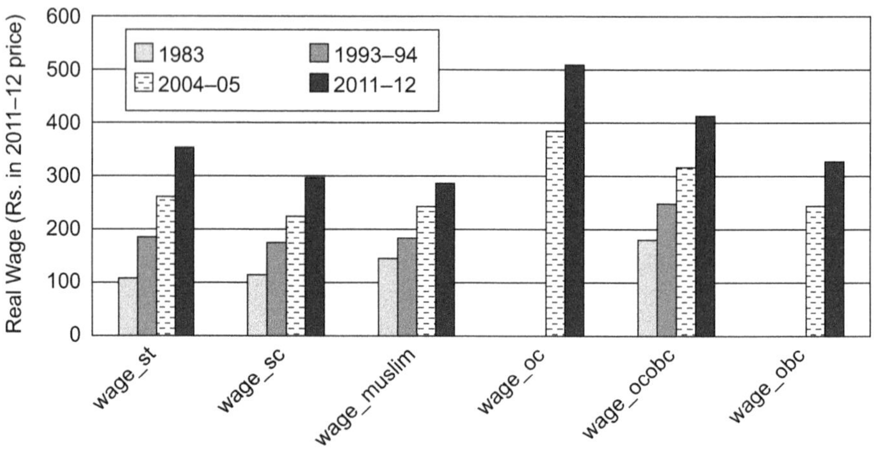

Figure 7.2 Trends in Real Wages by Social Group, 1983–2012
Source: Duraisamy and Duraisamy (2017)

This is indeed a cause for concern and the cause needs to be examined. Is it because females/lower caste groups are discriminated against in the labour markets or do such groups enter labour markets with lower skills (education or experience), which segregates them into low paying jobs?

A comparison is valid for homogenous groups in narrowly defined occupations or jobs in which characteristics such as education, age or professional experience and other skills are the same. However, the individuals are different in terms of caste, religion or gender, which forms the basis for discrimination. If the individuals vary by productive characteristics, then it can be controlled.

Wage or earnings function method

The wage function to analyse discrimination is specified as:

(2) $\ln W_i = \alpha + \beta X_i + \delta D_i + u_i$, i = 1,2, . . . T individuals.

where lnW is the logarithm of wage rates (daily or monthly or annual), X is the set of productive characteristics of the individual (education, labour market experience, ability etc.) and occupational and industry category, D is a dummy variable which takes the value of 1 if the individual belongs to the non-discriminatory group (male or forward Community) and 0 if he/she belongs to the discriminatory group (female or SC/ST) and the coefficient of the dummy variable δ is the average percentage difference in the wages between the groups which is considered as a measure of discrimination.

Several studies show evidence that a semi-log form (logarithm of wages) with non-linear term in labour market experience is the preferred specification for equation (1).

Duraisamy and Duraisamy (1997), based on the above approach, estimated the male-female wage difference controlling for education and labour market experience and found that females on an average earn 21% less than males in the S&T labour market and the gap narrows down to 14% if occupation and quality of education measured by division obtained in the highest degree are controlled for.

The above methodology presumes that the effect of the characteristics (X) across the two groups is the same but that may not be true. Hence, it is necessary to unconstraint the effects of the characteristics, which can be done using the decomposition method.

Wage decomposition (at mean) method

The method was first proposed by Oaxaca (1973) and Blinder (1973), which suggests that the earnings of two groups should be compared based on two separate earnings functions. Briefly, let the earnings function of the two groups be:

$$(3)\quad \ln W_{ij} = \alpha_j + \beta_j X_{ij} + u_{ij},\ i = 1,2,\ldots T \text{ individuals},\ j = n \text{ and } m \text{ (groups)}.$$

It can be shown that:

$$(4)\quad (\ln W^{*}p - \ln W^{*}q) = (\alpha_p - \alpha_q) + \Sigma(\beta_p - \beta_q)\, X^{*}_{q} + \Sigma(X^{*}_{p} - X^{*}_{q})\beta_p$$

where W* is the mean wage and X* is the mean value of the human capital variables and α and β are the parameter estimates of the wage equation (3). The logarithmic wage difference between the two groups is expressed as three components: (i) differences in the intercept, which is the entry-level wage difference, (ii) wage differences due to differential reward for the same characteristics or credentials and (iii) wage differences due to differences in characteristics of the two groups. The first component, the wage differential at the entry-level, is one form of discrimination and the second component is the unexplained or residual wage difference which is attributed to labour market discrimination and the third component is the differences due to productive characteristics (human capital endowments) between the two groups.

The methodological question is why we compute the third component using the reward to group 'm' (males or forward caste) but not 'n' (females or others) as the base. There are several alternatives proposed in the early literature on discrimination. Oaxaca (1973) suggested using both male and female wage coefficients. However, Cotton (1988) is of the view that either male or female wage structure is discriminated for or against and thus suggested to use the non-discriminated wage structure, which is the wage estimates based on the pooled sample of both the groups. This will enable one to compute the wage differences due to male advantage and female disadvantage separately. Neuwark (1988) and Oaxaca and Ransom (1994) suggested using the wage function estimated pooling the data for both the groups. The latter also derived the standard errors for the discrimination component, which will enable us to test whether the discrimination component of wage is statistically significant from zero.

The Oaxaca and Ransom wage decomposition method can be written as:

$$(5)\quad \beta^* = \Omega\, \beta_p + (1 - \Omega)\, \beta_q$$

where β^* is the non-discriminatory wage coefficient, β_p and βq are the estimated coefficients from the wage equation (2), and Ω is the weight estimated using the sample of both the discriminatory and non-discriminatory groups.

Gender discrimination in the Indian labour markets

Gender-based labour market discrimination has been extensively studied in the Indian context. In one of the earliest study, Usha (1983) applied the decomposition method and estimated the male-female wage differentials. The discrimination component ranges 10.4% to 39.5% by estimating the discrimination component using female and male wage structure respectively as non-discriminatory wage.

Duraisamy and Duraisamy (1995, 1996, 1998, 1999a, 1999b, 2004/5) extensively analysed the DHTP data. The male-female earnings difference is decomposed into explained (by human capital) and unexplained (attributed to discrimination) components. The model is estimated for two specifications with and without controls for occupation and quality of education. The unexplained component of the earnings differential based on the four methods described above and the standard errors of the discrimination component using the Oaxaca and Ransom (1994) method are estimated and the estimates are given in Table 7.2.

The results enable us to draw two important inferences: (i) there is strong empirical evidence of wage discrimination against women in the Degree Holders and Technical Personnel labour market and the discrimination coefficient is statistically significant at 1% level irrespective of the method of estimation; (ii) the discrimination ranges between 10–33% (column 2) and 13–21% (column 3) with and without controlling for the distribution of males and females across occupations and quality of education.

The major source of discrimination is through entry-level wages, which accounts for 78% of the male-female wage differentials. The education and labour market experience reduces while occupation increases the labour market discrimination against women in India. To sum up, the major source of sex discrimination in India is by self-selection of the minority group (women) into certain occupations and entry-level wages.

Table 7.2 Discrimination against Women in DHTP Labour Market in India

Method	*Discrimination*	
	% (SEE)	*% (SEE)*
1	*2*	*3*
Oaxaca (1973)		
Male Wage Structure	33.6 (0.59)	20.5 (0.0095)
Female Wage Structure	16.3 (0.01)	13.5 (0.0078)
Cotton (1988)	17.9 (0.11)	14.2 (0.0074)
Neumark (1988) and Oaxaca and Ransom (1994)	9.5 (0.0056)	12.7 (0.0067)

Note: SEE – Standard error of the discrimination coefficient

Source: Duraisamy and Duraisamy (1997)

A recent study by Dutta and Reilly (2008) analyse the NSS data for the period – 1983, 1993/4, 1999/2000 and 2004/5 and find discrimination components comprise about one-half of the overall gender pay gap. The industry-level analysis reveals that openness to trade is an important determinant of the industry-level gender pay gaps.

Migrant labourers at a disadvantaged position and they are being discriminated against in urban labour markets. Narasimhan (1994) examined wage discrimination against migrants using primary survey data from Chennai city and found that 38–56% of the wage differential between migrants and non-migrants is due to discrimination.

Caste-based discrimination in the Indian labour markets

There is ample empirical evidence on caste discrimination in the Indian labour markets. In one of their early works, Banerjee and Knight (1991) examined caste discrimination in the Indian context and more recently Madheswaran and Attewell (2007) extensively studied caste discrimination using the above method and showed a wage discrimination of 21% against SC/STs and 32% against OBCs for urban regular wage workers in 1999–2000. Geetha (2002) examined gender discrimination among caste groups in the secondary school teachers' labour market in Chennai city based on the decomposition method described above. Her findings reveal that discrimination against female teachers ranges between 16–22% in the case of 'forward' community and 45 to 59% in the case of 'Other' communities.

Mariappan (2009) using primary survey data of migrant workers in the unorganised sector of Chennai city showed evidence that 62% and 89% of the wage differentials between caste groups among migrant and non-migrant workers respectively was due to discrimination. Caste discrimination in the unorganised labour market is very high (81%).

Table 7.3 Wage Discrimination Among Social Groups, 2004–05

Social Group	*Mean Wage (Rupees per day)*			*Difference Due to*	
	Social group in Col. 1	*Comparison group**	*Difference* *Col. (3)–(2)*	*Productivity or Human Capital Characteristics (%)*	*Discrimination (%)*
1	2	3	4	5	6
ST	59.78	98.009	38.22	75.97	24.02
SC	68.16	103.61	35.45	88.04	11.95
OBC	82.93	100.55	17.62	75.22	24.77

Note: *Comparison group is the average wage of all wage earners excluding the social groups given in Column 1.

Source: Duraisamy (2009)

Duraisamy (2009) examined wage discrimination among social groups based on the decomposition method using NSS data for the year 2004–05. The results are summarised in Table 7.3.

These estimates indicate that the extent of wage discrimination is 24% between the ST and Others, and it is 12% in the case of SC and Others. It should be noted that discrimination is high between OBC and Others. Further analysis of discrimination within the group will enlighten our understanding on wage discrimination in the Indian labour markets.

In a recent study by Duraisamy and Duraisamy (2017), based on the above method, it was reported that wage discrimination for 2012 ranges from 9 to 25% based on OC wage structure and from 27 to 40% based on respective social group wage structure. The percentage of wage gap due to discrimination in 2012 compared to 1983 has increased for all social groups based on the social group wage structure and the same pattern is found for SCs and Muslims when OC wage structure is used. The discrimination component for OBCs is the highest among all social groups based on both the wage structures.

Wage decomposition across the wage distribution

There are several methods proposed in the literature to decompose the observed gender or caste wage gap. The method proposed by Machado and Mata (2005) and Melly (2006) has been widely used to decompose the gender or caste wage gap over the wage distribution based on quantile regression. Duraisamy and Duraisamy (2016, 2017) applied the above method to estimate the wage discrimination over the wage distributions. The Machado and Mata (2005) decomposition of log gender wage gap across the distribution can be written as:

$$(6)\ \ln\hat{W}_m(\theta) - \ln\hat{W}_f(\theta) = [\ln\hat{W}_m(\theta) - \ln\hat{W}_{cf}(\theta)] + [\ln\hat{W}_{cf}(\theta) - \ln\hat{W}_f(\theta)]$$

where $\ln\hat{W}_m(\theta)$ $[=X'_m\beta^*_m(\theta)]$ and $\ln\hat{W}_f(\theta)$ $[=X'_f\beta^*_f(\theta)]$ are the estimated wage densities of males and females and $\ln\hat{W}_{cf}(\theta)$ $[=X'_m\beta^*_f(\theta)]$ is the counterfactual wage density of females at the θth quantile of the quantile regression.

The results using the NSS data for the period 1983 to 2012 reported in Duraisamy and Duraisamy (2016) revealed that the gender wage gap, adjusted for differences in human capital endowments between men and women, based on Machado-Mata-Melly method, is more at the bottom than at the top of the wage distribution in all, and also in six segments of the labour market, except in rural segment in 2012 where the wage gap is also higher at the top of the distribution. This reinforces the existence and persistence of widespread gender discrimination in all segments of the Indian labour market. Importantly, low-wage earning women face higher discrimination than high-wage earning women. Over time, the adjusted wage gap has increased and the difference in human capital endowments has narrowed. Our results support the sticky floor hypothesis in 22 out of 26 estimates of adjusted wage gap profile and there is no evidence of glass ceiling, as observed for several Asian countries.

Duraisamy and Duraisamy (2017) examined the wage discrimination among caste and religious groups at mean and over the wage distributions using the methodology discussed above. The empirical results based on NSS data for the period of 1983 to 2012 revealed certain interesting common features for all the four disadvantaged social groups (ST, SC, OBC and Muslims). The main findings are summarised below: (i) the total wage gap and the wage gap due to productive characteristics increase as we move from bottom to top of the distribution up to 70th or 80th percentile and thereafter remain stable or decline slightly; (ii) it can be inferred from the results that the differences in human capital attributes account for a larger part of the wage gap across the wage distribution compared to the discrimination (effect of coefficient) component for all the four social groups; (iii) the discrimination component is lower at the bottom than at the top of the distribution. The wage discrimination increases modestly or remains stable as we move from the lowest 10th percentile to the median and then increases steadily to the top of the wage distribution. The percentage of unexplained to total wage gap indicates that the discrimination part is positive for all social groups, except for STs at some percentiles, in all the four years. The discrimination component is higher at the top of the distribution compared to the bottom or the median. The profile of the unexplained wage gap exhibits a glass ceiling effect, a phenomenon observed for gender wage gap in many countries. That is, individuals from the disadvantaged groups find it increasingly difficult to go up the job ladder which fetches higher wages due to labour market barriers and discrimination. Overall, the discrimination component is higher in 2012 compared to 1983 for all social groups.

Job discrimination in the labour market

Job discrimination can be examined using several indicators like (i) Segregation and Disparity indices and (ii) Decomposition methods using the available data from the labour market surveys such as National Sample Survey (NSS) employment and unemployment surveys. The alternative is to use the methodology specifically designed to measure discrimination in hiring practices.

Segregation and disparity indices

The earnings gap documented above can be traced to differential access of women and men to occupations. It is generally held that women are pushed to low paying, less risky or risk-free jobs and those requiring routine tasks than the high paying fields like engineering and technology, law and management etc. The sociological literature provides ample evidence on this issue. To measure the magnitude of segregation we use a gender disparity index, known as Duncan index.

The Duncan index or index of dissimilarity can be used to measure the distribution of workers from two groups (by gender or caste) by occupation. The dissimilarity index (D) is defined as:

$$(7)\quad D = \Sigma(S_{pi} - S_{qi})/2, i = 1, 2, \ldots J \text{ occupations}$$

where D is the index of dissimilarity which ranges between 0–100, S_p and S_q are the percentage share of men and women in the ith occupation respectively. The dissimilarity index takes the value of 0 when there is perfect equality between the considered groups and in the extreme case of dissimilarity it equals 100.

From the Table 7.4 the segregation index ranges from 33% to 35% in the Indian Scientific and Technical labour market which indicates that about one-third of the female workforce should switch occupations to attain parity in occupation so that the job discrimination can be reduced.

Table 7.4 Segregation Index in the Scientific and Technical Labour Market

Year	*Segregation index*
1961	35.4
1971	33.0
1981	34.2

Source: Duraisamy and Duraisamy (1998)

Job discrimination: decomposition method

The wage difference may arise due to (i) wage discrimination and (ii) job discrimination reflected through occupational segregation. It is possible to decompose the total wage differential into job and wage discrimination using the method developed by Brown, Moon and Zoloth (1980). It can be shown that the wage difference between two groups can be written as:

$$(8)\quad (\ln W^{*}p - \ln W^{*}_{q}) = \Sigma_j(S_{qj}X^{*}_{qj}(\beta_{pj} - \beta_{qj}) + \Sigma_j(S_{qj}\beta_{pj}\,(X^{*}_{pj} - X^{*}_{qj}) + \Sigma_j(\beta_{pj}\,X^{*}_{pj}(S_{pj} - S_{qj}) + \Sigma_j(\beta_{pj}\,X^{*}_{pj}(S_{pj} - S_{qj}) = WU + WE + JU + JE$$

where W* and X* are the average wage and human capital variables, S* is the share of workers in the ith occupation and β's are the parameter estimates. The subscripts j represents the jth occupation (j = 1,2, . . . J occupations) 'p' and 'q' represents the two groups namely the non-discriminatory (males or forward community) and discriminatory (females and other community) groups. The wage difference between the two groups are decomposed into (i) explained (WE) and unexplained (WU) differences in wages within the occupation and (ii) explained (JE) and unexplained (JD) differential due to access to a higher paid occupation. The unexplained wage (WU) and job (JU) components denote the extent of wage and job discrimination respectively.

Divakaran (1996) examined the wage and job discrimination using a primary survey of households in Chennai based on the above methodology. The findings of the study are summarised in Table 7.5.

Consequences of discrimination

Discrimination, in general, has several impacts on the economy and society. The consequences of discrimination have been discussed in several works (Birdsall and Sabot, 1991; Thorat, 2008).

Reduction in output and economic growth

Thorat (2008) argues that the practice of fixing occupations according to the caste system hinders mobility of resources such as human labour, land,

Table 7.5 Wage and Job Discrimination against Gender and Caste in the Indian Labour Markets

Source	*Gender Discrimination*	*Caste Discrimination*
Wage discrimination	13%	21%
Job discrimination	38%	35%

Source: Divakaran (1996, p. 255).

capital and entrepreneurship across caste groups, thus creating segmented and imperfect markets. Labour and capital do not move from one occupation to another even if the wage rates and rates of return (on investments) are higher in the alternative occupations. Factor immobility thus results in gross inefficiencies in resource allocation and in economic outcomes (Ambedkar, 1936, 1987).

The theories of discrimination formulated by Becker (1957) and Arrow (1972) clearly bring out the effects of discrimination on wages, profits and efficient allocation of labour. It has been shown that discrimination impedes economic growth by reducing efficiency in the allocation of labour among firms and the economy. The discriminated groups which see themselves as victims of injustice eventually realise that wages are lower than what their counterparts earn and this reduces their commitment to work and level of effort which will eventually reduce productivity (Birdsall and Sabot, 1991). Since the marginal productivity of the discriminated group (females or persons from lower caste) is more than the wages paid in the presence of discrimination, fewer than the optimal number of persons from discriminated sex or caste is employed. The allocation of labour will thus not be efficient. This will lead to further discrimination, that is, a 'vicious circle' of discrimination (Birdsall and Sabot, 1991).

Societal unrest and conflicts

The consequences of caste-based job allocation and wage disbursement on equity and poverty are more severe than those for economic growth. Since access to the source of income and economic rewards under the caste system are determined by an unequal assignment of rights, the result is an income distribution that is generally skewed along caste lines (Thorat, 2008). Discrimination perpetuates inequality and the inter-generation inequality widens. This leads to conflict among groups similar to the one proposed between capitalists and labourers by Marx. Ambedkar (1936) argued that whatever may have been the original purpose behind the origin of the caste system, later as it evolved in its classical form, it had an underlying economic motive, the purpose of which is income maximisation through coercion rather than economic efficiency of any sort. Economic and educational disparities, in general, and poverty of lower castes like the former untouchables and OBCs, in particular, are a direct outcome of the unequal assignment of rights under the caste system (Thorat, 2008).

Role of state in reducing discrimination

How to reduce, if not eliminate, discrimination in the labour market? There are two strands of thought: (i) the competitive market will automatically eliminate discrimination in labour and capital market and (ii) intervention policies of the State are required to reduce discrimination. The latter view is more appealing than the former as we see the persistence of discrimination in labour market over a period of time and the evidence presented in the previous sections does not show any reduction in the magnitude of discrimination. Thus the State has a key role to play in reducing the age-old practice of discrimination in any form. As the present work focuses on the economics of labour market discrimination, we discuss possible policy alternatives to reduce discrimination against gender and caste in the labour market.

Laws on equality of opportunity and equal pay for equal work

The labour laws pertaining to equality of opportunity and equal pay for the same work irrespective of gender and caste do prevail in different forms but discrimination persists in an 'invisible' form. As we have shown evidence, labour market discrimination mainly happens through hiring practices, entry-level wages and through occupational segregation.

Reservations in education and employment

Reservations for certain caste groups have been in vogue since independence. Unfortunately, the benefits of reservation are yet to trickle down to the economically weaker sections due to lack of opportunity to invest in human capital in early childhood which, in turn, permeates to wages and employment when they enter into the labour market. The Right to Education Act is an important step to achieve the goal of universal education. It should be noted that the quality of education does matter and if the marginalised groups do not get equal opportunity to good quality education, it is hard to eliminate labour market discrimination. What is the role of the State? Appropriate legislation and regulations are needed to make admission to elite schools based on a random basis rather than on the basis of socioeconomic and caste considerations. School vouchers can help the poor to meet the school cost and hence the lower caste students from poor families will not be denied the opportunity of investing in good quality education. Alternative ways of overcoming deprivation have been suggested by social scientists engaged in the discussion, particularly, in the context of reservation in the private sector for SC and ST and the extension of the reservation policy in education for the OBCs, low-caste converts to Islam and Christianity, and certain religious minority groups such as the Muslims, including political reservation for women (Thorat, 2008).

Conclusion

The discussion presented in this chapter provides strong evidence on the existence of wage differentials across gender and social groups. The residual component of unexplained wage difference, which is attributed to discrimination, is by no means a small part of the total wage difference. We have also discussed the consequences of discrimination. Evidence suggests that discrimination leads to inefficiency in the distribution of labour across the sectors, which will hamper the economic growth of a nation. It will also lead to political unrest and social inequality and poverty. The role of the State and the policy options are also explored. We have shown that the reservation policy, which has been in existence for more than 50 years, does not seem very effective in producing the desired result of reducing discrimination in the labour market. This is perhaps due to the fact that only a small proportion of the labour is employed in government and public sector and a large section of our labour force is engaged in private/unorganised sector where there is still no reservation. Another issue is the skill difference between marginalised groups and others. Early childhood investment in education and health plays a vital role in improving the labour market performance of the individuals.

The hallmark of a just society is non-discriminatory treatment, which is similar to the social goal of ensuring equality before law and equality of opportunity. With more committed efforts of the State and better responsiveness of individuals/households and groups, we hope to achieve this goal soon.

References

Ambedkar, B. R. (1936), *Annihilation of Caste*, Jalandhar, Punjab: Bhim Partrica.

Arrow, K. J. (1972), "Models of Job Discrimination," in A. H. Pascal (ed.), *Racial Discrimination in Economic Life*, Lexington, MA: Lexington Books, pp. 83–102.

Banerjee, B. and Knight, J. B. (1991), "Caste Discrimination in Indian Urban Labour Markets," *Journal of Developing Economies*, 7, pp. 277–307.

Becker, G. S. (1957), *The Economics of Discrimination*, Chicago: University of Chicago Press.

Birdsall, N. and Sabot, R. (eds.) (1991), *Unfair Advantage: Labour Market Discrimination in Developing Countries*, Washington, DC: The World Bank.

Blinder, A. S. (1973), "Wage Discrimination: Reduced Form and Structural Estimates," *Journal of Human Resources*, pp. 436–455.

Brown, R. S., Moon, M. and Zoloth, B. S. (1980), "Incorporating Occupational Attainment in Studies of Male-Female Earnings Differentials," *Journal of Human Resources*, pp. 3–28.

Cain, C. G. (1986), "The Economic Analysis of Labour Market Discrimination," in Orly Ashenfelter and Richard Layard (eds.), *Handbook of Labour Economics*, Amsterdam: Elsevier Science Foundation, pp. 3–20.

Cotton, J. (1988), "On the Decomposition of Wage Differentials," *The Review of Economics and Statistics*, 70(2), pp. 236–243.

Divakaran, S. (1996), "Gender-Based Wage and Job Discrimination in Urban India," *The Indian Journal of Labour Economics*, 39(2), pp. 235–257 [Based on her PhD Thesis, 1995].

Duraisamy, M. and Duraisamy, P. (1995), "Implications for Structural Reforms for Public-Private Sector Wage Differentials in India," *The Indian Journal of Labour Economics*, 38(4).

Duraisamy, M. and Duraisamy, P. (1996), "Sex Discrimination in Indian Labour Markets," *Feminist Economics*, 2(2), pp. 41–61.

Duraisamy, M. and Duraisamy, P. (1998), "Sex Segregation and Discrimination among Scientific Personal," in Maithireyi Krishnaraj, Ratna Sudarshan and Abusaleh Shariff (eds.), *Gender, Population and Development*, New Delhi: Oxford University Press, pp. 159–184.

Duraisamy, M. and Duraisamy, P. (1999a), "Gender Bias in the Scientific and Technical Labour Market: A Comparative Study of Tamil Nadu and Kerala," *Indian Economic Review*, 34(2), pp. 149–169.

Duraisamy, M. and Duraisamy, P. (1999b), "Women in the Professional and Technical Labour Market in India: Gender Discrimination in Education, Employment and Earnings," *The Indian Journal of Labour Economics*, 42(4), pp. 599–612.

Duraisamy, M. and Duraisamy, P. (2004/5), "Labour Mobility in the Scientific and Technical Labour Market," *Indian Economic Journal*, 53(3–4), pp. 53–62.

Duraisamy, M. and Duraisamy, P. (2016), "Gender Wage Gap across the Wage Distribution in Different Segments of the Indian Labour Market, 1983–2012: Exploring the Glass Ceiling or Sticky Floor Phenomenon," *Applied Economics*, 48(43), pp. 4098–4111.

Duraisamy, P. (2002), "Changes in Returns to Education in India, 1983–94: By Gender, Age-Cohort and Location," *Economics of Education Review*, 21(6), pp. 609–622.

Duraisamy, P. (2009), "Inequality among Social Groups in Education and Labour Market Outcomes in India," Paper presented in the National Conference on '*The Challenges in Human Development in India*' organised by the Centre for Development Studies, Thiruvananthapuram, January 24–25.

Duraisamy, P. and Duraisamy, M. (1997), "Male-Female Earnings Differentials in the Scientific and Technical Labour Market in India," in Solomon W. Polachek (ed.), *Research in Labor Economics*, Emerald Group Publishing Limited, 16, pp. 209–234.

Duraisamy, P. and Duraisamy, M. (1998), "Accounting for the Wage Differential in the Indian Labour Market," *Indian Journal of Labour Economics*, 41(4).

Duraisamy, P. and Duraisamy, M. (2005), "Regional Differences in Wage Premia and Returns to Education by Gender in India," *Indian Journal of Labour Economics*, 48(2), pp. 335–347.

Duraisamy, P. and Duraisamy, M. (2017), "Social Identity and Wage Discrimination in the Indian Labour Market," *Economic & Political Weekly*, LII(4), pp. 51–60.

Dutta, P. V. and Reilly, B. (2008), "The Gender Pay Gap in an era of Economic Change: Evidence for India, 1983 to 2004," *Indian Journal of Labour Economics*, 51(3), pp. 341–366.

Edgeworth, F. Y. (1922), "Equal Pay for Men and Women for Equal Work," *Economic Journal*, 32, pp. 431–457.

Geetha, N. (2002), *Wage Differentials and Discrimination by Gender, Sector of Employment and Caste: A Study of Secondary School Teachers in Chennai*, PhD Thesis, Department of Econometrics, University of Madras.

Govt. of Maharashtra. (1987). *Dr. Babasaheb Ambedkar: Writings and Speeches*, Vol. 3, Bombay.

Gunderson, M. (1989), "Male-Female Wage Differentials and Policy Response," *Journal of Economic Literature*, 24(1), pp. 46–72.

Lawrence Summers. (1991), Former Vice-President, Development Economics and Chief Economist, The World Bank, Personal Communication, 1991.

Machado, J. A. F. and Mata, J. (2005), "Counterfactual Decomposition of Changes in Wage Distributions Using Quantile Regression," *Journal of Applied Econometrics*, 20, pp. 445–465.

Madheswaran, S. and Attewell, P. (2007), "Caste Discrimination in the Indian Urban Labour Market: Evidence from the National Sample Survey," Special Issue, *Economic and Political Weekly*, 42(41), pp. 4146–4153.

Mariappan, R. (2009), *Labour Market Behaviour of the Workers in the Unorganised Sector: With Reference to Job Search, Wage Discrimination and Remittances*, PhD Thesis, Department of Econometrics, University of Madras.

Marshall, R. (1974). "The Economics of Racial Discrimination: A Survey," *Journal of Economic Literature*, 12(3), pp. 849–871.

Melly, B. (2006), "Estimation of Counterfactual Distributions Using Quantile Regression," *Review of Labor Economics*, 68, pp. 543–572.

Narasimhan, S. (1994), *An Economic Analysis of Labour Out Migration into the Metropolitan City of Madras*, PhD Thesis, Department of Econometrics, University of Madras.

Neumark, D. (1988), "Employers Discriminatory Behaviour and the Estimation of Wage Discrimination," *Journal of Human Resources*, 23, pp. 279–295.

Oaxaca, R. L. (1973), "Male-Female Wage Differentials in an Urban Labour Market," *International Economic Review*, 14(3), pp. 693–709.

Oaxaca, R. L. and Ransom, M. R. (1994), "On Discrimination and the Decomposition of Wage Differentials," *Journal of Econometrics*, 61, pp. 5–21.

Phelps, E. S. (1972), "The Statistical Theory of Racism and Sexism," *American Economic Review*, 62(4), pp. 659–661.

Robinson, J. (1933), *The Economics of Imperfect Competition*, London: Macmillan.

Rustagi, P. (2005), "Understanding Gender Inequalities in Wages and Incomes in India," *The Indian Journal of Labour Economics*, 48(2).

Terrel, K. (1992), "Female-Male Earning Differentials and Occupational Structure," *International Labour Review*, 131(4–5), pp. 387–404.

Thorat, S. K. (2008), "Labour Market Discrimination: Concept, Forms and Remedies in the Indian Situation," *The Indian Journal of Labour Economics*, 51(1).

Thorat, S. K. and Newman, K. S. (2010), *Blocked by Caste: Economic Discrimination in Modern India*, New Delhi: Oxford University Press.

Usha, S. (1983), "Labour Market Discrimination against Women," *Indian Journal of Industrial Relations*, 18(4), pp. 569–584.

Webb, W. (1891), "The Alleged Differences in the Wages Paid to Men and Women in Similar Work," *The Economic Journal*, 1, pp. 635–662.

8 Social discrimination and suicides in higher educational institutions

Role of state

K. Laxminarayana

The Indian economy and society are predominantly organized on the basis of caste. The ancient Indian society was a Hindu society. This society has never been united as a whole.

> The Ancient world may be said to have been guilty for failing to take the responsibility for the education of the masses. But never has any society been guilty of closing to the generality of its people the study of the books if its religion. Never has society been guilty of prohibiting the mass of its people from acquiring knowledge. Never has society made any attempt to declare that any attempt made by the common man to acquire knowledge shall be punishable as a crime. Manu is the only divine law giver who has denied the common man the right to knowledge.
>
> (Ambedkar, 1987)

Brahminism, through the agency of predominantly Brahmins and others, saw to it that the Scheduled Castes (SCs) and Scheduled Tribes (STs) were kept out of education and not allowed to own property or to bear arms. Ambedkar further writes that "Manu Smriti prescribes such heavy sentences as cutting off the tongue or pouring of molten lead in the ears of the shudra, who recites or hears the Veda". In the so-called ideal kingdom of caste Hindus, Eklavya had to sacrifice his thumb and donate, as gurudakshana, to Dronacharya, the so-called Guru, so that the bright tribal boy could be deprived of archery. In the so-called ideal kingdom of Rama Rajya, Rama killed Shambuka, the shudra, who had transgressed his Varna/caste and wanted to be a Brahmin. This situation remained more or less unchanged until the British rule in India.

This chapter is divided into five sections. The first section is an introductory one. The second section defines the concept of social discrimination. In the third section, change in the social composition is discussed broadly in the last 100 years. In the fourth section, caste-based prejudices towards Dalit students are shown clearly and the fifth section addresses concrete measures that a state can take, in order to help eliminate discrimination.

Introduction

British colonial Government affirmed in the report of Indian Education Commission of 1882 that all government aided schools should be opened to all castes and communities. However, the same report mentioned that "the principle affirmed by us must be applied with caution. It is not desirable for masters or inspectors to endeavor to force on a social change . . . It is however undesirable to urge them to claim a right about which they are themselves indifferent" (Philip Constable, 2000). In 1892 a group of retired Mahar and Chambhar army officers in Dapoli sent a petition to the Dapoli Municipal Council in Ratnagiri District to allow their children to study in Municipal Primary School. Then the council replied by saying if these untouchable children were admitted to the school, all the caste Hindu boys would have to abandon the school for religious reasons. The same council suggested that a separate class with a separate teacher would be opened for them, which the Dalit officers rejected. The officers represented to the Collector; then the municipality was forced to admit the children but they were made to sit on the veranda. Describing the situation of untouchability and caste discrimination towards the children of military officers during the British colonial period, Philip Constable writes, "In the final analysis, this municipal comprise of sitting untouchable students on the school Varandah was as much a rejection of the parents wish for the education of their children as denying them entry to the school altogether". This is how, although there is some change with regard to the entry of Dalit children into education, the situation did not change drastically compared to the pre-British period. Because of centuries-old, most atrocious discrimination of the lower sections of Hindu society, SCs/STs and even OBCs (Other Backward Classes) are lagging behind even after seven decades of independence, compared to upper castes with regard to access to education, in general, and higher education, in particular.

SC/ST students who enter Higher Education Institutions (HEIs), have been facing social discrimination and are being forced to commit suicide by academic and administrative bodies filled with people of a pernicious, casteist mentality. In this context, understanding the forms of social discrimination in HEIs, particularly central universities, is important. An attempt is made in this paper to recognize the forms of discrimination and need for a role of the state, taking the case of Hyderabad Central University.

Concept of social discrimination

Social discrimination in HEIs is discrimination practiced by the administration, teachers and even students, based on caste, gender and such other categories. According to UGC Regulations (2012), the meaning of discrimination is as follows:

> Discrimination means any distinction, exclusion, limitation or preference which, being based on caste has the purpose or effect of nullifying

or impairing equality of treatment in education and in particular: Equality of treatment also does not help in eliminating discrimination. In an unequal society, one has to give unequal treatment to bring about equality. One has to offer special help to the socially and academically disadvantaged classes. However, for the immediate purpose, the following definition of UGC Regulations may be adopted.

a) Of depriving a student or a group of students belonging to Scheduled Castes and Scheduled Tribes of access to education of any type or at any level;
b) Of limiting any student or group of students belonging to Scheduled Castes and Scheduled Tribes to education of an inferior standard;
c) Of inflicting on any student or group of students belonging to Scheduled Castes and Scheduled Tribes conditions which are incompatible with the dignity of man;
d) Of subjecting to the provision of establishing or maintaining separate educational systems or institutions for students or groups of students belonging to Scheduled Castes and Scheduled Tribes.

Change in the social composition of students in HEIs

The composition of students in HEIs has changed drastically in the last 100 years. From 1980 onwards, there is a rapid change from elite higher education to mass higher education on the one hand, and growth of for-profit private educational institutions on the other. (Paradoxically, the privatization of education and its ill effects on the marginalized sections also started since then). At the beginning of the 20th century, students in HEIs were overwhelmingly Brahmin, urban and male. In marked contrast to this trend, at the beginning of the 21st century, a large number of the students who were entering these institutions were from the untouchable castes, women and from a rural background.

In the erstwhile Andhra Pradesh State, from 1970s onwards, the depressed class students got support from Ambedkarites, radical and progressive student organizations. It was also a time when a good number of students from depressed classes left studies and joined revolutionary movements. In Andhra Pradesh, because of powerful Dalit assertions especially after the Karamchedu massacre in 1985, the pressure on public elite institutions to implement reservation policy started growing. As a result, HEIs were forced to implement the existing reservation policy. The implementation of the Mandal Commission Report, reserving 27% reservations for OBCs, significantly changed the student composition. From one dominant class and caste classroom, it changed to multiple-caste (SCs/STs/OBCs) and class classroom by the beginning of the 21st century. On the whole, the number of students from marginalized groups reaching public universities significantly increased. The Gross Enrolment Ratio (GER) increased from 5% in 1999–2000 to 8% in 2004–2005 and further increased to 11% in 2009–2010.

The GER for STs increased from 6% in 1999–2000 to 8% in 2004–2005 and further to 9% in 2009–2010. The GER for OBCs increased from 7% in 1999–2000 to 10% in 2004–2005 (Rao, 2015).

Instead of welcoming these students from the downtrodden castes, HEIs were rejecting them due to their exclusionary and casteist mindset. One of the crucial reasons was that the change in composition of students was not accompanied by a change in composition of teachers, change in content, and pedagogy and the casteist mindset of administrators, teachers and non-teaching staff.

In fact, there has been sparse entry of teachers from marginalized sections. For instance, in the Hyderabad Central University, the number of SC/ST faculty constitutes just 13% as against the constitutional requirement of 22.5%. If one considers the number of professors from these communities, it is a microscopic minority.

Discriminatory approach of faculty members and administrators

Ambedkar said caste is a notion. It is a state of mind. It is a tendency of the mind to look at the people in terms of caste. According to casteist mind of Brahmins and other upper caste people, members of the SC community are fit only to do manual and menial jobs as serfs, agricultural laborers, cobblers, pig-rearers and unorganized manual workers in urban areas. They look at the STs, as people living in remote homelands, in the forests and hills. Socially and educationally backward classes are seen as self-employed artisans, services providers, suppliers of marine food and tenants without any rights. All of them should be tied to do those hereditary occupations.

Despite the regressive attitude of the upper castes, because of reservation policy in the post-independence period, and especially after the 1980s and 1990s, these historically discriminated and educationally deprived sections are entering HEIs in a good number.

Evidently, teachers of these elite educational institutions and administrators, predominantly coming from upper castes, feel threatened, afraid of losing their monopoly over the institutions. Krishnan (2016) notes:

> Their entry into professional institutions (or HEIs) with the aid of reservations and in some institutions, through merit which is growing, made the upper caste elites feel threatened. They could not bear children of erstwhile laborers and bonded laborers, denizens of forests and remote plateaus and of providers of services, becoming their equals.

Added to this, were the discriminatory values of neo-liberal capitalism, which do not allow diversity. It is marked by a bureaucratic, technocratic, managerial approach. It emphasizes on standardization, homogenization of education, and rules out diversity and difference (Marginson, 2007). It excludes the people under the garb of excellence, quality and merit. It encourages individualism, propagating uncurbed self-centeredness in knowledge creation and dissemination.

The mixture of a new form of the Indian caste system and neo-liberalism together are accelerating caste discrimination, leading students from marginalized sections to suicides in HEIs. Hyderabad Central University is a case in point.

Caste-based discrimination and student suicides: a case of Hyderabad Central University

Senthil Kumar

Senthil Kumar, a PhD Scholar in the Physics Department, committed suicide in February 2008. The teachers are reported to have said, "Your community is a pig-rearing community. Why do you require a PhD?"[1] These kinds of prejudices are due to age-old entrenched caste hierarchies amongst the Indian upper castes. The second kind of caste discrimination is a little more sophisticated, originating from neo-liberalism. It emphasizes standardization and excellence. If you were to ask those who believe in this discourse, they would act as if they had no caste. They are educated in the western countries. They give out an appearance as if they are only interested in making the institution excellent. With these attitudes, they redefined what "pass mark" was in the case of Senthil. The following were the conditions:

a First, they said, it is 50% marks for "Pass" and in this calculation of 50%, internal marks were not taken into account. Normally, internal assessment marks are added to end-semester marks to calculate the percentage.
b Secondly, even if a student passes with 50% marks, "The school had decided that the course instructor would merely hand over the evaluation to the Dean and the Doctoral Committee of the particular student would determine whether the student's performance was good enough (50% also) to merit a pass." (Report of the Fact Finding Committee, 2008)
c Thirdly, they had a comprehensive viva exam and one had to successfully pass this exam. Then only a supervisor would be allotted.[2]

Because of this atrocious casteist mentality and subsequent introduction of new criteria of "Pass" system, Senthil did not pass in one course titled 'Statistical Mechanics'. Following this, they stopped his fellowship. This stoppage of fellowship had specific significance for him. He carried the responsibility of looking after his family. When his fellowship stopped, he was not able to send money to his parents. Additionally, he failed in the subject. So, no supervisor was allotted to him.

As mentioned in a report (PIL in AP High Court, 2013) submitted to the High Court of Andhra Pradesh by 29 teachers:

> Failure has a specific meaning for these students. Due to many reasons 'discontinuing' and going back home is not a viable option for poor, rural students, who may choose death over failure in which they must stare at their inability to provide for miserably poor families that have staked everything to educate them. In many cases, they were also the academic 'toppers' in a village or a community and the ignominy of returning as failures would also be unbearable.
>
> (PIL in AP High Court, 2013)

Because of similar situation Senthil could not go home with a "bad name" as a failed student and he committed suicide. Nobody involved in this perpetration of caste discrimination was given any punishment.

P. Raju

Mr. P. Raju joined in 2009 as an Integrated Masters (IMA) student. He committed suicide on March 19th, 2013. He had not been promoted to the 8th semester because of backlogs from his earlier semesters. Subsequently, he passed those subjects. In one course, the concerned teacher did not correct the answer script and as a result, the academic branch did not notify the results of the other papers. The facts are as follows:

a) The result of the course he passed in 2011, i.e. IL.105, was not notified until 2013. It is indeed shocking that the result of that course was not declared for two years. The Centre for Integrated Studies and the Office of the Controller of Examination are guilty of this grave mistake.
b) He cleared the other course in January 2013 but results were notified only after his suicide, i.e. on 20th March, 2013. The paper was corrected and submitted after 56 days of examination, held up by one faculty member. Following is the recommendation given by the fact-finding committee:

"Appropriate action may be initiated against concerned faculty and officials at the level of CALT, CIS and CE office for the various procedural lapses." (Report of the Committee, 2013, University of Hyderabad).

However, not only was there no punishment to the culprits but, in fact, they were promoted. The concerned faculty who did not submit the results in time became in-charge of the Vigilance Committee, the official in CE office who was responsible for the delay in results that led the student to take the fatal action went on to become the Controller of Examination.

It emerges clearly from the above instance that rules are there but they were not implemented in this case. Committees are appointed to probe suicides but their recommendations are not taken seriously and not implemented.

M. Venkatesh

M. Venkatesh joined PhD in 2011. He committed suicide in November 2013. He was in Advanced Centre for Research in High Energy Material (ACRHEM), a recently established interdisciplinary centre. The Centre initiated the PhD programme without proper preparation. It was funded by Defence Research and Development Organisation (DRDO). ACRHEM had to admit Venkatesh as per the recommendation of SC/ST admission committee. However, discrimination soon began in following forms:

a) He was not allotted a supervisor.
b) There was no doctoral committee for him while all other students had supervisors and doctoral committees.
c) Consequently, there was no laboratory space to work. In the beginning, the Director acted as a guide. When he retired, he did not arrange for any other guide, nor did he guide him as he was guiding other students even after retirement. He retained his office space. Some of these centres became rehabilitation centres for retired professors. There have been several violations of rules. Firstly, just three years before retirement, one is not eligible to be the sole guide as per the rules. So Venkatesh's assigned guide had violated this rule. Secondly, because of the interdisciplinary nature of his topic, he had an ad-hoc arrangement with a teacher in the School of Chemistry but not a carefully worked out co-supervisor. So nobody came forward as the supervisor from Chemistry after the retirement of the director who acted as supervisor. Under the circumstances, and considering the plight of the student, he could have acted as a guide for some more time and tried to arrange a supervisor in the meanwhile.
d) The Research Advisory Body (RAB), which is a body like the School Board in other schools, did not meet for a long period. Normally, it should meet twice a year. The RAB did not meet from November 2011 to November 2013. It is supposed to look after allocation of guides. It did not take up this matter even in November 2013 when it met. For Venkatesh, two years went by without a guide. There appeared to be no possibility of getting a guide. That meant no laboratory to work in, unlike his fellow students and under these conditions he was led to commit suicide. The fact-finding committee noted, "Glaring instance of insensitivity and the lack of diligence especially in attending to students who come from marginalized sections have been highlighted in all these reports on suicides in HCU" (Report of the Committee, 2013, University of Hyderabad).

E) There was no action taken on the Director of ACRHEM. In Senthil's case also there was no action taken on the person responsible.

Rohith Vemula

Rohith Vemula, a brilliant Dalit research scholar, was institutionally murdered by the discriminatory university administration in collision with Brahmanical Hindutva leaders .[3]

The incident started on August 3rd, 2015, when Ambedkar Students Association (ASA) held a protest demonstration against the disruption of a screening of "Muzaffarnagar Baaqui Hai" by the ABVP in Delhi. On the same evening, after the protest was over, the ASA students learned that there was a Facebook post by the UOH ABVP leader, Susheel Kumar, in which he had called activists of the ASA "goons". Several members of ASA went to Susheel Kumar and made him write a letter apologizing for his comments. But Mr. Susheel Kumar complained that he was beaten up by ASA students and forced into writing the letter. If we went into the sequence of facts and circumstances that led to the institutional murder of Rohith Vemula, it would run into dozens of pages. Therefore, we will confine to those few very important facts and circumstances which led to the suicide of Rohith Vemula are below.

The first report of the Proctorial Board (PB) released on August 12th, 2015 found no evidence of beating Susheel and therefore just issued stern warnings to both Susheel Kumar and the ASA students. There was no punishment to ASA students at that time. Had there been no interference by the BJP leaders and BJP led MHRD into internal affairs of University, the matter would have been closed there. However, in a subsequent report on August 31st, 2015 following a second meeting, the PB reversed its earlier decision and unilaterally punished the Dalit students by completely suspending them for the ongoing semester.[4] What transpired between the first and the second meeting? "Nothing has changed in between these two meetings except Susheel Kumar appeared in the second meeting and given a statement that he was beaten? The concerned students of the ASA were never called for cross-checking his version" (Laxminarayana, 2017).

The reasons for the reversal of its own decision and its implementation by the same PB are basically due to enormous pressure put by the Brahmanical Hindu upper caste party namely BJP and its ministers particularly MHRD ministers. The following facts indicate the interference of the BJP government into the autonomy of University:

a) On August 10th, 2015, Nandanam Diwakar, Vice President of the BJP, Rangareddy district, wrote a letter to Bandaru Dattatreya, State Minister for Labor and Employment.
b) On 1August 17th, 2015, BJP minister Mr. Dattatreya wrote a letter to Smriti Irani, the then MHRD minister, insisting on action against ASA students.

c) MHRD wrote five emails to the University between September 3rd–November 19thto look into the matter.[5]
d) On August 4th, 2015, BJP MLC Mr. Rama Chandra Rao threatened, in an email, to the then Vice Chancellor Mr. R.P. Sharma to take action against ASA students.

All these letters and emails were sent by MHRD and leaders of BJP, belonging to a political party in power at the centre which is wedded to the task of maintaining and strengthening caste system and caste discrimination. With the support of the administration, Proctorial Board members in the University, the MHRD got the ASA students suspended. [see the letters by MHRD to the University of Hyderabad]. However, the suspended students of ASA raised the glaring contradictions in the reports of PB and appealed for revocation of suspension. The Vice-Chancellor (VC) convened a meeting of Heads and Deans and revoked the suspension on September 11th, 2015 and announced that a new committee would look into the matter afresh.

Mr. Appa Rao was appointed VC on September 21st, 2015 and he immediately constituted a sub-committee headed by Prof. Vipin Srivastava. Naturally, the sub-committee did not look into the matter afresh as decided in the Heads and Deans' meeting. Rather, it manufactured more evidence against ASA and neglected unfavourable evidence with the sole purpose of punishing ASA students[6]. The following facts need to be mentioned to explain the casteist character of sub-committee and VC backed by BJP leader Bandaru Dattatreya and MHRD minister:

a) By using administrative power, the sub-committee made Duty Security Officer, Dileep Singh, counter-signed the letter by Susheel Kumar in September which said that he was forced to write an apology letter.
b) The sub-committee did not take into account the counter affidavit filed by CV Anand, the Commissioner of Police, in the High Court on October 3rd, 2015.[7]
c) The MHRD headed by Smriti Irani wrote five letters/emails by way of reminder to the University between September 3rd and November 19th, 2015, which only encouraged the casteist administration to act against the ASA students.
d) Last but not the least, the VC of the University, wilfully and criminally neglected Rohith's letter of December 18th, 2015. The letter proposed that the VC should serve 10mg Sodium Azide to all Dalit students at the time of admission, "supply a nice rope to the rooms of all Dalit students and provide the facility of euthanasia for students alike".

All these things clearly showed that the MHRD, University VC and EC sub-committee together punished Dalit students and Rohith was one of those five students. Failing to get sufficient support from the students and teaching community to face the coercive power of the BJP led MHRD minister and University administration, Rohith committed suicide on January 17th, 2016.

Role of state to prevent suicides of Dalit students

The pro-active role of the state is very important in reducing the caste discrimination in educational institutions. Of course, the Indian state in the post-independence period has been broadly a Hindu majoritarian state. In the current situation, the state has been strengthening and perpetuating Hindu communalism and caste system as discrimination is amply clear from Rohith's institutional murder.[8] At present, under a parliamentary democracy, there is scope for public discussion, mobilization and actions. It is necessary to build strong public opinion to convince the caste Hindus about evil influences of the caste system and discrimination. There is no option other than taking up patient and painstaking campaigns in the form of writing books and articles, delivering lectures, conducting discussions and participating and mobilizing people into democratic actions.

Simultaneously, one has to take up activities which can force the government to bring about specific policies resulting in laws to fight discrimination. I broadly agree with S.K. Thorat in his speech[9] delivered at the University of Hyderabad suggesting certain measures, of course with some modifications and additions:

1 Set up a committee at the university level to bring out the nature and extent of discrimination, that Dalit, OBC, and women students are facing in the campus and its harmful effects on personality and performance of the people concerned.
2 Ask MHRD to set up a committee at the national level to understand the nature and extent of discrimination and its evil effects by taking up thorough case studies of HEIs.
3 Need for the Rohith Act: There has to be a countrywide campaign by all HEIs involving well-known intellectuals of oppressed castes and other democratic-minded intellectuals' civil society organizations to force the governments to accept discrimination as a punishable crime. After the Karamchedu massacre of Dalits by landlords belonging to Kamma caste of Andhra Pradesh in 1985, the oppressed caste launched a massive national-level campaign which forced the government to enact the SC/ST (Prevention of Atrocities) Act. Similarly, a national level campaign has to be launched across the country at every level to force the central government to bring about the Rohith Act.
4 A new course on civic and democratic education and egalitarian values has to be introduced with a well thought-out curriculum of contents. This course should be made compulsory for all students with at least one-month classes for teachers and administrators including Registrar, Pro-Vice-Chancellor and Vice-Chancellor. The purpose is to make them

understand historical socio-economic conditions that gave rise to discrimination based on caste and other relevant categories and suggest measures to eliminate those socio-economic conditions.

5 There is a need to establish socially relevant centres/departments. The centres and departments like Women's Studies and Centre of Exclusion and Inclusive Policy, Dalit and Adivasi Studies which teach and research into discrimination based on caste, gender, class, tribe, disabled and other relevant distinctions need to be nurtured carefully and developed.
6 Give more weightage to those teachers taking Dalit students, students from rural areas and other first generation academically disadvantaged sections and making them complete Ph.D. degrees, similar to weightage given for writing articles in refereed journals and publishing books. The weightage should also give to those teachers, helping students coming from similar background in Integrated M.A. and M.A./M.SC Courses.
7 Last but not the least, a common school system should be established where every child from oppressed castes is ensured quality education, in the real sense of the term. The textbooks to be taught in schools, colleges and universities should be written incorporating knowledge about our country and its diverse population and with a perspective that is free of caste, communal and religious prejudices.

Although the University administration has responded to UGC (Promotion of Equity in Higher Educational Institutions) Regulations Act, 2012, and appointed anti-discriminatory officer, it is not in the spirit of the act. It is also said in the notification (2016).

> In case of students, the officer shall submit her/his recommendations to the institutions for taking appropriate follow of action . . . in case of teachers and non-teaching staff, the officer has to submit an inquiry report to the competent authority of the university to take appropriate actions in accordance with the provision of the statutes or ordinances or regulations of the University or the UGC regulations.

This competent authority is the VC or other administrative officer. How can a professor go against the decisions of the VC of the same university? There is no appointment of an Ombudsman by the university which is suggested by UGC. It should be made mandatory to appoint an Ombudsman in every university. There is another committee constituted by the administration, viz. Equal Opportunity Cell. There is a university-level grievance cell, but that has remained on paper. The Chair Person of these committees have neither interest in the Committee's work or nor have time to spend. The only qualification is they are either silent spectators or active supporters of VC, whenever and whatever he does.

In the context of violations of UGC guidelines and half-hearted functioning of existing committees, the inappropriate selection of Chair Persons, members of committees, the role of the state is of utmost importance. The state has to pro-actively ensure the implementation of measures mentioned above. Since the state is under the strong influence of Hindu communal fascist forces, there is pressing need for students, teachers and civil society to play an active role in making/forcing the state to take up these measures in order to eliminate social discrimination and caste system, on the basis of which social discrimination thrives.

Notes

1 Report of the Fact-Finding Committee Appointed in the Wake of the Death of Mr. Senthil Kumar, a PhD. Student in the School of Physics, University of Hyderabad, April 2008.
2 See Section 1.4, page3 and 4, of the Fact-finding Committee Appointed in the Wake of the Death of Mr. Senthil Kumar.
3 K. Laxminarayana, "Why Justice Roopanwal's Report in the Rohith Vemula Case Is a Travesty," November 17th, 2017. www.epw.in/engage/article/why-justice-roopanwals-report-rohith-vemula-case-travesty?0=ip_login_no_cache%3Dcf553de27177923c9727da6b3292372f
4 The proctorial board interim report submitted on August 12th, 2015. The same proctorial board gave a subsequent report on August 31st, 2015.
5 Mayank Jain, "Read the Letters HRD Ministry Sent Hyderabad University About 'Anti-National' Activities on Campus," January 19th, 2016. https://scroll.in/article/802107/read-the-letters-hrd-ministry-sent-hyderabad-university-about-anti-national-activities-on-campus
6 "Prepare for Dalit Euthanasia, said Rohith Vemula in Searing Letter to University of Hyderabad VC, Just Weeks Before his Death," January 19th, 2016. www.india.com/news/india/dalit-euthanasia-rohith-vemula-letter-to-university-of-hyderabad-vc-873626/
7 T.S. Sudhir, "How Rohith Vemula's 'Dalit Identity' Has Been Milked by All," *Daily O*, January 23rd, 2016. www.dailyo.in/politics/rohith-vemula-caste-politics-dalit-suicide-hyderabad-central-university-ambedkar-student-association/story/1/8622.html
8 "Vemula's Suicide an 'Institutional Murder': Satchidanandan," *The Hindu*, September 23rd, 2016. www.thehindu.com/news/national/Vemula%E2%80%99s-suicide-an-%E2%80%98institutional-murder%E2%80%99-Satchidanandan/article14015950.ece
9 Speech delivered by Professor Sukhadeo Thorat at University of Hyderabad on January 25th, 2016. https://youtu.be/hE_iyqsl6tQ

References

Ambedkar, B. R. (1938). *Annihilation of Caste* (1st ed.). Reproduced in 2008 by Gautama Book Center, New Delhi.

Ambedkar, B. R. (1987). Philosophy of Hinduism. In *Dr. B.R. Ambedkar Writings and Speeches* (Vol. 3). Education Department, Government of Maharashtra.

Constable, P. (2000). Sitting on the school verandah: The ideology and practice of 'untouchable' educational protest in late nineteenth-century western India. *The Indian Economic & Social History Review*, 37(4), 383–422.

Government of India. (2014). *Educational Statistics at a Glance*, Government of India, Ministry of Human Resource Development Bureau of Planning, Monitoring & Statistics, New Delhi.

Krishnan, P. S. (2016). Dalit suicides: Socio-historical facts and remedial and corrective measures: A note. *Indian Express*, January 29.

Laxminarayana, K. (2017). Why Justice Roopanwal's report in the Rohith Vemula Case is a travesty. *Economic and Political Weekly*, 52(46).

Marginson, S. (2007). *Globalization and Higher Education*. Retrieved from www.oecd.org/edu/research/37552729.pdf.

Rao, S. (n.d.). *Student Suicides in Elite Higher Educational Institutions*. An Unpublished Paper, Center for Zakir Hussain Studies, Jawaharlal Nehru University.

Report of the Committee Appointed to Inquire into the Circumstances Leading to the Demise of Mr. P. Raju. (2013). University of Hyderabad, Hyderabad.

Report of the Committee Appointed to Inquire into the Circumstances Leading to the Demise of Mr. M. Venkatesh, PhD Scholar, ACRHEM. (2013). University of Hyderabad, Hyderabad.

Report of the Fact-Finding Committee Appointed in the Wake of the Death of Mr. Senthil Kumar, a PhD Student in the School of Physics. (2008). University of Hyderabad, April.

Report Submitted to Andhra Pradesh High Court in the Context of Public Interest Litigation. (2013).

Sudhir, T. S. (2016). How Rohith Vemula's 'Dalit identity' has been milked by all. January 23. Retrieved from www.dailyo.in/politics/rohith-vemula-caste-politics-dalit-suicide-hyderabad-central-university-ambedkar-student-association/story/1/8622.html.

UGC Regulations on Prevention of Caste Based Discrimination/Harassment/Victimization and Promotion of Equality in HEIs. (2012).

9 Between beef and carrion

The politics of food consumption

Gayatri Nair

The recent legislation enforced by the Maharashtra government on the ban of beef has evoked a range of responses. Social media sites emerged as one of the prominent locations where the ban was ridiculed, discussed and debated. In an earlier version of this paper (Nair, 2016), I had argued that much of the antagonistic response to the ban arose from the anxiety of the liberal middle class. They construed the ban as a curb on their exercise of choice – as a limit to their consumption – at a time when what they consume has come to define who they are. Significantly, missing from this discourse at the time was the voice of the Dalits who too for long have come to be defined by what they consume and whose complex relationship with the consumption of beef is one marked by caste, poverty and memories of hunger.

This paper aims to explore this complex relationship through two ways – through a historical reflection on the political significance of rejecting work with, and the consumption of carrion; and an examination of the real implications of a ban on beef in terms of consumption practices for Indians in general but for the working class population in particular. Mapping the distinct and complex relation that Dalits have had with carrion and beef both, and the influence of Ambedkar in shaping it, particularly through his insistence on ending the consumption of carrion, should not be construed as an attempt to condone the ban. Rather the centrality that carrion and beef played in Dalit lives is highlighted to reflect on how the ban has worsened conditions for Dalits and the working classes. I argue that marking a distinction between carrion and beef was critical to establish material well-being and by extension to secure self-respect for a community shunned for its association with carrion. A shift from carrion to beef consumption signified an improvement in circumstances but more importantly constituted a bare minimum for Dalits, who have been historically sunk into poverty, destitution and hunger through the caste system; rising above it thus is essential for the self-respect of the community.

Oral histories and autobiographical accounts have been used here to foreground the complex manner in which beef and carrion feature in everyday lives of Dalits. This lies in stark contrast to the middle and upper class consumption of beef rooted in notions of pleasure and more significantly distanced from stigma. It is through a focus on the Dalit experience with beef and a history of carrion consumption that we can engage with the ban as more than just a curb on choice. Instead it allows us to think about the practise through the prism of hunger and destitution, and the role that consumption of beef plays for a population for whom even subsisting was made difficult.

The first half of this paper will draw from Dalit autobiographies such as Om Prakash Valmiki's Jhootan and Baby Kamble's *Jinne Amuche* to draw attention to how the community had a trying relation with carrion. It also explores this relation through a project undertaken by the 2009 batch of master's students in sociology (the author included), under the guidance of the eminent sociologist Sharmila Rege, at the Savitraibai Phule Pune University. The project sought to document the culinary life and memories around it of Dalits – a subject that was conspicuously absent from other such documents of food practices (such as recipe books). The second half of the paper will examine the political project of distancing Dalits from carrion, the continued links with beef and the inextricable links this had with Ambedkar's vision of the annihilation of caste rooted in the aims of building self-respect of a broken people.

Caste and carrion

Guru in his searing work on humiliation argued that there is a social cost to be borne by some for differential statuses accorded in society. The recognition and elevation of worth of some resulted in a loss for others. In bearing this cost, he posits, the reduction in the worth of others can often work through reducing humans to the level of animals and making them appear comparable[1] (2009, pp. 209–212). In caste society however, the Dalit is not merely reduced in worth but is in fact outrightly rejected. Curiously, this rejection occurs through an asymmetry of worth – an elevation of the animal, more specifically the (sacred) cow takes place alongside the rejection of the Dalit. This rejection of the Dalit and the repulsion their bodily being causes is reinforced through their link with carrion. The purity-pollution ideology bestows great worth only on the living cow, condemning the dead cow to a source of pollution so high that in its dissipated forms – meat, hide, leather – it continued to spread its pollution and mark all those who were forced into contact with it.

The social order of caste demanded that those who lay outside the *varna* order – i.e. the 'untouchable' castes – be forced to work in the most demeaning and 'polluting' of jobs. This particularly included work with carrion. For caste Hindus the cow was both sacred and an integral part of the agrarian economy, but its death signalled a potent moment of pollution, one which had to be contained by the Dalit. The cow was significant in agrarian work and animal husbandry but was also deemed productive in death, where farmers often sold cows that had stopped producing milk for slaughter. The ban effectively ended this practice by outlawing the sale of cows meant for slaughter. The death of the cow thus was both economically significant and socially damaging for the farmer unless the Dalit stepped in to perform the labour needed. The work of slaughter (also historically performed by the butcher caste community among Muslims), skinning, tanning the hide etc. is all work that is marked by caste. The ignominy that this work conferred was constantly impressed upon Dalits by the social structure which used their link with carrion to reiterate their low status. This was a distinct form of humiliation and Dalit memoirs such as Valmiki's dwell on what this meant for an individual and the larger community.

> My hands were trembling as I held the knife. I was trapped in a hard place. Chacha taught me how to ply the knife. That day something broke inside me. I skinned the bullock under chacha's guidance. I felt I was drowning in a swamp. I was being drawn into the very quagmire that I had tried to escape from. The wounds of the torment that I suffered with chacha on that hot afternoon are still fresh on my skin.
>
> (2003, p. 35)

Valmiki's reflection of his first encounter of work with carrion demonstrates how even as a child he is immediately aware of the humiliation that will come his way through his association with carrion. The association with carrion and the humiliation it carried for the Dalits was not only because disposing carrion was their caste-ordained duty but also because it was performed without adequate facilities and in unhygienic conditions, similar to manual scavenging. It was work that crushed their self-respect and subjected them to deep humiliation reiterating their low status. A narrative recorded as part of the Dalit Histories and Memories of Food project reveals this:

> Meat is usually bought, not taken from dead cattle because this is associated with a low caste status. Salim can thus recall how a Mahar man in his village was usually entrusted with carrying away and disposing the carcass of dead animals, which he did by carrying it over his head to a shop where he would sell the hide and bones. This man he vividly remembers as stinking immensely owing to the smell of the carcass. Pointing out that the business of selling the hide, meat and bones of these animals yields a lot, Salim claims, his son [the Mahar man's son] does the same job, running through the village with the dead animal on his head. Nothing much has changed, Salim wistfully points out.
>
> (2009, p. 104)

Yet as Salim's account highlights, the link with carrion was not one that could be easily severed by the community. Despite a certain material improvement in circumstances that could take place through a livelihood association with carrion, its caste connotations rarely went away. This can be especially seen through the economic mobility that a section of the Chamar community gained in Uttar Pradesh by entering leather manufacturing (Jaffrelot, 2002, p. 200) but which has done little to erode the low status accorded to them.

Carrion was used in addition for the hide, also for its meat. This meat provided basic albeit rare sustenance to Dalits, for whom hunger was a persistent reality. It was because of the use of carrion to mark caste status that Ambedkar while recognising the link of poverty and carrion consumption,[2] remained insistent that Dalits must reject the consumption of carrion, if self-respect in the community was to be cultivated. It was towards this end that he addressed the Mahad conference in 1927 with a specific appeal to Dalits to stop consuming carrion.

> No lasting progress can be achieved unless we put ourselves through a three-fold process of purification. We must improve the general tone of our demeanour, re-tone our pronunciations and revitalise our thoughts. *I therefore ask you now to take a vow from this moment to renounce eating carrion. It is high time that we rooted out from our mind the ideas of highness and lowness among ourselves. Make an unflinching resolve not to eat thrown out crumbs. We will attain self-respect and gain self-knowledge.*
>
> (Ambedkar, 2003, p. 4) (emphasis mine)

Throughout his address at Mahad, Ambedkar emphasized how the community needed to build its self-respect, on the foundation of rejection. This was not a rejection of a people, but of the values that denigrated the Dalit. Dalits rejecting the crumbs handed down to them by caste society was central to this. While several scholars, such as Jaffrelot (2005a, p. 47), have read this as a move to Sanskritisation, it could be read differently. Rejecting carrion was integral to the political project of rejecting caste, not an attempt to gain mobility within the system. Furthermore, inculcating the practice of rejecting carrion was essential also not just for political reasons but also for the physical health of the community especially when most often the cause of death of the cow was not known.

However despite Ambedkar's call and the vow taken at the Mahad conference, the same patterns of consumption continued for the most part. For most Dalits who could ill afford vegetables and other sources of meat, carrion provided a rare luxury and was an essential source of protein. Rege (2006) draws from Baby Kamble's autobiography *The Prisons We Broke* to note that instances of cattle epidemics were a time of feasting amongst the Dalit households. Somewhere between fresh beef and the compulsions of carrion, strategies for consumption were also evolved. Kamble points out that at times when there weren't enough cattle dying, men armed with medication would be on the lookout for stray cattle and would feed it drugs, following which they would eagerly wait to be called on to dispose of it when the animal died. Rege adds, "The women queued up for their share and sometimes if there was not enough firewood to cook the meat, it would be eaten almost raw." (2006, p. 203)

Meat therefore was a critical resource for a community that was ravaged by hunger. However, as the study on Dalit food practices highlighted, memories of hunger and what was eaten in times of crisis such as carrion could also transform into active food choices. Ambedkar's call for giving up the consumption of carrion was therefore not one met with absolute agreement and conviction by the Dalit community. Baby Kamble's account is noteworthy because it recounts anecdotes of how carrion was acutely desired despite political impulses running in the opposite direction. Improving economic conditions, if they occurred, were marked by a transition to the purchase of meat (as opposed to the consumption of carrion, as was the case with Salim) and not always by a move to vegetarianism, as is generally assumed. Joan Mencher documents the same in Tamil Nadu and Kerala, where interviews with Dalits revealed that beef consumption was central to their food practices and that gradually many made an attempt to move away from the consumption of cattle that died of disease and began procuring it from markets (1974, p. 246).

The politics of consumption

It is critical here to note that in highlighting the politics of consumption, for Ambedkar as well as the larger Dalit community, a distinction is maintained between beef and carrion. This distinction holds relevance to how the project of self-respect is conceived of by Ambedkar and can help understand the relevance of the beef ban imposed in many states today. The distinction is important to examine so that Ambedkar's progressive call is not collapsed into the political project of Hindutva.

When Ambedkar asks for Dalits not to consume carrion he is doing so to centre the politics of caste, not to obscure it. Its foundation is not the consumption of beef but beef as carrion; what was discarded by the upper castes had to be consumed by the Dalits. Noteworthy is that whenever Ambedkar has touched upon the issue, particularly in the Mahad address and the resolutions passed at the conference following that, it was always the term carrion that was used to mark what had contributed to injuring the spirit of the community. A rejection of 'the thrown out crumbs' that are forced on them by the structures and relations of caste was treated as an essential part of the Dalit political project of 'raising themselves' (Ambedkar, 2003, p. 34).

This distinction lies at complete variance with how the ban is conceived of by the Hindu right. Through the ban and the acts of vigilantism that have followed for the last two years, Hindu right groups are concerned only with the symbolic and moral worth of the cow as an essential symbol of the Hindu community. But while previously the marking of the cow as sacred heightened the divisions between caste Hindus and 'untouchables', in its more recent avatar, there have been desperate attempts to overlook the caste dimensions of the problem. In blurring the lines between beef and carrion, there is a refusal to acknowledge the distinct role played by the latter in creating the material and social conditions for the subjugation of the Dalit community.

In his exposition on the historical transformation of the Brahmins and their adopted practice of vegetarianism and cow worship, Ambedkar argues that the cow, while it was venerated, continued to be an item of consumption for Brahmin and other high castes. What marked the difference between the upper and lower castes was that while the upper castes consumed fresh beef, the lower castes consumed carrion. As the Brahmins under pressure from the growing influence of Buddhism changed their practices and shifted away from consumption of beef, other caste Hindus followed suit. It was only the 'untouchable' castes who did not and in fact could not do so, out of both poverty and owing to the caste obligations enforced on them.

There was therefore a difference between the upper and lower castes mapped neatly over the life and death of a cow. The sacredness of the cow was maintained by the upper castes and the pollution of its death managed by the lower castes. The recent move of the ban, however, conflates the difference between beef and carrion, by making it uniformly sinful for everyone to partake in the consumption of the dead cow – fresh or otherwise. This is not, however, directed toward progressive political ends of doing away with caste. For it to be so, the move should have acknowledged the difference between beef and carrion and in fact should not have banned the consumption of fresh beef at all.[3] Instead, the construction of the moral equivalence of all members of the Hindu community, undifferentiated by caste and centred on their uniform belief in the sacredness of the cow, is essential for the larger project of Hindutva politics. In order for the Hindu Right to consolidate politically, it has to forge a united Hindu community pitted against a common enemy of the Muslim 'other'. Caste is a constant obstacle in its path,[4] and yet Hinduism without caste is too radical in its import; the middle-ground here is an obscuring of caste, a sleight of hand to make it seem irrelevant to how the Hindu community forges its most critical social practices.

It is here that attention must be paid to the ban and the response it evoked. This is particularly observable when food practices are always explained away as an act of 'choice'. This is not to make the case that food consumption can never involve choices exercised by individuals. However, to view these choices as operating free from the exertions of a social structure is problematic. Especially in the Indian context, food and caste have come to be enjoined in a way that allows for food practices to be considered as markers of particular castes/caste status, as Ambedkar had also argued. At a time when caste is seen as only marking the lower castes,[5] the food practices of upper castes, although rooted in cultural, caste borne practices, are often termed as an exercise of choice and not tradition. Thus upper castes and classes will often claim to be vegetarian 'by choice'. This situation can lead one to conclude that there are no hierarchies in food practices similar to other social practices and leads to situations where caste can operate in significant but insidious ways.[6] In a political climate which frowns upon overt mentions of caste whilst permitting veiled discrimination based on it, food practices have emerged as codes for determining an individual's caste[7] (Nair, 2016).

Yet for a consolidated Hindutva ideology to emerge, as discussed above, an ideological understanding of Hinduism rooted in a Brahmanical view of the sacred cow must be reconciled with the entry of those who treated it as most profane – the Dalits. The ban which directly attacks the consumption habits of the Dalits highlights that the Dalits may still enter the Hindu fold only on the terms determined by the upper castes. The symbolic value of the cow protection campaign which can earn the BJP the support of the middle and upper caste Hindus have thus been chosen over the long term political gains they may receive with Dalit support to the party. It is the absence of a concerted voice against the ban from the Dalits owing to their marginal status in social and political life that enables such trade-offs to be made. Further, since the practice of beef consumption is more widely prevalent in the western and southern parts of the country and not as much in the North, where Hindutva politics currently reigns dominant, it may have contributed to the strident manner in which the BJP has thrown its weight behind the move. This is especially so since local units of the party in Kerala have not yet attempted to make an issue out of beef consumption where it is a popular practice. There is therefore a carefully constructed strategy at work, at the heart of which lies an attempt to draw a veil over the link between the cow and caste.

Yet caste cannot be so simply obscured from view. The very act of the ban, marking as illegal what was always conceived of as illegitimate and of which the Dalit regularly partook will only contribute to the worsening conditions amongst the poor, who are most likely to be Dalit.[8] Indeed the Dalit food memories project highlights how beef and pork are regular items of consumption in Dalit households. A practice borne of caste continued not only because of food choices having been cultivated over the years but also because beef is a much more affordable meat in comparison to chicken or mutton. It provides essential proteins particularly to a community that is largely engaged in hard physical labour and in much need of it. Forcing beef out of the food basket for Dalits not only criminalises their food practices but directly injures them by forcing them to now shift to more expensive sources of protein or away from it completely.

The tragic implications of caste, class and consumption

To imagine that the loss of an affordable protein can be easily compensated through the consumption of other items is to be misguided about the degree of poverty in India. The implications of this ban are gravest for the poor of the country. In the Indian context, however, it could be argued that everyone suffers from the ban, with the poor receiving the worst end of the deal.

Mapping protein consumption in India, scholars such as Utsa Patnaik (2007) have argued that India's slow agricultural growth, combined with an export oriented policy, have resulted in the net availability of food grains remaining fairly stagnant over time, marked with instances of significant falls in particular years.

Trends in per capita protein consumption (NSS 68th Round, Nutritional Intake Report) indicate that there is a decline in per capita protein intake per day in rural India from 1993–94 when it stood at 60.2 gm to 52.5 in 2011–12. In urban India the intake in 1993–94 stood at 57.2 gms which came down to 55.2 gms per day in 2011–12. Patnaik argues that the drop in protein intake is indicative of widespread poverty in the country particularly in the post liberalisation period. She clarifies (2007, p. 251) that the drop in consumption should not be read as an instance of Engel's law which states that as incomes rise, people move out of direct consumption of food grains to richer sources of proteins such as meat, eggs etc. Instead Patnaik argues that if one is to look at both direct and indirect consumption of food grains, then as incomes rise in a country, the total consumption of food grains should always rise since it includes both direct and indirect means of consumption.[9] The Indian scenario however highlights that there is a steady drop in both the direct and indirect consumption of food grains, indicative according to Patnaik of widespread poverty and hunger.

The debate about whether these figures demonstrate widespread hunger prevalent in India or an exercise of choice by Indians in moving away from protein rich food to other sources of energy such as fats, sugars and carbohydrates, is one which I shall refrain from entering at this juncture. What remains of importance is the implication of the beef ban in such a context. Reports published in the Indian Medical Gazette by Mahajan (2015), and trends observed by Nutritional Foundation of India point to a severe protein deficiency that the Indian population is suffering from. News reports[10] indicate that over the last two decades, eight per cent of the rural population and 70 per cent of the urban population suffer from a protein deficiency. Prema Ramachandran, Director of the Nutritional Foundation of India argues it is necessary in light of this trend to bring back "pulses and coarse grains into the policy ambit to arrest this trend. According to the NFI study, from 3.4kg of rice and wheat a month, the consumption of rice and wheat by the poorest classes went up to 8.3kg in 1999–2000, while consumption of coarse cereals went down from 2.4kg to 1.4kg."[11]

These are troubling numbers for any state to tackle, especially in light of the nutritional importance of proteins. The NSSO reports on nutritional intake make a strong case for the importance of proteins for the healthy development of the body irrespective of the kind of work performed by humans. In this context it can be argued that the beef ban only injures the ability of an already protein deficient population to access protein by curtailing its ability to access one of the cheaper sources of it available to them. State policy should ideally be focussed on boosting protein consumption by seeking to subsidise pulses through the PDS system (which has been introduced already in the states of Karnataka, Tamil Nadu and Orissa), as well as maintaining access to cheaper animal proteins. The Indian state would thus also have to focus on making meat consumption more viable in domestic markets as opposed to eyeing foreign earnings that come with increases in meat exports.[12]

The needs of the agrarian and urban working classes ought to be addressed adequately and a state that privileges the protection of cows over the basic needs of its citizens would need to carefully consider where its priorities lie.

An onslaught on self-respect

For the impoverished and hungry millions of this country, most of whom comprise the Dalits, the ban is not just an assault on their ability to gain sustenance but is also an onslaught on their struggle to gain self-respect. In order for the lower castes to gain self-respect, Ambedkar argued that it was critical that they reject carrion and refuse the 'thrown out crumbs' of caste society. With the ban in place, Dalits will be left unable to consume the cheapest of meats available to them. The ban has reiterated old codes of caste behaviour that in fact destroy their self-respect by sinking them further into abject poverty and hunger.

If the state is truly concerned with development it ought to recognise the politics of food and acknowledge the role of caste in shaping practices. Securing economic gains through India's high ranking in beef exports does little to attack the structure of caste. The consumption of beef for lower castes, although marked by caste, has also now come to be exercised as a choice of a kind. The implications of a ban on cow slaughter are not however limited to a stripping away of this choice but can be seen as the privileging of consumption practices of the upper castes along with presenting a ready weapon with which vigilantes can attack Dalits not just for their consumption practices but also for their work with carrion.

The ban thus flies in the face of public policy which must seek to forward an agenda of welfare for the people this can be achieved through twin objectives of widening access to proteins through availability of cheap meats such as beef, as well as by ensuring the basic sustenance of the poor creating conditions for their self-respect to be cultivated.

Notes

1 He cites the example of Black people being compared to animals – in strength, virility as well as in behaviour (Guru, 2009, p. 211).

2 The link between poverty and carrion consumption was historically established, argued Ambedkar. He notes in his work on the origin of the untouchable category that it was precisely poverty that prevented the Dalits from giving up on carrion consumption and shifting to other meats or vegetables.

3 A progressive call should be recognising its significance in Dalit food practices as well as through the work in carrion that Dalits must either participate in owing to direct enforcement of the caste obligations or owing to economic necessity. It should have called therefore for a ban on consumption and work by Dalits on carrion.

4 The violence at Una where Dalit men working with carrion were flogged by vigilante *gau rakshaks* (saviours of the cow), points to how Hindutva politics tackles the politics of caste.

5 As Deshpande and John (2010) argue upper castes having secured their access to resources of wealth, education, even health through now apparently 'legitimate' means where they no longer need to explicitly state their caste has meant that upper castes have come to believe that caste holds no value in the 'modern' world and thus these castes now sanitise themselves as being modern classes. This has resulted in the impression that caste belongs to the lower castes alone.

6 Real estate markets, where buildings are identified as being 'exclusively vegetarian' are a good indication of how caste discrimination can be practiced through the use of such codes.

7 The case of the canteen of the newspaper *The Hindu* prohibiting the consumption of meat immediately comes to mind, not only because of their call for the prohibition but also because the management explained their position as stemming not from a caste bias but owing to environmental concerns.

8 In looking at caste inequality, the data journalist Roshan Kishore draws from consumption expenditure data to point out how more than half of the SC population belongs to the poorest two quintiles based on consumption expenditure data. (www.livemint.com/Politics/ino3tfMYVsd6VVGUdWXB8H/The-many-shades-of-caste-inequality-in-India.html)

9 The direct consumption of food grains refers to its consumption in the form of cereals and pulses; its indirect form refers to cereals and pulses that are used as animal feed and which is then consumed by humans in the form of meat. Engels' law argues that with rising income individuals switch to more expensive sources of protein such as meats. Patnaik is making the point that even with rise in income therefore there is an overall rise in consumption of food grains which should take place, in this case through its indirect consumption via meat. In India though what is observable is that there is a severe decline in the availability and consumption of food grains, undifferentiated across direct and indirect means.

10 See, 'Protein intake in India dips 10%; oil, fat consumption' for a discussion on the protein deficiency. Available from: http://timesofindia.indiatimes.com/india/Protein-intake-in-India-dips-10-oil-fat-consumption-up/articleshow/47169586.cms. See also 'Protein deficiency in Rural India worrying', available from: www.livemint.com/Politics/fIf5xU1F83eGZ5FV1vfPcP/Protein-deficiency-in-rural-India-worrying.html.

11 Ibid. Available from: www.livemint.com/Politics/fIf5xU1F83eGZ5FV1vfPcP/Protein-deficiency-in-rural-India-worrying.html.

12 India is currently ranked as the third highest exporter of beef according to the FOA-OECD report and is to hold this position for the coming decade as well. For more see, https://indianexpress.com/article/world/india-third-biggest-beef-exporter-fao-report-4772389/.

References

Ambedkar, B. R. (2003). The Mahad Satyagrah. In *Dr. Babasaheb Ambedkar, Writings and Speeches, Vol. 17. Dr. B.R. Ambedkar and His Egalitarian Revolution; Part One: Struggle for Human Rights*. New Delhi: Dr. Ambedkar Foundation.

Deshpande, S. and John, M. E. (2010). The Politics of Not Counting Caste. *Economic and Political Weekly*, 45(25), 39–42.
Guru, G. (2009). The Rejection of Rejection: Foregrounding Self Respect. In G. Guru (ed.), *Humiliation*. New Delhi: Oxford University Press.
Jaffrelot, C. (ed.). (2002). *Pakistan: Nationalism Without a Nation*. Zed Books.
Jaffrelot, C. (2003). *India's Silent Revolution: The Rise of the Lower Castes in North India*. New Delhi: Orient Blackswan.
Jaffrelot, C. (2005a). Analysing and Ethnicising Caste to Eradicate it More Effectively. In *Dr. Ambedkar and Untouchability: Analysing and Fighting Caste* (pp. 31–51). London: C. Hurst and Co.
Jaffrelot, C. (2005b). *Dr. Ambedkar and untouchability: Fighting the Indian Caste System*. New York: Columbia University Press.
Mahajan, M. (2015). Protein Consumption in Diet of Adult Indians: A General Consumer Survey (PRODIGY). *Indian Medical Gazette*, 149(4), 149–150.
Mencher, J. P. (1974). The Caste System Upside Down, or the Not-so-Mysterious East. *Current Anthropology*, 15(4), 469–493.
Nair, G. (2016). Bitter Aftertaste of Beef Ban; 'Choice', Caste and Consumption. *Economic and Political Weekly*, 51(10).
Patnaik, U. (2007). *The Republic of Hunger and Other Essays*. Three Essays Collective.
Rege, S. (2006). Baby Kondiba Kamble; Jine Amuche. In *Writing Caste/Writing Gender* (pp. 194–226). New Delhi: Zubaan.
Rege, S., Tak, D., Thosar, S., and Aranha, T. (2009). *Isn't This Plate Indian? Dalit Histories and Memories of Food*. Gender Studies: Student Project Series. Pune: Krantijyoti Savitribai Phule, Women's Studies Center.
Valmiki, O. (2007). *In Jhootan* (p. 35). Kolkatta: Samya.

10 Changing context of caste, gender and land relations in India

Dontha Prashanth, Patturi Balaji and Matta Srinivas

Introduction

Empowerment is a multi-dimensional process involving civil, political, social, economic and cultural participation and rights. It is a process which enables people to make strategic choices in areas that affect their lives. The key factors for empowerment are access to resources and agency, which provides impetus to make choices using these resources: helps challenge the regressive structures and the patriarchal power relations (here) by women. Ambedkar quotes "Religion, social status and property are all sources of power and authority" (Rodrigues, 2017). In order to maintain control over the society, Hindu social order had confined the ownership and access to property to twice-born men (Brahmin, Vaishya and Kshatriya) while forcing a majority of women and Shudras to live in destitution. Women and Shudras were denied from their rightful share in the property, education and employment. Under the system of caste, there would be no room for the empowerment of women and Shudras. As a matter of fact caste structure in India is responsible for subordination of women and one of the routes through which it controls women is the '*superposition of endogamy on exogamy*'* (Indian Antiquary, 1917) that prohibits inter-caste marriage.

The practices of endogamy combined with the customary rules of inheritance limits property to the caste and social group. Endogamy limits the consequences of transmission of property through women, and maintains the property through marriage with families of one's own kind (Goody and Goody, 1976). Such limitation of property to social groups coupled with the exploitative tendencies of caste which left the rights to acquisition of property with Caste-Hindus while restricting women and Shudras from acquiring property had perpetuated inequality in the society. Dr. B. R. Ambedkar was a firm opponent of such iniquitous social formations and remained relentless in his struggle for annihilation of such forms of inequality. He advocated against perpetuation of iniquitous social practices, in which process while serving as Law Minister of Government of India, he introduced Hindu Code Bill aimed at granting equal rights in share of property for both men and women. By taking a comprehensive view on penetration of inequality through religious customary practices, he said "To leave inequality between class and class, between sex and sex, which is the soul of Hindu Society untouched and to go on passing legislation relating to economic problems is to make a farce of our Constitution and to build a palace on a dung heap. This is the significance I attached to the Hindu Code."[1] His advocacy on doing away with caste in marriage and adoption through Hindu Code Bill was aimed at preventing forfeiture of one's inheritance on account of inter-caste marriages. Under the Shastric law, the loss of caste through inter-caste marriage entails forfeiture of inheritance (Gour, 1919). However the reforms in equalizing the rights in property amongst men and women were defeated by dominant caste representatives in parliament which subsequently led to the resignation of Dr. B. R. Ambedkar as Minister for Law in 1951. It took more than 55 years to make an amendment in Hindu Succession Act to guarantee equal rights in inheriting the ancestral property by women.

In present context, caste and gender roles still have a stronger hold in the society with unequal distribution of property and unequal representation in workforce as against their demographic proportions of populations. Caste System in today's context still has a stronger hold in the hegemony of customary relations over constitutional provisions. In India, about 90.1% of the marriages are of same caste, about 5.1% of women married men lower than her caste, and 4.8% of woman married men higher than her caste (Kumudin Das et al., 2011). The demographic composition from 68th NSSO Round for Employment and Unemployment amongst various social groups for 2011–12 reveal that Scheduled Castes who constitute 18.85% of total population of India reside predominantly in rural areas, accounting for 78.1% of the total SC population, while amongst non SC/ST/OBC's a considerably higher proportion resides in urban areas who constitute 41.42% of their total population, which is greater in comparison with Scheduled Castes whose proportion of urban population constitutes for 21.95% of total SC population.

In terms of occupational engagement in rural areas, Scheduled Caste households operate predominantly as casual labour in agriculture and non-agricultural tasks accounting for 52.6% of their total working households, as against 21% in the case of non SC/ST/OBC's. To sum up a majority of non SC/ST/OBC's in rural areas are engaged as self-employed in agriculture and a majority of Scheduled Castes are engaged as casual labour in agrarian and non-agrarian tasks. The heavy engagement of Scheduled Castes in performing casual labour is not natural but is a result of denial of access to land ordained by the system of caste.

The available evidence on ownership of land amongst various social groups suggests that there is a skewed distribution of land. NSSO 70th Round Report on Household ownership and operational holdings – 2013 in India reveals that in rural areas, Scheduled Castes who constitute 20.06% of total households, own 9.2% of total land, which does not even constitute half of their proportion to total households, while Non SC/ST/OBC's who constitute 23.23% of total households owns a share of 32.03% of total land. These latest trends reflect skewed distribution of land amongst various social groups.

In addition, the structural transformation which happened in the post-1990's has resulted in caste translocation from public institutions to private sphere (which was traditionally dominated by Caste-Hindus but got strengthened further) as indicated by a study conducted by D. Ajit, Han Donker and Ravi Saxena (2012) on Caste-Wise distribution of Indian Corporate Board Members for the year 2010 which revealed that 92.6% of Corporate Board members are Forward Castes, of which Brahmins occupy a share of 44.6%, Vaishyas occupy a share of 46.0%, Kshatriyas and others with a share of 2%, rest 7.4% of corporate members are constituted by SC/ST/OBC.

Given the picture of the persisting inequalities amongst various social groups, the present paper would explore the role of customary practices of caste determining occupational stratification and accumulation of wealth amongst few social groups in today's context. The following paper attempts to analyze at present through a comparative analysis of the inter-connectivity of caste, gender and asset holding over the years.

Demography and changing patterns of occupational engagement and land ownership

The numbers as per the Census 2011 concerning the demographic composition of India, reveals that 51.4% of the total population are males, while 48.5% of the population is constituted by females. The majority of the population, around 69%, of the total resides in rural areas. The composition of Scheduled Castes and Scheduled Tribes reveals that Scheduled Castes form 16.6% of the total population, while Scheduled Tribes stands at 8.6%. Within Scheduled Castes and Scheduled Tribes, gender composition reveals that about 48.6% of Scheduled Castes are females, while amongst Scheduled Tribes 49.7% are females.

Nearly about 72% of India's working population resides in rural areas, amongst which males constitute 62% of rural working force, while females constitute 38% of rural working force. In urban pockets, where 28% of total working population of India resides, the proportion of males constitute 79% of the total urban working population while the proportion of females constitute 21%. The figures reveal an unequal distribution of workforce amongst males and females as against their proportion of population, whereas in the proportion of workforce amongst females in rural areas stands at 38%, while their proportion of population in rural remains to be 49%. In urban areas the situation is much worse, wherein females constitute 21% of total urban working population, as against their population in urban area with a share of 48% in the total urban population. The proportion of non-workers amongst males and females suggests that it is higher amongst females than males, with females constituting 60% of non-workers as against 40% of non-workers amongst males.

Occupational diversification

The effect of the caste system on agriculture clearly depicts the patterns of relegation of Scheduled Castes to agricultural labour, while a majority of Caste-Hindus were demarcated as self-employed cultivators. The occupational patterns amongst various social groups suggests that the dependancy of Scheduled Castes as agricultural labor and casual labour is higher in proportion as compared with the dependancy of non SC/ST/OBC's as agricultural labour.

Occupational patterns amongst males and female working population suggests that more than half, i.e. 55%, of them are dependant on agriculture, while the rest (42%) are engaged as other workers, leaving about 4% engaged in household industry. Amongst the rural agrarian working population, cultivators constitute 46% of the total agrarian working population (within which are 32% males and 14% females, together 46%), while agricultural laboureres constitute 54% (within which 31% are males and 23% is the female population). The trends reveal that amongst the female agrarian working population, there is a higher proportion of engagement as agricultural labourers than cultivators. However, as against their proportion of population, said engagement is lower, further analysis on the patterns exhibited by Scheduled Caste women's engagement as agricultural labour can present a better picture.

In rural areas, amongst Scheduled Castes as a proportion of rural SC agrarian working population, 25% of them operate as cultivators (with 17% male, and 8% female) and the rest (75%) are engaged as agricultural labourers (with 44% males and 31% females). The trends on occupational diversification in rural areas amongst Scheduled Castes exhibit the feature of higher dependancy of both male and female population in rural areas on agricultural labour. The proportion of SC female agricultural laboueres to total female agricultural labour in rural areas suggest that SC women constitutes 25% of total female agricultural laboureres (rural), whereas when the proportion of SC woman (rural) is accounted for as a proportion of total female population (rural), it stands at 18%, indicating that the magnitude of participation of Schedule Caste (female) as agricultural labour stands higher in comparision with overall female population. The analysis suggests that Scheduled Castes and woman as social categories who were denied ownership of land shows a higher dependancy as is exhibited by being largely agricultural laborers than as cultivators.

Census 1991 suggests that the proportion of cultivators (including tenant cultivators) accounted for 25.44% of the total working population, while the proportion of agricultural laborers stood at 49.06%, with total agrarian working population accounting for 74.50%. The figures for 2011 shows that there is a further decline in the proportion of cultivators to 14.75%, and a slight decline in the proportion of agricultural labour to 45.92% with proportion of agrarian working population also witnessing a decline to 50.67%, however still largely significant. Over the years, it has been observed that the proportion of Scheduled Castes performing agricultural labour has been highly significant.

Land ownership: changing patterns of ownership

The available evidence on ownership of land amongst various social groups suggests that there is a skewed distribution of land. NSSO 70th Round Report on Household ownership and Operational Holdings – 2013 in India reveals that in rural areas, Scheduled Castes who constitute 20.06% of total households own 9.2% of total land which doesnot even constitute half to their proportion to total households; OBC's own 45.68% of land as against 44.82% of households, while non SC/ST/OBC's, who constittute 23.23% of total households, own a share of 32.03% of total land. These latest trends shows skewed distribution of land amongst various social groups. However over the years, the proportion of land owned as well as the proportion of households for non SC/ST/OBC has been on a decline in rural areas when compared with the figures of 2003. The proportion of non SC/ST/OBC households which constituted 26.26% of households in 2003 has declined to 23.23%; the same when observed on the proportion of land owned, it also shows that there is declining pattern, though not drastic it declined from 36.3% in 2003 to 32.03% by 2013. The trends for OBC's show a pattern of increase, OBC households which constituted 41.61% of total households in 2003, constitute 44.82% by 2013, at the same time the proportion of land also has increased from 43.51% to 45.68% of total land owned by all social groups.

As far the social structure of both Scheduled Castes and OBC's are concerned, both were graded lower than Caste-Hindus, viz., twice-born. However in terms of ownership of land, OBC's have occupied a greater share of land as compared to Scheduled Castes, ownership of land amongst OBC's is at least proportionate to their households share. But ownership of land amongst Scheduled castes presents an overview that the ownership is less than their proportion of households.

As a comparative analysis what could be observed is that there is not much drastic change in the proportion of ownership of land by Scheduled Castes. However there is a significant amount of ownership of land observed in the hands of OBC's. Nancharaiah (1988) explains the phenomenon of transfer of ownership of land from Brahmins to non-Brahmins, which also includes a section of OBCs. As he argues, in Andhra Pradesh, in the eve of introduction of Rent Reduction Act 1947 and Estate abolition act 1948, non-Brahmins have refused to pay the rents demanded by the Brahmin landlords and thus with low rents being collected and with the foreseeing of Estate Abolition

Act being enacted, the Brahmins sold their lands to non-Brahmins even at lower prices. Non-Brahmins could acquire the land because they were in a superior position than the Scheduled Castes in the order of caste, and the prevalence of untouchability against Scheduled Castes and their dependence as agricultural labourers denied an equal opportunity for them to earn and improve. Added to which, particularly, Brahmins have also opted for migrating to urban spaces, which not only dwindled their share in rural population, but at the same time on account of their sale of lands to non-Brahmin powerful social groups, their share of land also has declined.

As an overall picture the access to land amongst various social groups presents a pattern of unequal distribution amongst various social groups, and asset holding being observed with the characteristic of graded distribution, with Caste-Hindus placed at top, OBC's in middle and Scheduled Castes in the last would only strengthen the argument of the accumulation of land being determined by the inter-connectivity of caste-endogamy rules of inheritance leading to concentration of land in the hands of few, while leaving a majority in destitution.

Caste: power and authority

Castes are exclusive endogamous groups of the society in which they operate as enclosed classes with specified occupational distribution graded as one above the other with graded inequalities and perpetuity of profession being determined by birth (Ambedkar, 1917, 1937).

Endogamy as a custom of marriage was considered as sacramental to the faith of Hindu religion, and stood as a base for the sustenance of caste system. Inter-caste marriages which violates the principle of endogamy were quite often treated with utmost contempt leading to social ostracization and elimination of the married couple. Even with the evolution of modern institutions of jurisprudence and justice during 19th century under colonial government with establishment of high courts and supreme courts, if marriages violating the principle of endogamy were declared null and void then the reason is to be found in the doctrine of inequality nurtured by Hindu Dharma Shastras which had legal sanctity. The feature of endogamy conjoined with the laws of inheritance of property becomes crucial in understanding the nature of accumulation of land/property in the hands of fewer social groups.

Intersectionality of caste and gender

First, Manu Smriti which served as legal doctrine[2] of Hindu socio-economic order has prevented Shudras to acquire property, by vesting a right with the Brahmin to snatch away whatever that is hard-earned by a Shudra.[3] It has ordained a Shudra to remain a slave only to eke out existence by way of accepting abandoned food,[4] left over clothes, while granting the right to acquire of wealth and education for the Caste-Hindus. By vesting the right to earn and accumulate wealth with twice-born or Caste-Hindus and denying any scope for Shudras to earn has laid the foundation for economic inequality. Alongside the laws of inheritance of said accumulated property have mandated for sacramental marriage as a necessary condition for the inheritance of the property for the off-spring of the married couple.

Mitakshara as a law of inheritance largely governs the inheritance rules of the country (Kumar, 1985). Under Mitakshara,

> the property of a Hindu is not his individual property. It is property which belongs to what is called which consists of father, son, grandson and great grandson. All these people have a birth-right in that property and the property on the death of anyone member of this coparcenary passes by what is called survivorship to the members who remain behind, and does not pass to the heirs of the deceased.
>
> (Ambedkar, 1951)

Here the property is inherited at the time of birth, birth being governed by the principle of begetting a child only through a marriage of the same caste results in perpetuity of the property in the hands of the same community. The transfer of the property is governed by rule of sacramental marriage.

In *Bai Kashi vs Jamnadas Mansukh Raichand on 5 March, 1912*, High Court of Bombay delivered a verdict declaring the marriage of a Brahmin Woman and a Shudra as illegal, null and void. In another case of *Swayampakula Subbaramayya And . . . vs Swayampakula Venkatasubbamma . . . on 5 February, 1941*, High Court of Madras declared 'anuloma' marriage, a marriage between a Brahmin man and Shudra woman, as illegal and declared that maintenance or share in wealth of an estate cannot be allowed to the children and wife since they were categorized as Shudras. Such were the rules of Hindu Dharma Shastra which continued even after the evolution of modern institutions of legal jurisprudence.

Added to the observance of such accumulation in the hands of Caste-Hindus, said accumulation was vested with Caste-Hindu men, while women were denied any share in the inheritance of ancestral property. In fact in the case of woman their relegation to household tasks[5] has defined the social status in a society immersed in caste-patriarchal notions of labour. However said notion was more applicable for woman of higher castes, while woman from lower social groups were ordained to be slaves.

Land accumulation by Caste-Hindus: a case for reforms

Religion which denied equality in terms of economic as well social equality ensured that a perpetual continuum of power is maintained through the control of woman's sexuality in a well-knitted inter-personal relations bounded by the rules of endogamy, which, as argued in previous section, determine the access to wealth accruing in the hands of Caste-Hindus.

Several studies also corroborate the fact of accumulation of a major portion of land in the hands of Caste-Hindus. Kumar Dharma (1962) asserts that around 1800, in the fertile regions of Malabar, Kanara and better irrigated fields of Tamil districts, significant proportion of lands were owned by Brahmins.

Census 1901 while elucidating the occupational engagement records that in Bengal Province, said

> Amongst Zamindars, the Brahmans, who number about 88,000, are most numerous; then follow the Kayasths with 73,000, the Babhans with 36,000 and the Rajputs with 25,000. Brahman zamindars are found all over the Province. They are especially numerous in the Orissa Presidency, Patna and Dacca Divisions, but they are outnumbered in the Presidency and Dacca Divisions by the Kayasths and in Patna by the Babhans and Rajputs, especially by the former, who are more than twice as numerous.[6]

Nancharaiah (1988) through the analysis of land records in a village of Kanchakoduru over the years of 1930, 1948, 1965, and 1982, reveals that for the year of 1930 the Brahmins controlled 77% of total land as they happened to be Inamdars, non-Brahmins about 21% and Scheduled Castes only about 2% of total land.

During the course of struggle for independence, several movements were initaited across the country against concentration of land in fewer hands under Zamindari system, and with a slogan of 'Land to the Tiller'. In the region of West Bengal, the alliance between Namasudras and Muslims against the Bhadralok Brahmins was launched on a programme for abolition of Zamindari System.[7] Several intermediary social groups who were predominantly non-Brahmin have had come together to resist forceful eviction from land by Zamindars. Since with the introduction of granting Occupancy Rights to the tenants who occupy the land for 12 years under the Bengal Rent Act 1859, the landlords kept on changing in order to ensure that occupancy rights were not granted to tenants who were cultivators of the land. In this moment, the intermediaries and agricultural labourers together fought against the landlord by forming ghettos and groups and avoiding payment of rents.[8] A letter communicated between *Mr. Surendra Prasad Lahiri Cltowdlturi, Zemindar to the President, Krisak Conference of Kishoreganj*[9] evidently captures the simmering tensions between the landed and tenants. Indian Freedom movement also incorporated a language against Zamindari system, in order to galvanize the support of a larger section of masses. However, landlords were keen on stressing Gandhian view of negotiations, as against a call for revolution against the system of Zamindari.[10] The same class of Zamindars who wanted a peaceful settlement on Zamindari system, were advocating for continuation of the practice of untouchability in open. Mr. Dharani Mohan Roy, a Zamindar and Senior Member of Chandra Pratapa Sanatana Hindu community, openly advocated for the retaining of untouchability, and firmly states that any opposition to said practice is against Smritis and Shastras.[11]

Against the backdrop of several movements across the country Zamindari Abolition legislations were introduced. Indian National Congress realizing the importance of the demand of larger masses, incorporated Land to Tiller as one of its objective in its election manifesto and under the unanimous suggestion of the revenue ministers conference in December 1947, formed a committee under the chairmanship of J. C. Kumarappa, to examine and make recommendations about agrarian reforms arising out of Zamindari abolition.[12]

The committee recommended for agrarian reforms by way of abolition of intermediaries and proposed for Land to the Tiller. It also recommended prohibiting subletting of land except in the case of widows, minors and other disable persons. The committee while observing a large scale dependency of labour on agriculture phased out a need for driving out agricultural labour from agricultural to non-agricultural occupations. However with the prevalence of strong customized structure of caste, the institutions having got controlled by Caste-Hindus prevented the scope of reforms. The next section deals with the numbers related to occupational structure and access to land amongst various social groups, with an analysis on how caste leaves no space for reforms towards attainment of equality in economic sense.

Institutionalized caste: interrogating failed reform process through institutions

Census 1951 records that amongst Scheduled Castes, 67.1% of working population was dependant on agriculture, in which 10.4% of them were cultivators of land, wholly or mainly owned, 17.6% of them were cultivators of land wholly or mainly unowned, and 33.0% of them were cultivating labourers, while rest 6.1% were non-cultivating owners of land. An implementation of Land Reforms should result in the granting of ownership of land to unowned land cultivated by Scheduled Castes and distribution of lands to landless agricultural labourers and should subsequently result in a change in the occupational dependency in agriculture. Land should belong to the tiller gets more applicable in the case of agricultural labourers and more particularly in the case of Scheduled Castes given the scale of operations in which they are involved beginning with tilling of land to harvest, and the supervision of the farms by permanently attached labourers.

Land reforms and the positioning of scheduled castes

In the light of said context about the precarious situation of untouchables in the socio-economic sphere, several committees, such as Committee on Untouchability 1969 recommended for reserving 50% of the total surplus land to be reserved for Scheduled Caste landless agricultural labourers because they constitute 50% of the total landless population. Added to which it was also recommended that the state governments should reclaim the inferior lands and allot them (Murdia, 1975). In light of the recommendations on several committees on land to the tiller approach, the following paragraph explains on how systematically caste-structures avoided for transfer of land.

NSSO Report 1954–55, while placing its observations on availability of surplus land with a ceiling fixed at 20 acres had observed "If the ceiling limit is fixed at 20 acres, and all households holding more than 20 acres are required to hand over the area held by them in excess of 20 acres, then the amount of land which becomes available for distribution in this way would be about 63 million acres." The discussion on land reforms which was initiated in 1948 could only reach it's finality by 1972, where the ceiling limit was proposed at 10–18 acres for irrigated land with two crops, 27 acres for irrigated land with one crop and 54 acres for dry land.

However in terms of implementation the process of distribution was a failure. The working group on Development and Welfare of Scheduled Castes during the eighth five-year plan (1990–95) in their report (August 1990) observed that "agricultural ceiling laws have been a mere failure. As against the estimated availability of surplus land of about 30 million hectares, only a little over 7 million acres had been declared surplus so far. Against this, 4.5 million acres of land was distributed to about 4 million beneficiaries" (Pg. No 149, Fourth Annual Report, National Commission for SC/ST, 1996–97).

Caste obstructs socio-economic reform

One of the reasons for the failure of the reform process was the institutionalization of caste system in occupational structure, where at the revenue departments which were supposed to collect and furnish the information on land records were dominated by Caste-Hindus, particularly Brahmins. On one hand, the legal systems of Land Tribunals were established; on the other hand, the revenue departments were depending upon the information passed on by the local bodies of Patwaris, Kulkarnis and Karanams. Mearns (1999) cited in Deshpande (2003) writes "Various exemptions and loopholes left by individual states allowed landlords to retain control over land holdings, most infamously through benami (nameless entity) transactions, whereby village record keepers (patwaris) could be bribed to register holdings in the names of deceased or fictitious persons". The incidence of manipulation by the local level officers was of such height that the lands were registered as Benamis in the names of servants, unborn children, cows, horses and dogs. It even took the form of registering the lands on the names of Hindu deities (Sinha, 1978).

NSSO 37th Round report –1982 on ownership holdings, had brought down the figures on the ownership of land by Scheduled Castes, where it observed that Scheduled Castes who constitute 19.71% of total households (rural) owned 7.89% of total land (rural), as against non SC/ST households with a proportion of 70.55% households (rural) owning 82.01% of land (rural). The figures by 1982 stand self-explanatory on the skewed distribution of land in comparison with the proportion of households. Scheduled Castes who are positioned at the bottom of caste hierarchy were the ones who depended heavily on agriculture by performing all tasks within agriculture. However caste which leaves no scope for reform has even prevented for transfer of land despite the presence of several legislations.

Conclusion

Caste obstructs economic progress by not allowing efficient allocation of resources. Land to the tiller as an objective was aimed at attaining a higher productivity in agriculture, but caste defeated the objective through the access of Caste-Hindus to various state institutions. Such non-implementation of a reform in place has become the source of perpetuation of an inequality based on a foundation of caste. It has a large bearing on economic outcomes, as non-access to land eventually entails higher dependence as agricultural labour particularly in rural economy. Ambedkar conceived emancipation of women is imperative for equal and just society and favoured positive discrimination for their upliftment. His concept of ideal society was based on social justice that saw unity and equality of all human beings, between man and man and between man and woman. Therefore, he emphasized on ideal society based on the principle of justice that values liberty, equality and fraternity. He, however, calls for the change in the state of mind that brings forth the social equality and provides dignity to women. This is possible when social relations that form our conscience changes us as humans and emancipates us through self-realization.

Notes

* B. R. Ambedkar said this quote in a paper written by him on "Castes in India: Their Mechanism, Genesis and Development" which got published in 1917 by Indian Antiquary.

1 *Dr. Babasaheb Ambedkar: Writings and Speeches*, Vol. 14 (Part-2, p. 1326).

2 Manu Dharma Shastra served as the Legal Document before the Constitution of India was adopted. Manu Dharma Shastra was observed to be the constitution of India on a custom mode Beteile in (Thorat and Kumar, 2008), (M.V. Nadkarni, 2007, p. 1847).

3 Chapter 8, Verse 417: *A Brahmana may confidently seize the goods of (his) Sudra (slave); for, as that (slave) can have no property, his master may take his possessions.*

Chapter 10, Verse: 129 "*No collection of wealth must be made by a Sudra, even though he be able (to do it); for a Sudra who has acquired wealth, gives pain to Brahmanas.* The Laws of Manu (1886) Ch. X, verse 129,"

4 "Manusmriti, Chapter X: 125 reflects on how abandoned food is: The remnants of their food must be given to him, as well as their old clothes, the

refuse of their grain and their old household furniture" The implementation of this rule in villages is testified by various studies by anthropologists, Wiser (1936) records in his book "The Hindu Jajmani System" on how the aforementioned clause is observed in practice, and noted *"A Sweeper (bhangi) if he attends a marriage for the duties of sweeping he is made to collect the food which is leftover on the leaf plates"*

"The Poorer of the Kam-Karnewalas when not otherwise occupied spend a share of their time during September and October in the low marshland near the village harvesting wild rice. No figures for the actual amount harvested are available but we found that the sweepers for instance, were using this wild rice almost exclusively during September and October. In their usual Sunday grain offerings to the local church they contributed mostly wild rice".

5 Census 1931 states "It is certainly regarded as much more socially respectable for a wife to be engaged at home on household duties than to labour in the fields, and there is a generally increasing tendency, as castes aspire to a higher social standing, to keep their wife at home" (J.H. Hutton, 1933).

6 (H.H. Risley, 1903, p. 218).

7 (Omvedt, 1979).

8 (Anand V. Swamy, 2010, p. 9).

9 *"The atmosphere was surcharged with keen anti-landlord feelings, which manifested themselves in the rankest form in the Fiery speeches delivered by some fire-brands. The Pandal was resounded from time to time with the loud deafening shout of the slogan "down with the Zamindars down with the capitalists'.' The atmosphere was too hot for representatives of zamindars not to speak of the zamindars themselves, who would have cut a very sorry figure if they had appeared personally."* Zamindars Vs Kishan Agitators, 1939 Published by Land Holders Journal.

10 Congress Leaders on Zemindari Institution, Land Holders Journal, 1939.

11 Touchability and Untouchability, Dharani Mohan Roy, Land Holders Journal, 1932.

12 Report of the Congress Agrarian Reforms Committee, 1949.

References

Ajit, D., Donker, H., and Saxena, R. (2012). Corporate Boards in India: Blocked by Caste? *Economic and Political Weekly*, 39–43.

All India Congress Committee. (1949). *Report of the Congress Agrarian Reforms Committee*. Madras: Madras Publishing House.

Ambedkar, B. R. (1917, May). *Castes in India: Their Genesis, Mechanism and Development* (Vol. XLI). New York: Indian Antiquary.

Ambedkar, B. R. (1937). *Annhilation of Caste*. http://ccnmtl.columbia.edu/projects/mmt/ambedkar/web/.

Ambedkar, B. R. (1948). *The Untouchables Who Were They and Why They Became Untouchables*? (Vol. 7). Maharashtra, India: Maharashtra Government.

Ambedkar, B. R. (1951). *Hindu Code Bill*. Ambedkar.org.

Bai Kashi vs Jamnadas Mansukh Raichand Verdict. (1912, March 5). Bombay High Court.

Buhler, G. (1886). *The Laws of Manu*. Oxford: Clarendon Press.

Census of India – 1991, Office of the Registrar General & Census Commissioner, India, Government of India.

Census of India – 2011, Office of the Registrar General & Census Commissioner, India, Government of India.

Chowdary, S. L. (1939). Zemindar vs Kishan Agitators. *Land Holder's Journal* (Vol. VII, Issue 7). Calcutta: Macson Press, pp. 482–484.

Congress Leaders on Zamindari Institution. (1939). *Land Holders Journal* (Vol. VII, Issue 7). Calcutta: Macson Press, pp. 505–507.

Das, K., Das, K. C., Roy, T. K., and Tripathy, P. K. (2011). *Dynamics of Inter-Religious and Inter-Caste Marriages in India*. Washington, DC: Population Association of America.

Deshpande, R. S. (2003). Current Land Policy Issues in India. *Land Reform, Land Settlement and Cooperative*, 155–174.

Employment and Unemployment Among Social Groups in India (July 2011–June 2012), National Sample Survey 68th Round. Ministry of Statistics and Implementation, Government of India.

Fourth Annual Report, National Commission for Scheduled Castes and Scheduled Tribes (1996–97 & 1997–98), Government of India.

Goody, J. and Goody, J. R. (1976). *Production and Reproduction: A Comparative Study of the Domestic Domain* (No. 17). Cambridge: Cambridge University Press.

Gopalaswami, R. A. (1951). *Census of India, 1951 Special Groups*. New Delhi: Managaer of Publications.

Gould, H. (1986). The Hindu Jajmani System: A Case of Economic Particularism in Approaches to Culture and Society. Selected Articles, 1945–1985. *Journal of Anthropological Research*, 42(3), 269–278.

Gour, H. S. (1919). *The Hindu Code*. Calcutta: Butterworth & Co (India), Ltd.

Household Ownership and Operational Holdings in India (January–December 2013), National Sample Survey 70th Round. Ministry of Statistics and Implementation, Government of India.

Household Ownership Holdings in India (January–December 2003), National Sample Survey 59th Round. Ministry of Statistics and Implementation, Government of India.

Hutton, J. H. (1933). *Census of India, 1931* (Vol. 1, Part 1). New Delhi: Managar of Publications.

Kumar, D. (1962). Caste and Landlessness in South India. *Comparative Studies in Society and History*, 4(3), 337–363.

Kumar, D. (1985). Private Property in Asia? The Case of Medieval South India. *Comparative Studies in Society and History*, 27(2), 340–366.

Mearns, R. (1999). *Access to Land in Rural India*. The World Bank.

Murdia, R. (1975). Land Allotment and Land Alienation: Policies and Programmes for Scheduled Castes and Tribes. *Economic and Political Weekly*, 1204–1214.

Nadkarni, M. V. (2007). Does Hinduism Lack Social Concern? *Economic and Political Weekly*, 1844–1849.

Nancharaiah, G. (1988). *Land and Caste*. Himalaya Publishing House.

Patankar, B. and Omvedt, G. (1979). The Dalit Liberation Movement in Colonial Period. *Economic and Political Weekly*, 409–424.

Report on Land Holdings (July 1954–April 1955), National Sample Survey 8th Round. Manager of Publications, The Cabinet Secretariat, New Delhi.

Risley, H. H. (1903). *Census of India, 1901* (Vol. 1, Part 1). Calcutta: Office of the Superintendent of Government Printing.

Rodrigues, V. (2017). Ambedkar as a Political Philosopher. *Economic & Political Weekly*, 52(15), 101.

Roy, D. M. (1932). Touchability and Untouchability. *Land Holders Journal* (Vol. I, Issue VI). Calcutta: Macson Press, pp. 380–386.

Sinha, A. (1978). Legal Loopholes: To Landlords' Rescue. *Economic and Political Weekly*, 1758–1760.

Some aspects of Household Ownership Holding (January to December 1982), National Sample Survey 37th Round. Department of Statistics, Government of India, New Delhi.

Swamy, A. (2010). *Land and Law in Colonial India* (No. 2011-03). Department of Economics, Williams College.

Swayampakula Subbaramayya and vs Swayampakula Venkatasubbamma (5 February 1941), Madras High Court.

Thorat, S. and Kumar, N. (2008). *In Search of Inclusive Policy: Addressing Graded Inequality*. Rawat Publications.

Wiser, W. (1936). *The Hindu Jajmani System*. New Delhi: Munshiram Manohar Lal Publishers Pvt. Ltd.

11 Inter-group inequality in Punjab

Does caste matter?

Nitin Tagade, Ajaya K. Naik and Chandrani Dutta

Introduction

Dr. B. R. Ambedkar, more than a century back in 1916, wrote a pioneer paper on castes in India to understand its genesis, mechanism and development. In this, he remarks that the caste is a superimposition of the endogamy on the exogamy (Ambedkar, 1916). The caste in India defined in this way, Ambedkar points out that various tools were utilised to maintain the caste system such as the Sati practice, widowhood and child marriage. The outcome of this age old primitive system has yielded a system of graded inequality where one caste is placed above other; and the rights and privileges have been assigned at higher proportion to those who are on the higher ladder and the duties are assigned at higher level to those who are on the lower ladder (Ambedkar, 1936). Thus, the inequality is an integral part of the caste system where the assets in terms of rights and privileges and liabilities in terms of duties are disproportionately assigned across different groups. Ambedkar further argues that the occupational segregation is not the product of the division of labour, but it is of the division of labourers (Ambedkar, 1936). The system has yielded an inefficient system where the workers are not bound by the individual choices but they are bound towards the codes and conducts of their own castes. What are those codes and conducts which have made the caste system so integral to this land. These codes and conducts, as Ambedkar illustrates, controls economic rights of each caste group and invariably impacting the economy. This could be understood from fundamental features of the caste system (Ambedkar, 1936; Thorat, 2005). These features are: first, fixation of economic rights meaning that the occupation is fixed by birth to the members of a particular caste; and the continuation thereof by heredity; second, unequal distribution of economic rights related to occupation, property rights, employment, wages, education etc., among the caste groups; third, occupation are not only fixed and unequal in their distribution, but some occupations are treated superior and the others as inferior, thus maintaining a hierarchy of occupations based on the social stigma of the high and the low; fifth, provides for a comprehensive system of social and economic penalties to enforce the caste-based economic order;

and sixth, provides a philosophical rational and justification in the Hindu religion, to the caste system. Thus, the outcome of combined effect of the elements of the caste system is the inequality in wealth ownership and income productivity (see, Tagade et al., 2018; Thorat and Tagade, 2018; Naik and Tagade, 2018); and occupational segregation and unequal wages (Thorat and Madheswaran, 2018). The benefit of the improved economic development is ensued largely to those who are privileged in the caste system rather than by those who are in lower rung of the society.

In this background, this paper is an attempt to understand whether caste-based discrimination would decline to an insignificant level due to the high rate of economic growth. An attempt has also been made to understand whether caste-based discrimination is weakening from the point of view of Sikhism, a religion which was initially propagated to remove the caste-based divisions in the Hindu society. The analysis is carried out using linear regression and Oaxaca-Blinder decomposition method. The case of Punjab has been analysed as it is one of the high-income states in India, while it is also one of the states exhibiting the highest degree of disparity between social groups (Chakraborty, 2001). The analysis in this paper is carried out based on 68th National Sample Survey Organisation (NSSO) on Consumption Expenditure conducted during 2011–12. The paper would also analyse whether the philosophical tenets of Sikhism have been able to reduce the influence of caste in Punjab. This paper is divided into seven sections. Following the introduction in the first section, the second section provides a brief review on the inter-linkages between caste and economic development in the context of Punjab following the inter-group disparities in MPCE in the state are highlighted in the third section. The factors influencing inter-group differences in consumption expenditure are examined in the fourth section followed by the decomposition of MPCE in fifth section. The inter-group inequalities and their decomposition are discussed in the sixth section while the conclusion is presented in the last section.

The case of Punjab

Punjab is one of the most agriculturally as well as industrially developed states in India. According to Shergill and Singh (1995), rural poverty declined substantially in the early 1990s in Punjab largely due to the advent of the Green Revolution, while in the case of India as a whole, reduction in poverty became noticeable only after 2004 (Thorat and Dubey, 2012; Shukla and Mishra, 2014). In the rural agricultural belt, Jats control majority of the agricultural land, an outcome of the 1901 Punjab Land Alienation Act, which reserved landownership rights only to the agriculturalist castes of the state. Some of the communities like Mazhabis, Balmikis, Ravidasias and Chamars have historically denied of land ownership (Puri, 2003). In the aftermath of Green Revolution, mechanisation in agriculture led to many changes in traditional labour relations. It increased the demand for agricultural labourers. Wages also increased, thus augmenting the incomes of agricultural labourers in the state. Consequently, the Scheduled Castes (SCs), who were otherwise practising their caste-based occupations, joined in large numbers to meet the increasing demand of agricultural labourers. Studies undertaken by Jodhka (2000, 2002) corroborated Beteille's argument that occupations in the age of mechanisation and commercialisation have become mostly 'caste-free'. However, occupational mobility, which took place in Punjab, reinstated the existing labour relations between the dominant landowner Jats and the lower-caste agricultural labourers. Even with the agrarian change taking place in Punjab, Jodhka (2002) argued that Dalits in the state remained un-free and 'attached' with the landowner Jats on a long-term basis. Jats remained at the privileged position of being the landowners, while the Dalits, despite having numerical strength in the rural areas, only had control of three per cent of agricultural land (Singh, 2012). Therefore, subjugation of the SCs by the dominant landowner classes continued despite economic development.

Religious composition of Punjab society reveals Sikhs as the dominant religious group at the aggregate level. However, Sikhs are a majority in the rural areas and Hindus dominate in the urban areas. As it is generally perceived that discriminatory practices based on caste, are considered a rural phenomenon, being agrarian and traditional, compared to an urban set up, it is in this sphere that a contradiction arises in the particular state. In rural areas, Sikhism became popular among both the landowning dominant communities like the Jats and among many SCs. Therefore, rural Punjab included both high-caste Sikhs who owned agricultural lands, and the low-caste Sikhs and Dalits. A large proportion of SCs in the state comprise the Mazhabis, Chamars and the Ad Dharmis, of which the latter two have become more socially advanced as compared to the Mazhabis (Jodhka, 2000). The Sikh religion is distinct from the Hindu religion in terms of its philosophical tenets and, discrimination based on the caste of an individual, does not have any religious sanction in Sikhism (Jodhka, 2002). However, such practices continued in the villages of Punjab (Jodhka, 2006). Moreover, relations between the landowning class and the labourers did not change even with agricultural development, as discussed earlier. Therefore, small landowners in Punjab shifted from their erstwhile occupations like agriculture to other activities, and agricultural labourers, who were mostly Dalits, in rural Punjab diversified into non-farm activities like vegetable vending, rickshaw pulling, brick moulding and other forms of causal labour, which was also a consequence of the social boycott of the Dalits by the landowning Jats (Singh, 2012).

Apart from Jodhka's (2002) finding of the persistence of the practice of untouchability from a field survey of 51 villages in the state, there is little evidence to validate the argument that discrimination would weaken or end in the event of high economic growth. Therefore, this paper attempts to determine whether discrimination, which is widely prevalent in Hinduism, is less likely to occur in other religions, especially Sikhism, which does not sanction such practices.

Inter-group disparities in MPCE

The economic and non-economic features of the household by socio-religious groups in Punjab in 2012 are presented in Table 11.1. The total number of estimated households in Punjab is 56.8 lakh, among which 16.4 per cent are Hindu SCs (HSCs), 21.6 per cent are Sikh SCs (SSCs), 11.9 per cent are Other Backward Castes (OBCs), 19.8 per cent Hindu High Castes (HHCs), and 25.8 per cent Sikh High Castes (SHCs), while the rest fall in the 'Others' category. The rural areas of the state are dominated by SHCs and SSCs. Of SHC and SSC households, 75 per cent and 86 per cent live in rural areas, respectively. The size of households by socio-religious groups does not vary much with the average household in the state having 4.5 members. However, a systematic pattern can be discerned in terms of the average Monthly Per Capita Consumption Expenditure (MPCE), which is lowest among the Sikh and Hindu SCs, and highest among the Sikh and Hindu HC households. The economic asset ownership in terms of the share of households owning any land in the state is highest among SHCs (96.7 per cent), followed by

Table 11.1 MPCE and Economic and Non-economic Asset Distribution by Socio-religious Groups in Punjab

Background Characteristics	*HSCs*	*SSCs*	*OBCs*	*HHCs*	*SHCs*	*Others*	*Total*
No. of households (HHs) (in '0000)	934	1228	674	1123	1465	259	5683
Share of HHs (%)	16.4	21.6	11.9	19.8	25.8	4.6	100
Rural share of HHs (%)	55.3	85.8	54.8	20.9	75.0	55.2	60.1
Average HH size (in number)	4.23	4.76	4.76	4.02	4.72	4.55	4.51
Average MPCE (in Rs.)	1796	1656	2161	2829	3078	2194	2356
Share of HH's own land (in %)	81.4	93.9	89.6	71.8	96.7	81.1	87.1
Share of any literate in the HH (in %)	80.0	70.7	89.9	90.3	92.8	84.5	84.7
Share of highest education level of the HH at higher education level (in %)	19.7	19.1	30.0	56.6	45.5	29.3	35.0

Source: NSSO CE 68th round

SSCs (93.9 per cent), OBCs (89.6 per cent), HSCs (81.4 per cent) and HSCs (71.8 per cent). The trend observed with respect to economic assets is also replicated for the non-economic assets. Hence the share of any literate person in the households is substantially highest among the SHCs, followed by the HHCs, OBCs, HSCs, and SHCs. An analysis of the share of households with higher education levels (that is, 'higher secondary and above' level of education) clearly points to the prevalence of a disparity among socio-religious groups. At the higher education level, HHCs outnumber SHCs with the figures for both being 56.6 per cent and 45.5 per cent, respectively, while both these groups together outnumber SCs (comprising both Hindus and Sikhsat more than 19.1 per cent of the total, and OBCs (at 30.0 per cent).

The state of Punjab is somewhat different from others in its caste composition due to the dominance of Sikh religion unlike in other States in India where Hindus constitute the majority. In Punjab, 56 per cent of the population follows the Sikh religion, with the proportion being substantially high at 79 per cent in the rural areas of the state. The spread of Sikhism in the state is undeviating across social groups. Figure 11.1 shows the distribution of the population across social groups in 2012, wherein SCs, high castes and OBCs following the Sikh religion constitute about 23 per cent, 27 per cent and 7 per cent of the population, respectively. On the other hand, about 40 per cent of the population in the state is Hindu out of which SCs comprise 15.4 per cent and high castes 17.6 per cent of the total.

Figure 11.2 delineates a comparison of the MPCE across socio-religious groups in Punjab, which is disaggregated by rural and urban areas. The MPCE is highest among the SHCs at Rs. 3078, followed by Rs. 2829 among the HHCs, Rs. 2161 among the OBCs, Rs. 1656 among the SSCs and Rs. 1796 among the HSCs. The comparison between the HSCs and HHCs show that the MPCE of HHCs is 1.6 times higher than that of the HSCs. Similarly, the MPCE of SHCs is 1.9 times higher than that of the SSCs. Thus, the disparity between SHCs and SSCs is greater than the disparity between the HSCs and HHCs. A similar pattern is observed in the rural and urban areas with a higher disparity between the SHCs and SSCs in rural areas and urban areas, on one hand, and Hindus, on the other hand.

Factors influencing inter-group differences in MPCE

The salient features of sample households have been illustrated in terms of their demographic, social and economic characteristics. In this section, these characteristics have been employed to estimate the relative strength of different factors affecting the MPCE of the households of various socio-religious groups in Punjab. We exclude OBC households from the analysis because of the low sample size and confine the analysis SC and HC households belonging to the Hindu and Sikh religions at one place as well as separately in order to identify the differences between them on the basis of religion, which has an impact on social relations. It was hypothesised that

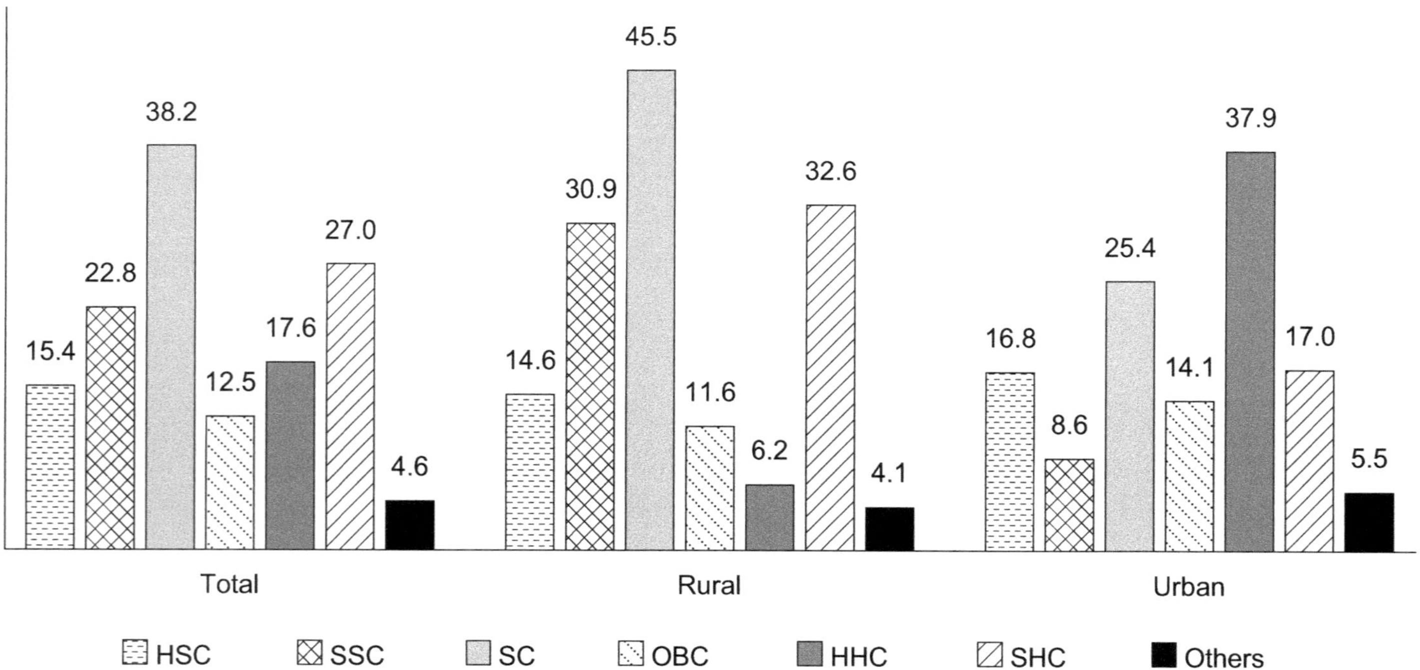

Figure 11.1 Share of Population by Socio-religious Groups in Punjab – 2012

Source: NSSO CE 68th round

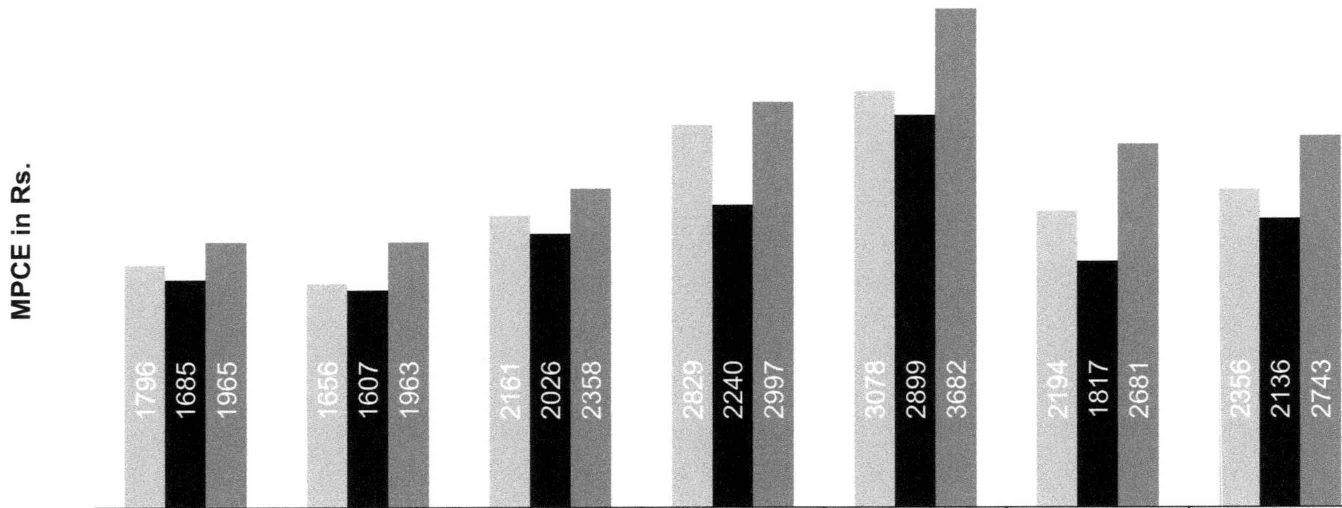

	HSC	SSC	OBC	HHC	SHC	Others	Total
Total	1796	1656	2161	2829	3078	2194	2356
Rural	1685	1607	2026	2240	2899	1817	2136
Urban	1965	1963	2358	2997	3682	2681	2743

Figure 11.2 Comparison of MPCE across Socio-religious Groups in Punjab (In Rs.) – 2012

Source: NSSO CE 68th round

the household's consumption expenditure (CE) would *inter alia* depend on the following factors:

1 The caste and religious background of the household: SCs and High Caste (HCs) in Model 1. It is to be noted that these social groups are bifurcated on the basis of the Hindu and Sikh religions for estimating Model 2 and Model 3.
2 Adult (aged 21 years and above) literate in the household: Yes=1; Otherwise 0
3 The highest education level of adults (aged 21 years and above) in the household.

   a Low, if up to middle school (reference category);
   b Medium, if higher than middle school but less than higher secondary; and
   c High, if higher secondary and above.

4 Place of residence: Urban=1; Otherwise 0.
5 Ownership of Land: Yes=1; Otherwise 0.
6 Total Land Possessed (in Hectares).
7 Total number of the members in the household.
8 Occupational Type of the Household

   a Self-employed (SE) – Includes SE in agriculture and non-agriculture in the rural areas and SE in non-agriculture in the urban areas;
   b Regular Wage/Salary earning – Includes households located in both rural and urban areas (Regular);
   c Casual labour – Includes both agriculture and non-agriculture; and
   d Others.

The coefficient on each of the variables listed above except the first was allowed to vary according to the caste of the households (as listed in variable 1). Consequently, if *Xi* represents the explanatory variables for the households *i*, *(i = 1 . . . N)*, then the equation is as follows:

$$CE_i = \alpha_1 \times HC_i + \alpha_2 \times SC_i + \beta_1 \times X_i + \beta_2 \times (X_i \times SC_i) + \varepsilon_i$$

where there are n households, indexed *i* = 1, 2, 3 . . . n such that:

CE is the monthly consumption expenditure of household *i*
HC*i* = 1, if the household *i* is a high-caste household, 0 otherwise
SC*i* = 1, if the household *i* is an SC household, 0 otherwise
X*i* is the value of the explanatory variable for household *i*
α and β are coefficients.

The interpretation of the coefficients in the above equation above is as follows:

1 The coefficients α_1 *and* α_2 are the intercept terms associated with HC and SC households, respectively. The presence of these terms ensures that the equation passes through the mean. In other words, if all the explanatory variables took as values their sample means, the predicted value of income would be the mean consumption.
2 The coefficient β_1 is the effect associated with the explanatory variable *for all households.*
3 The coefficient β_2 is the *additional* effect associated with the explanatory variable for *SC households only.*

> If β_2 is significantly different from zero, then this means that the variable has a (statistically significant) different effect on SC households as compared to its effect on HCH households. If β_2 is not significantly different from zero, then it means that there is no (statistically significant) difference in the variable's effect between SC and HC households.

Table 11.2 includes the following three models: for both Hindu and Sikh households in Punjab (1); separately for Hindu households (2) and; separately for Sikh households (3). The results in Model (1) using the households of both religions in Punjab reveals that the MPCE for HC living in urban area, engaged in casual labour, without land and with low educational levels would be Rs. 2550. Acquiring land assets would add Rs. 523 to the HC household. The acquisition of educational assets in terms of a literate person in the household would add Rs. 115 to this; and acquiring an educational asset in the form of an adult in the household educated to the level of matriculation or higher (the highest level of education) would add Rs. 1233. The change in the occupation also adds substantially to the income of HC households. Acquiring a regular salaried household status would add Rs. 814 to the MPCE of HC household.

The results shown in Table 11.2 ascertain the changes in consumption expenditure among HC and SC households in accordance with the changes in their attributes (see Table 11.3). In fact, they change substantially with varying degrees HC households with respect to the SC households in several aspects. These were examined by considering the educational level, place of residence and occupational type of the household.

1 The educational asset of the households impacts the MPCE of SC households more than it does MPCE of HC households in Punjab. As compared to the HC households, the return on the highest level of education (that is, education at the higher secondary level and above) is substantially low for SCs. For HCs, it adds up to Rs. 1233, whereas for the SCs, it adds up to Rs. 872.
2 As compared to HC households, the return on owning land is lower for SC households; for HC and SC households, owning land added Rs. 524 and Rs. 260, respectively, to the MPCE.

Table 11.2 Regression estimates for the MPCE generating equation

VARIABLES	*Model 1*	*Model 2*	*Model 3*
	Total	*Hindu*	*Sikh*
HC	2550*** (268.5)	3008*** (442.7)	2815*** (604.4)
SC	2526*** (225.0)	2659*** (327.9)	2353*** (403.0)
Literate in HH	115 (147.2)	69 (247.2)	55 (190.2)
HH size	-293*** (19.49)	-331*** (31.08)	-269*** (26.05)
Land possessed (in hectares)	147*** (18.89)	198*** (71.05)	129*** (19.40)
Land owned	524*** (172.0)	210 (222.1)	358 (517.9)
SC land owned	-264 (266.6)	39 (345.7)	29 (641.7)
Self-employed	726*** (218.1)	87 (412.9)	1249*** (292.0)
Regular salaried	814*** (229.3)	66 (415.3)	1598*** (318.1)
Others	1559*** (278.3)	1801*** (508.4)	1401*** (359.1)
SC Self-employed	-416 (268.7)	231 (488.5)	-918*** (351.4)
SC Regular salaried	-395 (279.5)	380 (490.3)	-1164*** (376.9)
SC Others	-1034*** (386.1)	-1145* (640.4)	-1142** (545.5)
Rural	-306*** (114.5)	-563** (230.5)	-400*** (153.5)
SC Rural	272 (179.9)	505 (314.1)	359 (256.1)
Medium education	380** (167.6)	740** (289.6)	41 (214.9)
Higher education	1233*** (161.8)	1930*** (278.2)	650*** (207.3)
SC Medium education	-224 (214.7)	-497 (352.9)	94 (283.2)
SC Higher education	-361 (227.5)	-939** (375.7)	176 (294.7)
Observations	2639	1201	1359
R-squared	0.696	0.661	0.738

Note: Standard errors in parentheses; and ***p < 0.01, **p < 0.05, *p < 0.1.

Source: NSSO CE 68th round

Table 11.3 Expected MPCE of Household (in Rs.)

Source	*Total*		*Hindu*		*Sikh*	
	HC	*SC*	*HC*	*SC*	*HC*	*SC*
Intercept	2550	2526	3008	2659	2815	2353
Literate in HH	115	115	69	69	55	55
HH size	-293	-293	-331	-331	-269	-269
Land possessed (in hectares)	147	147	198	198	129	129
Land owned	524	260	210	248	358	387
Self-employed	726	310	87	318	1249	331
Regular salaried	814	419	66	446	1598	434
Others	1559	525	1801	656	1401	259
Rural	-306	-34	-563	-58	-400	-41
Medium education	380	156	740	243	41	135
Higher education	1233	872	1930	991	650	825

Source: NSSO CE 68th round

3 Living in urban areas vis-à-vis living in rural areas reduces Rs. 306 and Rs. 34 to the MPCE for of HCs and SCs, respectively.
4 The returns on different attributes between HC and SC households are of mix in nature. The HC household living urban area, engaged in casual labour, with low educational level and with no land would have higher MPCE of Rs. 3008 among Hindu compared to Rs. 2815 among Sikh. The return on many of the attributes is higher for HC as compared to SC households, but in the case of a few attributes the rate of returns are higher for SC households. The return on self-employed and regular salaried is high for the SCs as compared to HC households belonging to Hindu; while in the case of Sikh the returns of the medium and higher education is high for SCs as compared to HC households.

Decomposition of the differences in MPCE between HCs and SCs

The relative strength of different economic and non-economic assets and place of residence show a differential impact on the consumption patterns of different socio-religious groups in the previous section. We have conclusively arrived at the significant differences in the MPCE due to the differential rate of returns on assets such as land ownership, education and place of residence for HCs, SCs and OBCs. The other reason could be the differences in their asset endowments. Therefore, it is necessary to distinguish between the rate of return on assets and ownership of assets. Since both these differ across socio-religious groups, we decompose the difference in MPCE between HCs and SCs by using the coefficient of both the groups. We consider the differences on the following bases; firstly, if the SC assets receive an HC coefficient; and secondly, if the HC assets receive an SC coefficient. The previous models also clearly brought out the differential rate of returns on economic and non-economic assets between Hindu and Sikh households. Therefore, the decomposition has also been made to compare the differences between HCs and SCs belonging to Hindu and Sikh households separately.

Table 11.4 shows the results from the decomposition of the differences in MPCE between the HC and SC households in totality, comprising both Hindu and Sikh households; whereas Tables 11.5 and 11.6 show these for Hindu and Sikh households, respectively. Each table has two decompositions. The first decomposition relates to evaluation of the difference that would have been achieved if SC assets had received an HC coefficient. The second decomposition relates to evaluation of the difference that would have been achieved if HC assets had received SC rate of returns.

Table 11.4 shows that when SC and HC assets were evaluated by using the HC coefficient (asset returns) vector, of the total difference of Rs. 1415 in MPCE between the HC and SC households (belonging to both Hindu and Sikh religion). Of the total differences, an amount of Rs. 925 (65 per cent) could be explained by asset endowments between these two groups

Table 11.4 Decomposition of the Difference in Mean MPCE between High Caste (HC) and Scheduled Caste (SC)

	Value	*SE*	*Z value*	*p* > |z|
Mean MPCE of HC	3345	66.67	50.18	0.00
Mean MPCE of SC	1931	35.67	54.12	0.00
Difference between HC and SC	1415	75.61	18.71	0.00
Decomposition of difference using HC coefficient vector				
Explained	925 (65.4)	101.27	9.13	0.00
Unexplained	490 (34.6)	116.10	4.22	0.00
Decomposition of difference using SC coefficient vector				
Explained	1251 (88.4)	201.90	6.19	0.00
Unexplained	164 (11.6)	207.23	0.79	0.43

Note: The figures in parenthesis indicate the contribution of explained and unexplained effect (%) in the MPCE differences.

Source: NSSO CE 68th round

Table 11.5 Decomposition of the Difference in Mean MPCE between Hindu High Caste (HHCs) and Hindu Scheduled Caste (HSCs)

	Value	*SE*	*Z value*	*p* > |z|
Mean MPCE of HHC	3254	110.20	29.53	0.00
Mean MPCE of HSC	2047	59.29	34.53	0.00
Difference between HHC and HSC	1207	125.13	9.65	0.00
Decomposition of difference using HHC coefficient vector				
Explained	842 (69.8)	163.39	5.15	0.00
Unexplained	365 (30.2)	186.74	1.96	0.05
Decomposition of difference using HSC coefficient vector				
Explained	1206 (99.9)	318.16	3.79	0.00
Unexplained	1 (0.1)	325.74	0.00	1.00

Note: The figures in parenthesis indicate the contribution of explained and unexplained effect (%) in the MPCE differences.

Source: NSSO CE 68th round

of households. However, when the SC and HC assets were evaluated by using the SC coefficients vector, an amount of Rs. 1250 (88 per cent) of the total differences of Rs. 1415 could be explained by differences in asset endowments between the two groups of households. In other words, the unexplained effect declined when the rate of returns of SCs was considered instead of the HC rate of returns to evaluate the difference in asset endowments.

In Tables 11.5 and 11.6, the differences in MPCE between HC and SC households are relatively higher for those following the Sikh religion

Table 11.6 Decomposition of the Difference in Mean MPCE between Sikh High Caste (SHC) and Sikh Scheduled Caste (SSC)

	Value	*SE*	*Z value*	$p > \|z\|$
Mean MPCE of SHC	3518	86.57	40.64	0.00
Mean MPCE of SSC	1834	43.05	42.61	0.00
Difference between SHC and SSC	1684	96.68	17.41	0.00
Decomposition of difference using SHC coefficient vector				
Explained	1069 (63.5)	169.98	6.29	0.00
Unexplained	615 (36.5)	185.23	3.32	0.00
Decomposition of difference using SSC coefficient vector				
Explained	1470 (87.3)	344.73	4.26	0.00
Unexplained	214 (12.7)	349.73	0.61	0.54

Note: The figures in parenthesis indicate the contribution of explained and unexplained effect (%) in the MPCE differences.

Source: NSSO CE 68th round

as compared to those following the Hindu religion, with the figure being Rs. 1207 and Rs. 1684, respectively. Of the total differences, the amounts of Rs. 841 (70 per cent) and Rs. 1069 (64 per cent) can be explained by the asset endowment between the HCs and SCs belonging to the Hindu and Sikh households, respectively. In other words, the differences between HC and SC households belonging to Sikh religion are higher than the corresponding differences for households belonging to the Hindu religion. In fact, the differences in the asset endowments account for the higher proportion of differences in MPCE amongst the Hindu households as compared to their Sikh counterparts.

Asset endowment and return breakdown

The findings delineated in Tables 11.4, 11.5 and 11.6 indicate that the aggregate results help to quantify the extent of the differences in asset endowments and differences in asset returns between any two groups of households, while also showing that these differences contributed to the aggregate differences in their respective MPCEs. However, the findings in the tables do not specify which assets and their returns have a larger impact on the aggregate outcome.

Table 11.7 breaks down the aggregate results for HCs and SCs belonging to both Hindu and Sikh religions while indicating the difference in the contributions made by the individual variables. Table 11.8 depicts the differences between the HC and SC households separately for the Hindu and Sikh religions. These estimates have been obtained by pooling the observations to estimate the common coefficient vector. Table 11.7 shows that when the observations were pooled to obtain a common coefficient vector, of the

Table 11.7 Individual Contributions to the Decomposition of the Difference in MPCE between High Castes and Scheduled Castes, Pooled Estimates

	Value	*SE*	*Z value*	*p* > |z|
Mean MPCE of HC	3345	66.48	50.32	0.00
Mean MPCE of SC	1931	35.53	54.33	0.00
Difference	1415	75.38	18.77	0.00
Decomposition of Difference Using the HC Coefficient Vector				
Any literate in the HH	21.3	13.09	1.63	0.10
Highest edu. In the HH medium	-8.8	6.39	-1.37	0.17
Highest edu. In the HH high	425.0	39.35	10.80	0.00
Family size	23.0	25.54	0.90	0.37
Land possessed	182.1	34.11	5.34	0.00
HH type – Self employed	2.0	25.66	0.08	0.94
HH type – Casual labour	188.2	25.42	7.41	0.00
HH type – Others	8.7	6.89	1.27	0.21
Sector	42.4	14.05	3.02	0.00
Any land owned	0.7	4.03	0.18	0.86
Total	884.7	52.83	16.75	0.00
Decomposition of Difference Using the SC Coefficient Vector				
Any literate in the HH	122.7	174.46	0.70	0.48
Highest edu. In the HH medium	76.9	54.58	1.41	0.16
Highest edu. In the HH high	100.8	74.66	1.35	0.18
Family size	-874.6	149.52	-5.85	0.00
Land possessed	-24.9	17.53	-1.42	0.16
HH type – Self employed	9.9	66.00	0.15	0.88
HH type – Casual labour	-86.9	36.12	-2.41	0.02
HH type – Others	19.0	31.50	0.60	0.55
Sector	85.2	68.20	1.25	0.21
Any land owned	412.5	202.56	2.04	0.04
Constant	689.5	304.02	2.27	0.02
Total	530.1	58.14	9.12	0.00

Source: NSSO CE 68th round

overall difference of Rs. 1415 in the MPCE between HC and SC households, Rs. 885 (63 per cent) could be explained by the inter-group differences in asset endowments while the remaining Rs. 530 (37 per cent) was the unexplained part due to differences in asset returns.

Half of the aggregate asset endowment effect of Rs. 1415, that is, Rs. 425 (30 per cent) was caused by differences between the HC and SC groups in proportion of their respective households, wherein the highest level of education of an adult was higher secondary or higher. The differences in the proportion of households comprising casual labourers contributed Rs. 188 (13 per cent) while the differences in terms of the land possessed contributed Rs. 182 (13 per cent).

The second panel of Table 11.8 details the contributions of the different assets to the unexplained contribution of Rs. 530 in the overall difference in the MPCE between the HC and SC households. In terms of the contribution

Table 11.8 Individual Contributions to the Decomposition of the Difference in MPCE between HCs and SCs (separately for Hindu and Sikh households), Pooled Estimates

	Hindu				*Sikh*			
	Value	*SE*	*Z value*	*p > |z|*	*Value*	*SE*	*Z value*	*p > |z|*
Mean MPCE of HC	*3254*	*109.49*	*29.72*	*0.00*	*3518.03*	*86.07*	*40.87*	*0.00*
Mean MPCE of SC	*2047*	*58.82*	*34.80*	*0.00*	*1834.37*	*42.72*	*42.94*	*0.00*
Difference	*1207*	*124.29*	*9.71*	*0.00*	*1683.66*	*96.09*	*17.52*	*0.00*
Decomposition of Difference Using the HC Coefficient Vector								
Any literate in the HH	13.7	8.62	1.59	0.11	28.88	17.73	1.63	0.10
Highest education in the HH -medium	−31.3	11.61	−2.69	0.00	10.10	8.66	1.17	0.25
Highest education in the HH -high	468.3	48.93	9.57	0.00	413.51	44.54	9.28	0.00
Family size	12.2	38.26	0.32	0.75	18.13	34.08	0.53	0.60
Land possessed	22.8	8.84	2.58	0.01	338.40	63.02	5.37	0.00
HH type – Self employed	1.4	17.78	0.08	0.94	2.67	34.43	0.08	0.94
HH type – Casual labour	144.1	22.28	6.47	0.00	242.23	33.17	7.30	0.00
HH type – Others	−8.5	9.77	−0.87	0.38	26.27	14.01	1.88	0.06
Sector	64.8	21.20	3.05	0.00	22.21	9.03	2.46	0.01
Any land owned	−4.4	7.66	−0.57	0.57	9.27	4.76	1.95	0.05
Total	683.1	61.90	11.04	0.00	1111.67	76.97	14.44	0.00
Decomposition of difference using SC coefficient vector								
Any literate in the HH	−71.7	195.38	−0.37	0.71	−164.74	326.12	−0.51	0.61
Highest education in the HH -medium	165.9	77.84	2.13	0.03	21.44	76.30	0.28	0.78
Highest education in the HH -high	522.1	140.88	3.71	0.00	−142.80	118.40	−1.21	0.23
Family size	−714.0	239.67	−2.98	0.00	−1147.04	197.47	−5.81	0.00
Land possessed	−17.6	9.84	−1.79	0.07	−66.87	32.04	−2.09	0.04
HH type – Self employed	86.8	84.67	1.02	0.31	−179.01	145.24	−1.23	0.22
HH type – Casual labour	−28.5	40.59	−0.70	0.48	−143.13	49.23	−2.91	0.00
HH type – Others	88.0	71.58	1.23	0.22	−61.41	29.02	−2.12	0.03
Sector	315.3	164.01	1.92	0.05	79.06	53.99	1.46	0.14
Any land owned	116.8	225.12	0.52	0.60	218.60	422.45	0.52	0.61
Constant	60.8	395.45	0.15	0.88	2157.89	521.82	4.14	0.00
Total	523.9	105.34	4.97	0.00	571.99	85.90	6.66	0.00

Source: NSSO CE 68th round

to the unexplained part stemming from asset ownership, the differences between the HC and SC groups are as follows: land ownership contributed Rs. 412 (29 per cent) followed by the highest level of education, which contributed Rs. 101 (7 per cent), place of residence, which contributed Rs. 85 (6 per cent), and the medium level of education, which contributed Rs. 77 (5 per cent) to the total difference.

Inter-group inequality

In the previous two sections, we observed how asset ownership and asset returns yield different MPCEs among the HCs and SCs. This inequitable distribution of the MPCE is because of asset ownership and asset returns. Therefore, an attempt has been made to measure the contribution of the various economic and non-economic factors in determining inequality, particularly the factors related to social and religious identity, land ownership, educational achievements, and the place of residence. These were explored on the basis of the decomposition of inequality.

In the beginning, we attempted to compare the distribution of households belonging to different socio-religious groups by MPCE quintile groups with their proportion in the total households. This would provide some insights on inequality between groups and also within each group. Table 11.9 shows the household size in the first row, the share of households by quintile groups in the second row (Row per cent) and the share of households by social groups in the third row (Col per cent). It shows that 9,34,000 households in Punjab are HSCs. Of this, 25 per cent were in Q1 and about 12 per cent were in Q5 (see Row per cent). Similar figures are given for the other six socio-religious groups. The third row (Col per cent) in case of HSCs indicates their distribution in each quintile group. The share of HSC households in Q1 was 25.4 per cent, of SSC households 30.4 per cent, and so on. Based on this table, we can also assess the over-representation and under-representation of each social group in different quintiles. First we examine the case of HSCs and HHCs. The share of HSCs in the total households is 16.4 per cent but their share is 25.4 per cent in Q1, 25 per cent in Q2, 18.4 per cent in Q3, 19.8 per cent in Q4, and 11.6 per cent in Q5. On the contrary, the share of HHCs in the total population is 19.8 per cent but their share is under-represented in the Q1 and Q2 quintiles and over-represented in the remaining quintile. Similarly, the share of SSCs is about 21.6 per cent but over-represented in the lowest three quintiles and under-represented in the highest two quintiles.

The mean MPCE varies across social groups in each quintile group. In the lowest quintile group, the average MPCE is Rs. 1066 among HSCs, Rs. 1099 among SSCs, Rs. 1129 among OBCs, Rs. 1152 among HHCs, and Rs. 1207 among SHCs. Similarly, in the highest quintile group, the average MPCE values are Rs. 4481, Rs. 4197, Rs. 4224, Rs. 5224, and Rs. 4544, for the HSCs, SSCs, OBCs, HHCs, and SHCs, respectively. Thus, the degree of inequality may differ across social groups in different contexts but it is certainly the

Table 11.9 Distribution of Population by Social Groups and MPCE Quintile Groups in Punjab – 2012

Social Group	*SRG*	*Q1*	*Q2*	*Q3*	*Q4*	*Q5*	*Total*
HSCs	Number	238	231	172	185	108	934
	Row%	25.4	24.8	18.4	19.8	11.6	100
	Col%	26.7	22.2	14.8	15.5	7.8	16.4
SSCs	Number	373	306	278	167	103	1228
	Row%	30.4	24.9	22.7	13.6	8.4	100
	Col%	41.9	29.3	24.0	14.0	7.4	21.6
OBCs	Number	101	157	123	164	130	674
	Row%	15.0	23.3	18.3	24.3	19.2	100
	Col%	11.3	15.1	10.6	13.7	9.3	11.9
HHCs	Number	87	155	288	256	336	1123
	Row%	7.8	13.8	25.7	22.8	29.9	100
	Col%	9.8	14.9	24.9	21.5	24.0	19.8
SHCs	Number	34	155	247	353	676	1465
	Row%	2.3	10.6	16.8	24.1	46.2	100
	Col%	3.8	14.9	21.3	29.6	48.4	25.8
Rest	Number	58	38	50	69	44	259
	Row%	22.5	14.5	19.3	26.6	17.0	100
	Col%	6.5	3.6	4.3	5.8	3.2	4.6
Total	Number	891	1042	1158	1194	1397	5683
	Row%	15.7	18.3	20.4	21.0	24.6	100
	Col%	100	100	100	100	100	100

Note: The rows indicate population size (in 000'), row per cent and column per cent, respectively.

Source: NSSO CE 68th round

lowest among SCs as compared to that for HCs, irrespective of any context such as place of residence or religious following. This can be better expressed through the Gini Coefficient.[1]

The decomposition of inequality

Inequalities are certainly observed in any population though they could be low, medium or high. However, it is important to understand the cause for inequality. Since the inter-group inequality is observed for distinct groups, it is imperative to determine both the between-group inequality and within-group inequality. Once these figures are determined, we can not only compare the within-group and between-group inequalities but also observe how between-group inequality differs as the dividing line of groups is changed besides clearly identifying the prominent group in predicting between-group inequality.[2]

Table 11.10 shows the results of the decomposition of the households' MPCE by sub-dividing the household sample in Punjab by the following variables: the caste, religion, highest education level of adults in households, land ownership, and place of residence.

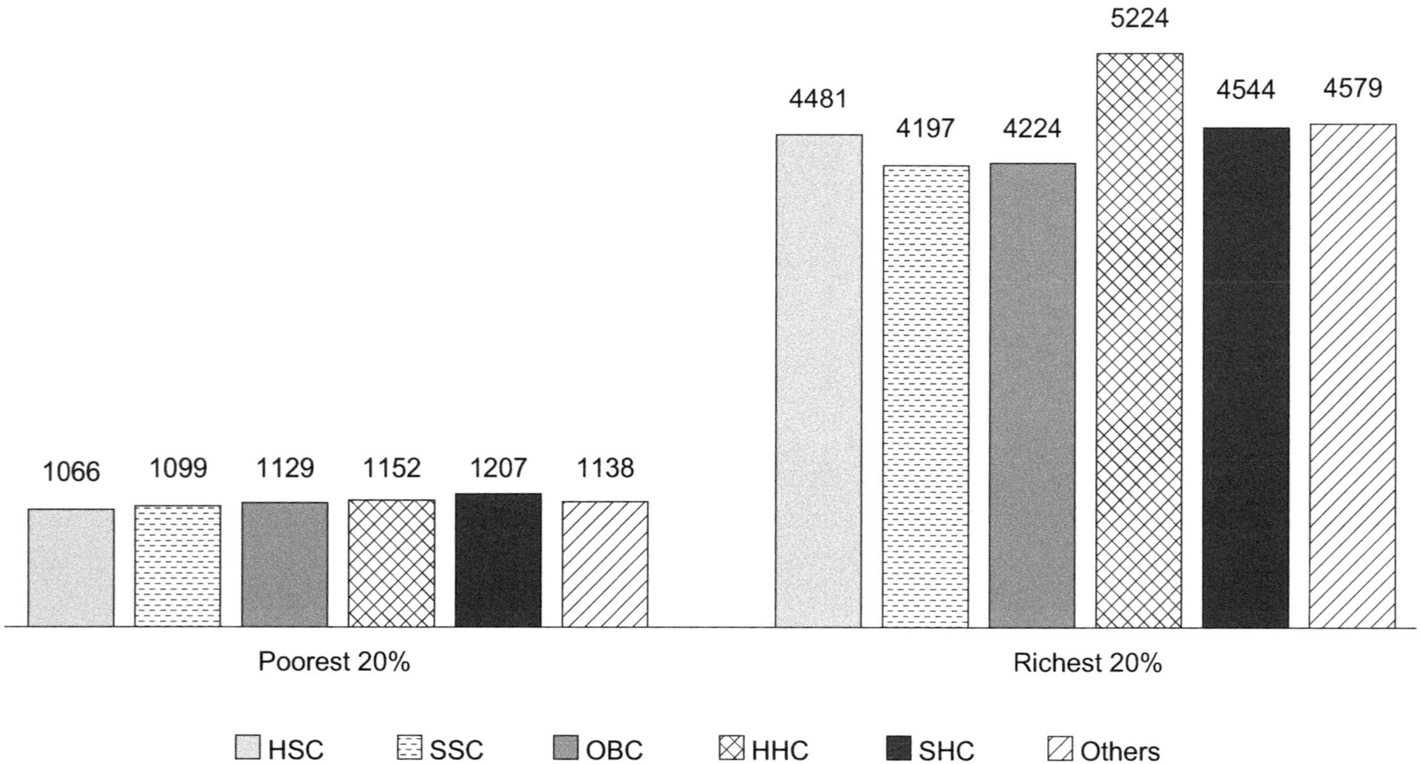

Figure 11.3 Comparison of MPCE among Social Groups by the Richest and Poorest Quintile Groups in Punjab

Source: NSSO CE 68th round

Table 11.10 Gini Ratio and Its Decomposition by Observable Characteristics in Punjab

Decomposition by	*Gini Value*	*GE(0) Value*	*Within Group Contribution*	*Between Group Contribution*
By Caste	0.321	0.168	80.3	19.7
By Caste within Sikh	0.313	0.159	73.4	26.6
By Caste within Hindu	0.329	0.179	87.8	12.2
By Caste within Urban	0.340	0.191	88.5	11.5
By Caste within Rural	0.290	0.136	75.9	24.1
By Religion	0.320	0.167	100.0	0.0
By Place of Resident	0.321	0.168	93.6	6.4
By Land own	0.321	0.168	98.5	1.5
By highest level of Education	0.312	0.160	84.5	15.5

Source: NSSO CE 68th round

The first point that is observed on undertaking this exercise is that the Gini Coefficient is the highest in urban areas as compared to the rural areas on the basis of caste. The second observation is that the inequality arrived at on the basis of the caste-based groups yields a slightly higher level of inequality as compared to that arrived at on the basis of religion, place of residence, land ownership and highest level of education. The third observation is that the highest proportion (19.7 per cent) of the overall inequality is explained by caste-based inequality, which further increases when it is applied only to the Sikh religion. The fourth observation is that caste is also an important predictor in rural areas, explaining more than 24 per cent of the overall inequality as compared to 11.5 per cent in urban areas. Thus, the contribution of between-group inequality is substantially high among the Sikh households and rural households, which clearly points to the prevalence of discriminatory practices against the SC households following the Sikh religion.

Conclusion

Dr. B. R. Ambedkar fought against the evil of caste system throughout his life and sought annihilation of caste through his writings and actions for the reason that it obstructing individual freedom leaving no space for individual choices, occupational mobility and scientific temper. The consequence of such an anti-democratic system has resulted in the hierarchical and graded inequality. This paper sought to investigate that does caste-based discrimination would decline with high economic growth to an insignificant level? Is the extent of caste discrimination lesser among households belonging to the Sikh religion as compared to that among their counterparts belonging to the Hindu religion? These are some of the questions addressed in this paper through an analysis of inter-group inequality and the relative strength of the demographic, economic and non-economic assets in predicting the consumption expenditure of households in Punjab. The first question has been addressed by exclusively taking the state of Punjab for the analysis, keeping in mind the success of Green Revolution in the agriculture sector with respect to India's development strategy in the initial phase. The second question has been addressed by analyzing the discrimination separately for Hindu and Sikh households. For the purpose, we have used the Blinder – Oaxaca (1973) decomposition method to explain the difference in consumption expenditure among HC and SC households.

The first point that emerges is that there is a substantial disparity in MPCE between HC households, on one hand, and SC and OBC households, on the other. In fact, the SC households are more likely to get over-represented in the low-MPCE quintile groups than while the HC households in the high-quintile group, irrespective of whether the household belongs to the Hindu or Sikh religion. The assessment of relative strength of the economic and non-economic assets clearly shows that the returns on these are relatively low among the SC households as compared to their HC counterparts. For example, the rate of returns on land ownership is Rs. 524 for HCs (Rs. 210 for HHCs and Rs. 358 for SHCs) as compared to that of Rs. 260 among SCs (Rs. 248 for HSCs and Rs. 387 for SSCs) and the rate of returns on higher education is Rs. 1233 for HCs (Rs. 1930 for HHCs and Rs. 650 for SHCs) as compared to that of Rs. 872 among SCs (Rs. 991 for HSCs and Rs. 825 for SSCs). However, the rate of returns between HC and SC are again differs between the Sikhs and Hindus. In some of the attributes, the HSCs have higher returns but SSCs does not. Similarly in a few attributes, SSCs have higher returns but HSCs does not. For example, the returns of the occupational type have higher returns for HSC households as compared to HHC households; but in the case of education SSC households have higher returns than SHC households.

The decomposition analysis shows that these factors do not explain the differences in the MPCE between HCs and SCs (combined as well as separately for the Hindu and Sikh households) completely, but some part remains unexplained, which may be attributed to the discrimination effect. For example, 35 per cent of the difference in the MPCE between HC and SC households is unexplained (the difference in MPCE between HHCs and HSCs is 30 per cent while that between SHCs and SSCs is 36 per cent). The decomposition of inequality also clearly brings out the 'between-group' contribution prominently in the case of caste, and shows that it is substantially high in the case of Sikh and rural households.

Thus, the results suggest that economic growth alone may not be a contributing factor for weakening caste-based discrimination. The prejudices based on social identity also account for the unequal outcomes stemming from caste-based discrimination.

Notes

1 The Gini Coefficient is computed as half the mean of the difference in consumption expenditure between pairs of households divided by the average score. The formulation is Gini is $G = \frac{1}{2N^2\mu}\sum_{i=1}^{N}\sum_{j=1}^{N}|C_i - C_j|$ where N is number of households, C_i is the MPCE of the households, and μ is the mean expenditure computed over all the households.

2 The decomposition of inequality is additive and therefore, overall inequality can be written as the sum of within-group and between-group inequality: $\underbrace{I}_{\text{overall ineqality}} = \underbrace{A}_{\text{within group inequality}} + \underbrace{B}_{\text{between group inequality}}$. In other words, the share of B represents the contribution of between-group inequality to the overall inequality, whereas the share of A represents the contribution of within-group inequality.

References

Ambedkar, B. R. (1916). "Castes in India: Their Mechanism, Genesis and Development", Paper read before the Anthropology Seminar of Dr. A. A. Goldenweizer at the Columbia University, New York, 9 May.

Ambedkar, B. R. (1936). *Annihilation of Caste*, Bhim Patrika Publication, Jalandhar, Punjab.

Borooah, V. K. (2005). "Caste, Inequality and Poverty in India", *Review of Development Economics*, Vol. 9, No. 3, pp. 399–414.

Chakraborty, A. (2001). "The Concept and Measurement of Group Inequality", Working Paper No. 315, Centre for Development Studies, Thiruvananthapuram, May.

Jodhka, S. S. (2000). "'Prejudice' without 'Pollution'? SCs in Contemporary Punjab", *Journal of Indian School of Political Economy*, Vol. 12, Nos. 3 and 4, July–December, pp. 381–402.

Jodhka, S. S. (2002). "Caste and Untouchability in Rural Punjab", *Economic and Political Weekly*, Vol. 37, No. 19, pp. 1817–1823.

Jodhka, S. S. (2006). "Beyond 'Crisis' Rethinking Contemporary Punjab Agriculture", *Economic and Political Weekly*, Vol. 41, No. 16, pp. 1817–1823.

Madheswaran, S. and Attewell, P. (2010). "Wage and Job Discrimination in the Indian Urban Labour Market", in Sukhadeo Thorat and Katherine S. Newman (eds.), *Blocked by Caste: Economic Discrimination in Modern India*, Oxford University Press, New Delhi, pp. 123–147.

Naik, A. K. and Tagade, N. Y. (2018). "Poverty and Inequality in Maharashtra: Intergroup Differentials and Its Determinants", *Journal of Social Inclusion Studies*, Vol. 4, No. 1, pp. 151–168.

Puri, H. K. (2003). "Scheduled Castes in Sikh Community: A Historical Perspective", *Economic and Political Weekly*, Vol. 38, No. 26, 28 June, pp. 2693–2701.

Shergill, H. S. and Singh, G. (1995). "Poverty in Rural Punjab, Trends over Green Revolution Decade", *Economic and Political Weekly*, Vol. 30, Nos. 24 and 25, pp. A80–A83.

Shukla, V. and Mishra, U. S. (2014). "Is the Recent Reduction in India's Poverty Inclusive?" *Economic and Political Weekly*, Vol. 49, No. 47, 22 November, pp. 70–75.

Singh, M. (2012). "Preferences for Migrant Agricultural Labour in Punjab", *Economic and Political Weekly*, Vol. XLVII, No. 29, 21 July, pp. 27–28.
Tagade, N., Naik, A. K. and Thorat, S. (2018). "Wealth Ownership and Inequality in India: A Socio-religious Analysis", *Journal of Social Inclusion Studies*, Vol. 2, No. 4, pp. 1–18.
Thorat, S. (2005). "Caste System and Economic Discrimination: Lessons from Theories", in Sukhadeo Thorat, Aryama and Prashant Negi (eds.), *Reservation and Private Sector: Quest for Equal Opportunity and Growth*, Rawat Publication, New Delhi, pp. 66–88.
Thorat, S. and Attewell, P. (2010). "The Legacy of Social Exclusion: A Correspondence Study of Job Discrimination in India's Urban Private Sector", in Sukhadeo Thorat and Katherine S. Newman (eds.), *Blocked by Caste: Economic Discrimination in Modern India*, Oxford University Press, New Delhi, pp. 35–51.
Thorat, S., Banerjee, A., Mishra, V. and Rizvi, F. (2015). "Urban Rental Housing Market: Caste and Religion Matters," *Economic & Political Weekly*, Vol. 50, Nos. 26 and 27, 27 June, pp. 47–53.
Thorat, S. and Dubey, A. (2012). "Has Growth Been Socially Inclusive during 1993-94-2009-10?" *Economic and Political Weekly*, Vol. 47, No. 10, 10 March, pp. 43–53.
Thorat, S. and Lee, J. (2010). "Food Security Schemes and Caste Discrimination", in Sukhadeo Thorat and Katherine S. Newman (eds.), *Blocked by Caste: Economic Discrimination in Modern India*, Oxford University Press, New Delhi, pp. 287–310.
Thorat, S. and Madheswaran, S. (2018). "Graded Caste Inequality and Poverty: Evidence on Role of Economic Discrimination", *Journal of Social Inclusion Studies*, Vol. 4, No. 1, pp. 3–29.
Thorat, S. and Tagade, N. (2018). *Maharashtratil Vishamta ani Garibi: Sampattik Vishamta va Jatiya Bhedbhavacha Prabhav* (Inequality and Poverty in Maharashtra: Impact of Wealth Inequality and Caste based Discrimination), Sugava Prakashan, Pune.

12 Dr. B. R. Ambedkar's view on agricultural holdings and collective farming

The case of Telangana state

Y. Sreenivasulu and Tajuddin Md.

Introduction

India is an agrarian society where more than 60 percent of its producers own holdings of less than one hectare of land. The structure of landholdings is pear in shape and moreover, Agricultural Census 2011, reveals that only a little over three percent of the producers own more than three hectares, while only 0.28 percent owns more than 10 hectares of land in the State of Telangana. It is noticed that the petty commodity producers are the extremely vulnerable, struggling to survive/sustain themselves in conditions where they cannot grow, and any surplus is accidental. Furthermore, rural banking is not in favour of the small and marginal farmers, tenant farmers, and other vulnerable groups. Narasimha Rao and Suri (2006) studied the dimensions of agricultural distress and found that about 70 percent of the farmers have borrowed from the fertilizer/pesticide traders at 24 percent interest rate during the cropping period. The small and marginal farmers are forced into the wage market because of their insufficient holding size. The NSS survey highlighted that over 60 percent of the farmers prefer to opt out of agriculture if they had an alternative. The numbers of non-cultivating landowners (non-residents) are increasing over time (Vijay, 2012) and such an absentee landlordism does not contribute to agricultural productivity and agricultural growth. These changing tendencies in agrarian structure might lead to further marginalization of agriculture.

Long ago Dr. B. R. Ambedkar had raised the issue of the consolidation of land holdings and tenancy reforms which helps to reduce unequal and informal institutions in the land market. The land control and ownership by higher caste depended on religious ideological notions, customary rules and norms (Ambedkar, 1936). These led to Dalits being excluded from land rights historically. "The consolidation of holdings and tenancy legislation are worse than useless. They cannot bring about prosperity in agriculture. Neither consolidation nor tenancy legislation can be of any help to the untouchables who are just landless labourers. Only collective farms can help them."[1] This essay tries to address the issues in agriculture through the thoughts of Dr. B. R. Ambedkar on agriculture. His vision on small agricultural holdings and collective farming is of more relevance at present context of agriculture.

Dr. B. R. Ambedkar's view on agricultural holdings

Dr. B. R. Ambedkar is one of the multi-dimensional personality and outstanding intellectuals of India. He is known as the architect of India's constitution and a doughty champion of the interests of scheduled castes. He analysed various social and political problems though economic dimension contributing much towards the development of India. His work on "small holdings in India and their remedies" in 1918 still reflects the present scenario on small holdings in Indian agriculture. Dr. B. R. Ambedkar strongly supported the land reforms, and wanted that land should be under the state control; where it provides secure and equitable rights to the rural masses those have the right to productive land under the principle of state socialism.[2] He argued that land is the only one of the factors of production and the productivity of one factor or production is dependent upon the proportion in which other factors of production are combined.[3]

He was of the opinion that if farming is an only occupation, then to possess a small piece of land is better than to have none. People cultivate in small piece of land is not because their standards of living is low but because it is the only profitable opportunity available to them and if they had better opportunity than this they would never prefer the small piece of land and this is just because of the petit culture due to enormous pressure on land.[4] The situation of the farmer without any other alternative source of employment leaves them with no other alternative but to depend on agriculture.[5] The problems those lying with the small holdings in the present context was explained by Ambedkar long back where he wanted that there should be a socialist pattern of control over the industry and land by the government so that it may be used for collective farming by the landless poor and only this pattern of farming can only solve the problem of landless poor.[6]

Agriculture at present still constitutes more than 45 percent of the workforce. Ambedkar long back identified the problems those related to agriculture by giving priority to the land and as a believer in state socialism he argued that "The consolidation of holdings and tenancy legislation are worse than useless. They cannot bring about prosperity in agriculture. Neither consolidation nor tenancy legislation can be of any help to the untouchables who are just landless labourers. Only collective farms can help them."[7] The land holding situation was elaborated by Ambedkar in 1918 and it got reflected in seventies in the planning commission documents referring to his work 'the total impact of land reforms has been less than had been hoped, for this there are several reasons. In the first place, there has been too little recognition of land reform as a positive programme of development, and it has been only too often regarded as extraneous to the scheme of community development and the effort to increasing agricultural production.'[8]

Sudha Pai (2010) has pointed out that traditionally Dalits/untouchables did not have access to agriculture land due to their social status. In post-independence many of these those deprived their right to processes land were given lands under various programmes and schemes but those who received these lands did not even know the existence of it and mostly the uncultivable land was distributed and they only possess part of the land without even knowing where their land is. Though under the legal frame work policies were initiated to improve the conditions of those who were historically deprived of their rights to land for production purpose, this issue is still at large to be addressed to remove the disparities (Thorat, 2009).

Avowed goal towards achieving the economic development of the Dalits along with other weaker sections has been the integral part of India's planning, though it is a political programme through which the state tries to impress the masses to get support (Mohanty, 2001). It is a well-known fact that the physical capital among the Dalits is limited as majority of them does not possess cultivable land. Even if it is there it is in a limited endowment (Suryanarayana, 2001). Land is an important asset which not only indicates economic position but also serves as proxy for social and political strength (Kamble, 2001), it is the historical impact of the customary restrictions on the ownership of agriculture land by large section of Dalits, even today most of them are wage labourers (Thorat, 2001). Ambedkar felt that neither consolidation nor tenancy legislation would help the landless agricultural labourers, it would be better where there would be collective farming which means nationalization of agriculture. But Govt. of India in order to reduce inequalities in land distribution pattern was opted for land reforms.[9] For the purpose of the study, we have collected information from various reports of Agricultural Census of Telangana and Andhra Pradesh, Published by Directorate of Economics and Statistics, Govt. of Telangana and United Andhra Pradesh.

Trends in agricultural holdings in Telangana

The state of Hyderabad was founded on the principle of pure despotism or autocracy the whole being considered as the private property of the ruler.[10] It is pointed out that unlike the Zamindars and Jagirdars of other parts of India, the Jagirdars of Hyderabad state had no proprietary rights over the land. They were only entitled to collect the revenue from the land which is under their supervision. Khusro (1958) sheds enormous insights on the land administration in Hyderabad state.[11] The land administration was divided into: the Nizam's *Sarf-e-Khas* (Crown Lands), the Paigahs, the other exempted Jagirs (Ilaqas), the Ordinary Jagirs and the Sub-Jagirs. They belonged to non-Brahmin upper castes Velama and Reddy with lands under their control. Satyanarayana (1993) points out that there was an emergence of the new rich rural peasant class after the abolition of Zamindari system after independence. He points that non-Brahmin upper castes (Kamma, Velama, Reddy and Kapus) have consolidated their position in Andhra

Pradesh (including the present Telangana), while those from backward class remained the poor peasants, and there was no change in the status of Dalits who were agriculture labourers. It indicated that consolidation of the land in few hands in village community and thus played crucial role in village economy.

After the Nizam's rule, the period of 1950s and 1960s, all farmers received permanent rights on lands, after the abolishing of the Zamindari system in India. Further, after the Green Revolution in the 70s, which has been the result of technological reforms in the region, the farmers used the new technologies to enhance productivity, and agriculture became more profitable. During this period, land under tenancy was very less. This resulted in traditional inputs being replaced by the modern inputs such as HYV seeds, bio-technically engineered seeds, fertilizers, pesticides, and agricultural implements such as harvesters, etc. Adoption of new technology increases self-cultivation, and as productivity increases, the average farm income increases significantly. As a result, the proportion of absentee landowners as well as tenants decreased in the region. Hence, from the subsistence economy, agriculture as an activity for producing for the market became more profitable. However, after the 1990s, productivity became stagnant, and agriculture was no more remunerative. Hence, farmers shifted to non-agricultural sectors, and after 2000, the farmers decided to search for other alternatives because agriculture was not at all remunerative. In this process, many large farmers shifted to urban areas and raising marginal, small and tenant farmers in the state.

Raising marginal agricultural holdings and extent of tenancy in Telangana

The present agricultural situation of India where it largely depends on small and marginal farmers those constitute nearly 80 percent thus making India to depend on these groups for agricultural growth and food security. Dev (2012) refer to Lipton (2006) where the roles of small farms were well recognized in development and poverty reduction. Majority of the farm holdings are small and marginal farmers and their sustainability is crucial for livelihoods in rural areas and for entire country. It is also observed that a monthly income and consumption figure varies from different size of land holdings.[12] Dev referring to the study of National Commission for Enterprise in the Unorganized Sector (NCEUS, 2008) says that

> some of the general issues that confront marginal-small farmers as agriculturalists are: imperfect markets for inputs/product leading to smaller value realizations; absence of access to credit markets or imperfect credit markets leading to suboptimal investment decisions or input applications; poor human resource base; smaller access to suitable extension services restricting suitable decisions regarding cultivation practices and technological know-how; poorer access to 'public goods' such as public

irrigation, command area development, electricity grids; greater negative externalities from poor quality land and water management, etc.[13]

It is evident that most of the farmers those belong to small and marginal farming though continue to be in large numbers are yet to receive their due share in development of the agriculture. Moreover, the NSS (2003–04) data analysis reveals that only a little over five percent of the producers own more than three hectares, while only 0.52 percent own more than 10 hectares of land. Thus in many parts of the country, agricultural bondage and attached labour have significantly declined, if not disappeared, while casual wage labour has increased. Tenancy has declined, according to NSSO 2003–04 – only 6.5 percent of the operated land was found to be under tenancy. Tenancy can be part and parcel of the capitalist-social relations, where people who have risen up against the class hierarchy and no longer wish to till their land themselves.

It is observed that multiple livelihood options are necessary for the sustenance of rural households. Thus, the rural economy has developed in complex ways. What are the means by which rural households reproduce themselves, and what kinds of differentiation might result? Mostly the petty commodity producers are extremely vulnerable, struggling to survive/sustain themselves in conditions where they cannot grow, and any surplus is accidental. "Challenges for Revival of Indian Agriculture", by Mahendra Dev (2008) pointed out that most of the fertilizer, irrigation and power subsidies go to the developed regions and to the large farmers; the small and marginal farmers are not among the beneficiaries of these development schemes. Furthermore, rural banking is not in favour of the small and marginal farmers, tenant farmers, and other vulnerable groups. As mentioned earlier, Narasimha Rao and K. C. Suri (2006) studied the dimensions of agricultural distress and found that about 70 percent of the farmers have borrowed the fertilizer/pesticide from traders at 24 percent interest rate during the cropping period. The small and marginal farmers are forced into the wage market because of their insufficient holding size (Rao, 2007). A few years back, a NSS survey highlighted that over 60 percent of the farmers prefer to opt out of agriculture if they had an alternative. The Book, *Five Big Questions about Five Hundred Million Small Farms*, by Peter Hazel, has pointed out that smallholding development is one of the main ways to reduce poverty. The present challenge is to improve the working of markets for output, input, land and financial services, and to overcome market failures that discriminate small farmers.

Structurally, in Telangana agriculture is known to be essentially poor peasant and tenant farmer based. The poor peasants account for 92.15 percent of the total farm households, accounting for 62.4 percent of area operated. In contrast, large farmers comprise only 0.28 percent of the total households, with 4.01 percent of the operated land in Telangana in 2011. Tenants account for 24 percent of the total farm households, and around 13.65 percent of the area of total cultivable land, which was not reported in the official records.

According to the Agricultural Census, in the Figure 12.1, there is a huge increase in marginal holdings, with small units of land, i.e., below one hectare, in Telangana. In 1970–71, there were 38.45 percent marginal holdings, which increased to 61.95 percent to total agricultural holdings in Telangana in 2010–11. Similarly, the area operated by marginal farmers has risen from 5.53 percent in 1970–71 to 25.28 percent in 2010–11. Family division is one of the reasons for sub-divided lands, while another reason, not reported is that the big landowners leased-out land to the landless and small farmers. We observe that there are significant raise marginal and small holdings, compared to other size holdings. According to VS Vyas (2007), there is stagnation in agricultural productivity and production. At the same time, there is also stagnation in the prices of output, and rise in the prices of the agricultural inputs over a period. This has seriously affected the economy of a large number of marginal, small and tenant farmers, and some landowners have shifted to non-agricultural activities. All landless agricultural laborers, female laborers, small, marginal and tenant farmers depend on agriculture for their livelihood. There are a number of small, marginal and tenant farmers committing suicides even in agriculturally progressed districts such as Warangal, Karimnagar and Nizamabad in Telangana (Revathi, 2014). This section of peasants has low income, lower capacity and weak assets. They

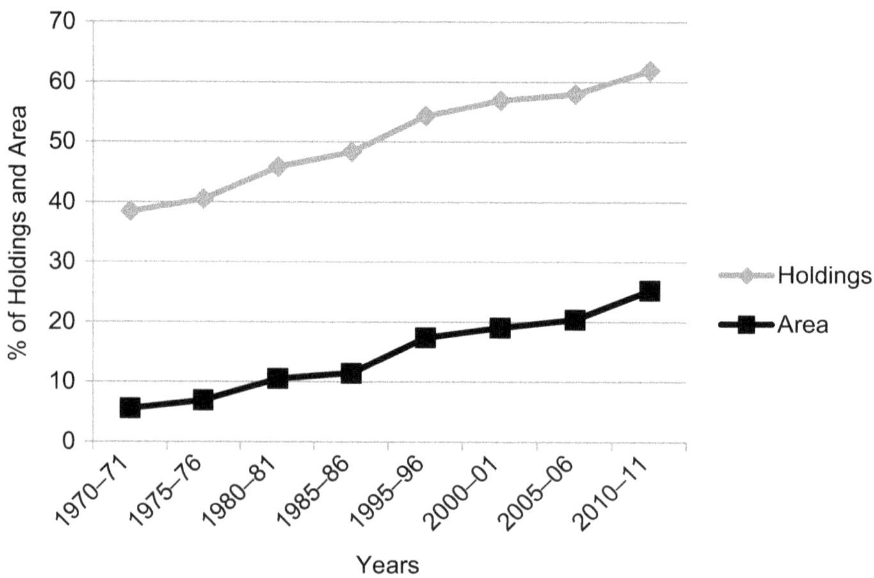

Figure 12.1 Trends in percentage of operational holdings and area by marginal farmers in Telangana

Source: Agricultural Census

cannot bear sudden shocks in agriculture and their capacity to participate in the development process is very low. The crisis in agriculture made a situation of suicidal in the farming community, where most of them are marginal and small holdings farmers. As per National Crime Records Bureau report (2014) where the status of land holdings of farmers those committed suicide reveals that 44.5 percent are small farmers and 27.9 percent are marginal farmers respectively, which accounts 72.4 percent of the total farmers committed suicide (4,095 out of 5,650). 53.1 percent and 14.5 percent of small farmers those committed suicide were reported from Maharashtra (1,135 out of 2,516) and Telangana (366 out of 2,516).[14]

The land holding data (Figure 12.2) shows that large holdings as well as area have declined in Telangana significantly. The large holdings have declined from 35.34 percent in 1970–71 to 4.01 percent in 2010–11; while medium holdings declined from 7.6 percent to 1.8 percent; semi-medium holdings declined from 12.7 percent to 5.8 percent; and small holdings declined from 17.3 to 13.7 percent in the Telangana. In the case of area operated by large farmers have been declining from 6.12 percent in 1970–71 to 0.28 percent only in 2010–11. The trends shows that marginal holdings accounted for more than 80 percent; while large holdings

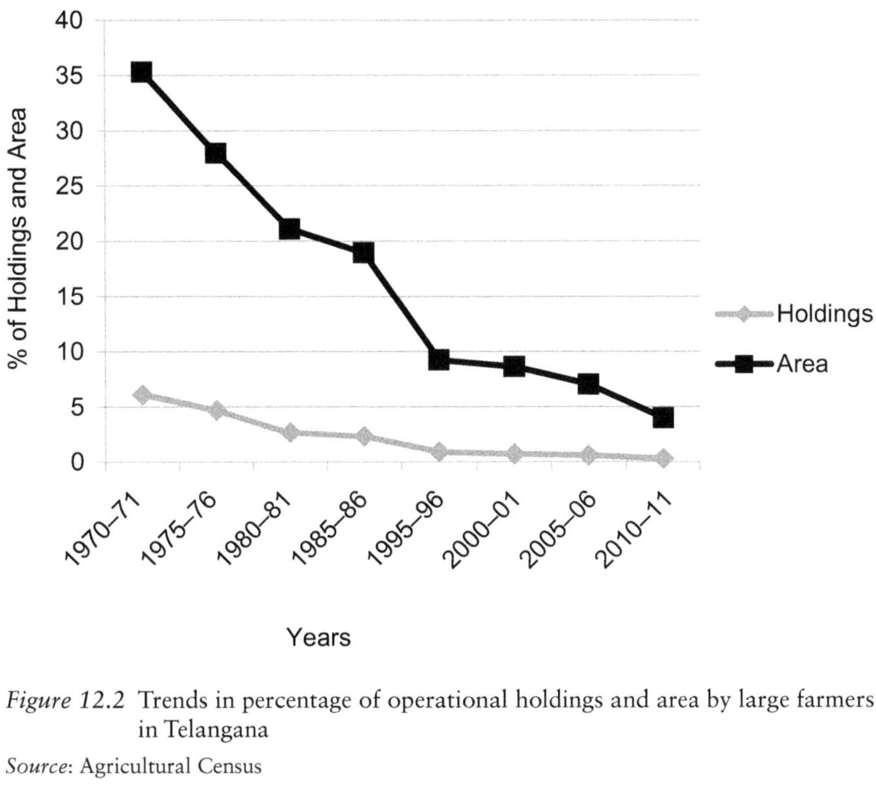

Figure 12.2 Trends in percentage of operational holdings and area by large farmers in Telangana

Source: Agricultural Census

accounted for less than 0.3 percent, and the marginal and smallholdings put together, accounted for more than 94 percent in all districts in Telangana. Among all categories of holdings, only the poor peasants and tenants operate more than 92 percent of the land – which is a significant amount of area.

Declining number of cultivators in Telangana

In 1971, from the Figure 12.3, about 15.03 percent of cultivators provided employment for 17.1 percent of the agricultural labourers. However, the proportion of the cultivators has been declining over the years, from 15.03 percent in 1971 to 9.02 percent in 2011; while the proportion of the total agricultural holdings has been increasing over the period by small and marginal holdings.

The big landowners were a major labour-demanding segment in the agrarian economy. The data from the Hand Book of Statistics of 2005–06 shows that, in Telangana 62.4 percent of area is operated under small and marginal holdings comprising 92.15 percent of total operational holdings.14.95 percent of area is operated under medium holdings which account for three percent of total holdings. Though the proportion of big landowners is very small, they operate more amount of land.

Rises in extent of tenancy

The Hyderabad Tenancy and Agricultural Lands Act of 1950 has protected nearly six lakh tenants and 33 percent of the total cultivated land under tenancy in 1950's in Telangana. After 1970's the share of leased-in area has

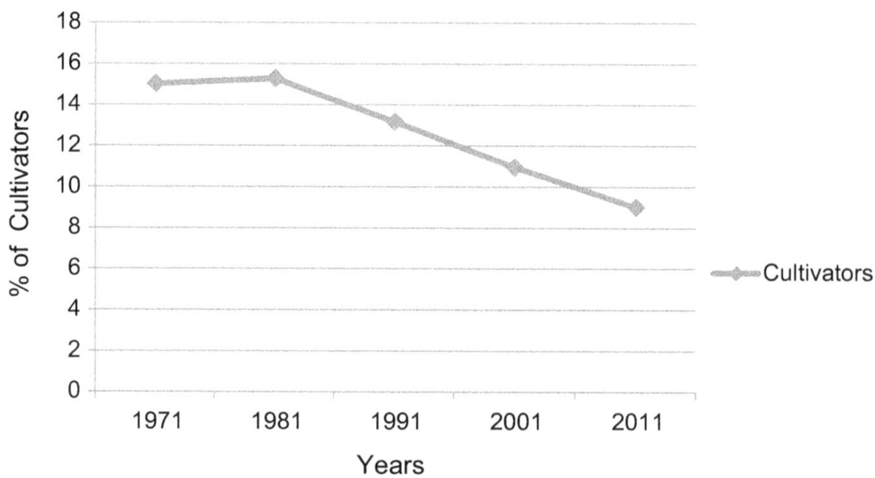

Figure 12.3 Trends in percentage of cultivators declining over period in Telangana

Source: Agricultural Census.

been declining due to increased profitability of agriculture through use HYV technology. Consequently, the medium and large farmers themselves cultivate their lands to enhance productivity. Recent data and studies shown that extent of land under tenancy have increased in Telangana (Sreenivasulu, 2015; Revathi, 2014). The nature and ownership of land is determined by the pattern of tenancy. When there is more land owned by absentee landowners, there is a high possibility to generate an informal pattern of tenancy. The high proportion of informal tenancy system is one of the major causes for farmers have committed suicide in the state (Revathi, 1998). The predominance of poor peasants and tenant households, as well as the area operated and land distribution is highly skewed and uneven; and the bottom 92.15 percent of the households account for 62 percent of the total operated area. The average size of marginal and smallholding farms are very low and cannot generate adequate employment and for their sustenance, if they depend only on crop cultivation (Haque, 1996). Hence, they are willing to take available land on lease for cultivation, as they do not undertake other farm or off-farm activities. The farmers, particularly small and marginal farmers, do not have the ability to invest in agriculture; due to this there is high investment and labour input. There is a need for the liberalization and legalization of land leasing for promoting agriculture efficiency, equity, occupational diversification and rural transformation. For example, take the case of the socialist countries (China and Vietnam), where liberalization of land leasing has shown a positive impact on economic growth.[15] Though leasing is not legal in Kerala but the Kudumbashree mission assist the poor women to lease in land in a joint liability group (JLG) for creating an income source for them. It is reported that a group usually consists 4–10 members with an area ranging from half an acre to 12 acres of leased in land, and around 2.3 lakh women have benefited from this model of collective farming. This model suggests the government to revisit the ban on land leasing.[16]

Dr. B. R. Ambedkar's views on collective farming and its relevance for contemporary times

From the centuries caste and class are correlated and in agriculture the labourers traditionally belong to Dalits, tribes or poorer members of other middle and lower castes. These are the groups who actually worked on the land but did not have any rights over the land; even today their proposition as owner of the land is much less. Regarding the ownership of the agricultural land and poverty among the SC agriculture labour households, it is being noticed that those from Schedule Caste in the states of Andhra Pradesh, Telangana, Bihar, Haryana, Gujarat, Jammu and Kashmir, Maharashtra, Punjab, Rajasthan, Tamil Nadu and West Bengal are having land which is lower in proportion than compared to all India. High levels of landlessness among the SCs made them depend on daily wage employment, making them to depend on low earning, which is the major cause of poverty among them (Thorat, 2009). The link between the women and agriculture is also very strong. Apart from this women constitute a special case in development studies because of their dual role; they are responsible for reproduction and maintenance of the future labour force as well.[17]

Policies and programmes of 1970's and 1980's saw women as objects rather than subjects to development. The notion of Mahila Samakhya (MS) which is more than a two decade old programme which carries the distinction of being large scale government programme committed to women's education especially poor, rural women. The vision of this programme came out in preview of 1986 national policy on education, which outlined on a broad concept of women's education and empowerment.[18] This organization since its inception is embedded in knowledge of the women's movement and struggles to establish the worth and value of women's work, to make their contributions visible.[19]

To enhance and empower the condition of the poor and rural women through financial inclusion approach the micro credit system was started among the groups, though there is still gap in reflecting their empowerment. This however made them to be involved in other livelihood models those functioning throughout the country. In Telangana the MS along with DPAP implemented "Smamata Dharini" programme under which the women from groups come together to cultivate the land by taking it on lease. This programme though was helpful but failed to continue because of lack of coordination between the MS and DPAP. The same initiative under the name of "Kudumbashree" in Kerala has done wonders in the terms of both employment and income for the groups those involved in collective farming by taking land in lease.[20]

Conclusion

From the view point of Dr. B. R. Ambedkar, the main drawback of those working in agriculture in Indian economy was that most of the land is in hands of few individuals with no access to land for the deprived classes. His contribution towards to overcome the crisis was nationalization of land, tenancy legislation and collective farming. This paper attempts to analyze the thought of Ambedkar on collective farming. The main objective of this paper is to address the vision of Ambedkar on small holdings and collective farming its relevance to Telangana state. It is being found that there is increase in marginal and small land holdings whereas there is a decline in the percentage of the large farmers holding. It is evident that the small and marginal farmers face lot of problems (informal institutional credit, improper markets and poor infrastructure at village level) to overcome this issues, the vision of Ambedkar is only the suitable remedy for this problem i.e., "Collective Farming" which now a days is being experimented by most of the SHGs in the country and has shown positive results (Kudumbashree model of collective farming of Kerala, collective farming by DDS in Telangana).

Notes

1 quote sited form Keer, *Ambedkar: Life and Mission*, p. 391 in Ishita Aditya Ray and Sarbapriya Ray (2011). "B.R. Ambedkar and His Philosophy of Land Reform: An Evaluation", *Afro Asian Journal of Social Sciences*, Vol. 2, No. 2, 1 Quarter 1. www.onlineresearchjournals.com/aajoss/art/60.pdf

2 Mohod Utkarsh (2015). "Ambedkar's Long Neglected Thoughts on Land Reforms and Agriculture", 4 March 2015. http://roundtableindia.co.in/index.php?option=com_content&view=article&id=8090:long-neglected-ambedkar-s-philosophy-on-land-reform-and-agricultural-development&catid=119&Itemid=132.

3 Jai Narayan Sharma (2010). "Economic Ideas of Dr. Ambedkar", in S.N. Mishra (ed.), *Socio-Economic and Political Vision of Dr. B.R. Ambedkar*. New Delhi: Concept Publishing Company, p. 134.

4 Ambedkar referring to Prof. Jevons on the small farming and its critique in his work small holdings in India and their remedies, see Ambedkar, B. R. (1918)."Small Holdings in India and Their Remedies", *Journal of the Indian Economic Society*, Vol. 1918.

5 P. Narasimha Rao and Kondaveeti Chinnaya Suri (2006). "Dimensions of Agrarian Distress in Andhra Pradesh", *Economic and Political Weekly*, April 22, pp. 1546–1552.

6 Ibid., pp. 135–136.

7 quoted sited form Keer, *Ambedkar: Life and Mission*, p. 391 in Ishita Aditya Ray and Sarbapriya Ray (2011), "B.R. Ambedkar and His Philosophy of Land Reform: An Evaluation", *Afro Asian Journal of Social Sciences*, Vol. 2, No. 2, Quarter 1. www.onlineresearchjournals.com/aajoss/art/60.pdf

8 Dr. Rashi Krishna Sinha (2011) quoting from the Planning Commission Report of 1972 in Agricultural Holdings in India and the Relevance of Dr. Ambedkar's Thoughts as a fellow Ambedkar Chair, Department of Economics & Rural development Dr. Ram Manohar Lohia Avadh University, Faizabad. www.rmlau.ac.in/pdf/ppt.pdf

9 Estharla Krishna Rao (2007). "Dalits' Entitlement to Land: An Agenda That Never Was!", in Fr. Thomas Pallithanam (ed.), *Rekindling Hope? Access, Retention and Development of Land: A Dalit Perspective*. Hyderabad: Andhra Pradesh Social Watch Report, pp. 63–65.

10 See A.M. Khusro (1958). *Economic and Social Effects of Jagirdari Abolition and Land reforms in Hyderabad*. Dept of Publication and University Press, Osmania University, Hyderabad.

11 Ibid.

12 Mahendra Dev (2012). *Small Farmers in India: Challenges and Opportunities*. WP-2012-014, June. www.igidr.ac.in/pdf/publication/WP-2012-014.pdf

13 Mahendra Dev, referring to the report of National Commission for Enterprise in the Unorganized Sector (NCEUS) (2012). *Small Farmers in India: Challenges and Opportunities*. WP-2012-014, June, p. 7. www.igidr.ac.in/pdf/publication/WP-2012-014.pdf

14 http://ncrb.nic.in/StatPublications/ADSI/ADSI2014/chapter-2A%20farmer%20suicides.pdf

15 Report of the Expert Committee on Land Leasing NITI AAYOG Govt. of India New Delhi March 31, 2016.

16 Ibid., referring to Haque and Nair (2014).

17 Joan P. Mencher and K. Sarodamoni (1982). "Muddy Feet, Dirty Hands: Rice Production and Female Agricultural Labour", *Economic and Political Weekly*, 25th December, pp. A149–165.

18 Dipta Bhog and Malini Ghose (2012) "Mapping the Multiple Worlds of Women's Literacy: Experiences from Mahila Samakhya", in Vimala Ramachandran and Kameshwari Jandhyala (eds.), *Cartographies of Empowerment: The Mahila Samakhya Story*. New Delhi: Zubaan, pp. 237–269.

19 Geeta Memon and Soma Kishore Parthasarathy (2012). "Embedding Economic Empowerment within an Education Process: The Mahila Samakhya Experience", in Vimala Ramachandran and Kameshwari Jandhyala (eds.), *Cartographies of Empowerment: The Mahila Samakhya Story*. New Delhi: Zubaan, p. 392.

20 The programmes on the collective farming however gave good results initially but it was unable to continue in case of Andhra Pradesh but the similar programme in Kerala under Kutumbashree is functioning very well and giving good results. It is noted that the members in the groups are more in AP than Kerala and the composition of the caste is also a factor as in AP most of the women were from SC and ST community in case of Kerala they belong to all the categories irrespective of caste. The crops cultivated were traditional those doesn't have much market value in case of Andhra and Telangana whereas in Kerala the groups cultivate market oriented crops along with traditional crops which gives them some profits. Refer Haque and Jaya Lekshmi (2014) for more details.

References

Ambedkar, B. R. (1918). "Small Holdings in India and Their Remedies", *Journal of the Indian Economic Society*, Vol. 1.

Ambedkar, B. R. (1936). *Annihilation of Caste*. Jalandhar: Bheem Patrika.

Dev, M. (2008). *Inclusive Growth in India: Agriculture, Poverty, and Human Development*. New Delhi: Oxford University Press.

Dev, M. (2012). *Small Farmers in India: Challenges and Opportunities*. WP-2012-014, June. www.igidr.ac.in/pdf/publication/WP-2012-014.pdf

GoI. (2016). *Report of the Expert Committee on Land Leasing*. NITI AAYOG, Govt. of India New Delhi, March 31.

Haque, T. (1996). *Sustainability of Small Holder Agriculture in India*. New Delhi: Concept Publishing Company.

Haque, T., and Lekshmi Nair, J. (2014). *Ensuring and Protecting the Land Leasing Right of Poor Women in India*. World Bank Conference on Land and Poverty, March.

Kamble, B. N. (2001). "Socio-Economic Development of the Scheduled Castes, with Special Reference to Agricultural Landless Labourers in Maharashtra", *Artha Vijnana*, Vol. XLIII, No. 1–2, March–June, pp. 208–232.

Khusro, A. M. (1958). *Economic and Social Effects of Jagirdari Abolition and Land Reforms in Hyderabad*. Hyderabad: Dept of Publication and University Press, Osmania University.

Lipton, M. (2006). "Can Small Farmers Survive, Prosper, or Be the Key Channel to cut Mass Poverty", *Journal of Agricultural and Development Economics*, Vol. 3, No. 1.

Mishra, S. N. (2010). *Socio-Economic and Political Vision of Dr. B.R. Ambedkar*. New Delhi: Concept Publishing Company.

Mohanty, B. B. (2001). "Economic Development of Scheduled Castes in Rural India: Rhetorics and Realities", *Artha Vijnana*, Vol. XLIII, No. 1–2, March–June, pp. 35–49.

National Commission for Enterprises in the Un-organised Sector. (2008). *Report on a Special Programme for Marginal and Small Farmers*. New Delhi.

National Crime Records Bureau. (2014). *A Report on Accidental Deaths and Suicides in India*. Ministry of Home Affairs, Govt. of India, New Delhi.

Pallithanam, T. (2007). *Rekindling Hope? Access, Retention and Development of Land: A Dalit Perspective*. Andhra Pradesh Social Watch Report, Hyderabad.

Ramachandran, V. and Jandhyala, K. (2012). *Cartographies of Empowerment: The Mahila Samakhya Story*. New Delhi: Zubaan.

Rao, N. P. and Suri, K. C. (2006). "Dimensions of Agrarian Distress in Andhra Pradesh", *Economic and Political Weekly*, Vol. 41, No. 16, April 22, pp. 1546–1552.

Rao, V. M. (2007). *Sustainability of Indian Agriculture: Towards an Assessment*. ISEC, ESS Working Paper, August.

Revathi, E. (1998). "Farmers' Suicide Missing Issues", *Economic and Political Weekly*, Vol. 33, No. 20, May.

Revathi, E. (2014). *Liberalizing Lease Market: The Andhra Pradesh Licensed Cultivators Act*. Working Paper No. 135, July, Centre for Economic and Social Studies, Hyderabad.

Satyanarayana, A. (1993). "Land, Caste and Dominance in Andhra Pradesh", *Proceedings of Indian History Congress*, Vol. 54, pp. 641–644.

Sreenivasulu, Y. (2015). *Functioning of Land Lease Market in Different Agro-Climatic Settings in India*. New Delhi: Serials Publication.

Sudha, P. (2010). *Developmental State and the Dalit Question in Madhya Pradesh: Congress Response*. New Delhi: Routledge.

Suryanarayana, M. H. (2001). "Scheduled Castes, Their Disadvantages and Deprivation: A Rural All-India Profile", *Artha Vijnana*, Vol. XLIII, No. 1–2, March–June, pp. 84–97.

Thorat, S. (2001). "Caste and Economic Discrimination: Theory and Evidence on Rural Labour Market", *Artha Vijnana*, Vol. XLIII, No. 1–2, March–June, pp. 123–146.

Thorat, S. (2009). *Dalits in India: Search for a Common Destiny*. New Delhi: Sage Publications.

Vijay, R. (2012). "Structural Retrogression and Rise of New Landlords in Indian Agriculture: An Empirical Exercise", *Economic and Political Weekly*, Vol. XLVII, No. 5, February 4.

Vyas, V. S. (2007). "Marginalized Sections of Indian Agriculture: The Forgotten Millions", *The Indian Journal of Labour Economics*, Vol. 50, No. 1.

Bibliography

Agarwal, S. (ed.). (1991). *Dr. BR Ambedkar: The Man and His Message: A Commemorative Volume*. Prentice-Hall.

Agriculture Census Division. (2014). *Agriculture Census in India (2010–2011)*. All India Report on Number and Area of Operational Holdings, Department of Agriculture & Co-operation, Ministry of Agriculture, Govt. of India.

All India Congress Committee. (1949). *Report of the Congress Agrarian Reforms Committee*. Madras: Madras Publishing House.

Ambedkar, B. R. (1915). *Administration and Finance of the East India Company*. New York: University of Columbia (republished in 1989) *Dr. Babasaheb Ambedkar Writing and Speeches* (Vol. VI), Government of Maharashtra.

Ambedkar, B. R. (1916). 'Castes in India: Their Mechanism, Genesis and Development', Paper read before the Anthropology Seminar of Dr. A. A. Goldenweizer at the Columbia University, New York, USA.

Ambedkar, B. R. (1918). 'Small Holdings in India and Their Remedies', *Journal of Indian Economic Society*, 1, 1900–1945.

Ambedkar, B. R. (1923). *The Problem of the Rupee: Its Origin and Its Solution*. Westminster, UK: P.S. King & Son Ltd (republished in 1989) *Dr. Babasaheb Ambedkar Writing and Speeches* (Vol. VI), Government of Maharashtra.

Ambedkar, B. R. (1925). *The Evolution of Provincial Finance in British India: A Study in the Provincial Decentralization of Imperial Finance*. Westminster, UK: P.S. King & Son Ltd (republished in 1989) *Dr. Babasaheb Ambedkar Writing and Speeches* (Vol. VI), Government of Maharashtra.

Ambedkar, B. R. (1936). *Annihilation of Caste*. Jalandhar: Bheem Patrika.

Ambedkar, B. R. (1937). *Annihilation of Caste*. http://ccnmtl.columbia.edu/projects/mmt/ambedkar/web/.

Ambedkar, B. R. (1939). *Federation versus Freedom*. R.R. Kale Memorial Lecture, Gokhale Institute of Politics and Economics, Pune.

Ambedkar, B. R. (1943). 'Post War Development of Electric Power in India', *Indian Information*, 15 November.

Ambedkar, B. R. (1943). 'First Session Plenary Labour', *Indian Information*, 15 July 1944.

Ambedkar, B. R. (1945). 'Dr. Ambedkar on Social Security', *Indian Information*, 15 September.

Ambedkar, B. R. (1945). 'Multipurpose Development of the Damodar Valley, 23 August 1945', *Indian Information*, 10 October.

Ambedkar, B. R. (1945). 'Multi-Purpose Plan for Development of Orissa Rivers. Presidential Speech, 8 November 1945', *Indian Information*, 15 December.
Ambedkar, B. R. (1947). "States and Minorities." In *Writing and Speeches of Dr. Ambedkar* (Vol. 1), Education Department, Government of Maharashtra, Maharashtra.
Ambedkar, B. R. (1948). *The Untouchables Who Were They and Why They Became Untouchables?* (Vol. 7). Maharashtra, India: Maharashtra Government.
Ambedkar, B. R. (1951). *Hindu Code Bill*. Ambedkar.org.
Ambedkar, B. R. (1955). *The Rise and Fall of the Hindu Women*. Ambedkar Publication Society.
Ambedkar, B. R. (1987). 'Philosophy of Hinduism', in *Dr. B.R. Ambedkar Writings and Speeches* (Vol. 3, Part 1, Chapter 1). Education Department, Govt. of Maharastra.
Ambedkar, B. R. (1989). 'Untouchables or the Children of India's Ghetto', in *Dr. Babasaheb Ambedkar Writings and Speeches, Government of Maharashtra, Maharashtra* (Vol. 5), pp. 4–5.
Ambedkar, B. R. (1989). *Writings and Speeches*. Education Department Government of Maharashtra, p. 329.
Ambedkar, B. R. (2003). 'The Mahad Satyagrah', in *Dr. Babasaheb Ambedkar, Writings and Speeches, Vol. 17. Dr. B.R. Ambedkar and His Egalitarian Revolution; Part One: Struggle for Human Rights*. New Delhi: Dr. Ambedkar Foundation.
Ambirajan, S. (1999). 'Ambedkar's Contribution to Indian Economics', *Economic and Political Weekly*, 34(46 & 47), 3280–3285.
Appu, P. S. (1975). 'Tenancy Reform in India', *Economic and Political Weekly*, 1339–1375.
ASER Centre. (2014). *Annual Status of Education Report 2014*. New Delhi.
Austin, G. (1966). *The Indian Constitution: Cornerstone of a Nation*. New Delhi: Oxford University.
Bai Kashi vs Jamnadas Mansukh Raichand verdict on 5 March, 1912, Bombay High Court Congress Leaders on Zamindari Institution. Land Holders Journal, 1939.
Banerjee, A. and Piketty, T. (2003). 'Top Indian Income: 1956–2000', Photocopy. Cambridge, MA: Department of Economics, Massachusetts Institute of Technology.
Banerjee, A. and Piketty, T. (2003). 'Top Indian Incomes 1956–2000', Working Paper 03–32. Cambridge, MA: Department of Economics, Massachusetts Institute of Technology.
Barnett, S. A. (1976). 'Approaches to Changes in Caste Ideology in South India', in Burton Stein (ed.), *Essays on South India*. New Delhi: Vikas Publishing House, pp. 149–155.
Bayly, S. (1988). *Indian Society and the Making of the British Empire*. Cambridge: Cambridge University Press, pp. 156–158.
Beteille, A. (1986). 'Individualism and Equality', *Current Anthropology*, 27(2), 212–234 and also Brown, D. E. (1988). *Hierarchy, History, and Human Nature: The Social Origins of Historical Consciousness*. The University of Arizona Press; Dirks, N. (1987). *The Hollow Crown: Ethnohistory of an Indian Kingdom*. Cambridge: Cambridge University Press; Barnett, S. A. (1976). 'Approaches to Changes in Caste Ideology in South India', in Burton Stein (ed.), *Essays on South India*. New Delhi: Vikas Publishing House, pp. 149–155.

Bhaduri, A. (2016). 'Danger Zones of High Economic Growth', *Economic and Political Weekly*, 51(43), 14–17.

Binswanger-Mkhize, H. P. (2012, May). 'India 1960–2010: Structural Change, the Rural Non-Farm Sector, and the Prospects for Agriculture', in *Center on Food Security and the Environment Stanford Symposium Series on Global Food Policy and Food Security in the 21st Century*. Stanford University.

Blyn, G. (1966). *Agricultural Trends in India 1891–1967*. Philadelphia: University of Pennsylvania Press.

Borooah, V. K. (2005). 'Caste, Inequality, and Poverty in India', *Review of Development Economics*, 9(3), 399–414.

Buhler, G. (1886). *The Laws of Manu*. Oxford: Clarendon Press.

Chakraborty, A. (2001). 'The Concept and Measurement of Group Inequality', Working Paper No. 315, Centre for Development Studies, Thiruvananthapuram.

Chakravarty, S. (1998). 'Development Planning: The Indian Experience', OUP Catalogue.

Chowdary, S. L. (1939). Land Holder's Journal.

The Collected Works of Mahatma Gandhi, Vol. LXXVII, p. 45.

Constable, P. (2000). 'Sitting on the School Verandah: The Ideology and Practice of "Untouchable" Educational Protest in Late Nineteenth-century Western India', *The Indian Economic & Social History Review*, 37(4), 383–422.

Das, K., Das, K. C., Roy, T. K., and Tripathy, P. K. (2011). *Dynamics of Inter-religious and Inter-caste Marriages in India*. Washington, DC: Population Association of America.

Desai, A. R. (1948). *Social Background of Indian Nationalism*, By Tarun Enterprises, Delhi and Published by Ramdas Bhatkal for Popular Prakashan Pvt. Ltd., Tardeo, Mumbai.

Deshpande, R. S. (2003). 'Current Land Policy Issues in India', *Land Reform, Land Settlement and Cooperative*, pp. 155–174.

Deshpande, S. and John, M. E. (2010). 'The Politics of Not Counting Caste', *Economic and Political Weekly*, 45(25), 39–42.

Dev, M. (2008). *Inclusive Growth in India: Agriculture, Poverty, and Human Development*. New Delhi: Oxford University Press.

Dev, M. (2012). 'Small Farmers in India: Challenges and Opportunities', WP-2012-014, June 2012. www.igidr.ac.in/pdf/publication/WP-2012-014.pdf.

Dev, M. (2016). 'Changes in Labour Market and Rural Non-farm Sector in India', in *Rural Labour in India: Processes and Policy Options*. Hyderabad: S. R. Sankaran Chair (Rural Labour), National Institute of Rural Development and Panchayati Raj, pp. 7–23.

Dirks, N. (1987). *The Hollow Crown: Ethnohistory of an Indian Kingdom*. Cambridge: Cambridge University Press, pp. 1–5, 126–129. See also Appadurai, A. (1981). *Worship and Conflict under Colonial Rule*. Cambridge: Cambridge University Press.

Dirks, N. (1987). *The Hollow Crown: Ethnohistory of an Indian Kingdom*. Cambridge: Cambridge University Press, pp. 19–54; for an elaboration of this argument see also Appadurai, A. and Brekenridge, C. (1976). 'The South Indian Temple: Authority, Honour and Redistribution', *Contributions to Indian Sociology*, 10(2), 187–211.

Dirks, N. (2003). *Castes of Mind: Colonialism and the Making of Modern India*. New Delhi: Permanent Black, pp. 3–19.

Dr. Ambedkar Foundation. (2013). *Dr. Babasaheb Ambedkar Writings and Speeches* (Vol. 14). Edited by V. Moon. New Delhi: Dr. Ambedkar Foundation.

Dr. Babasaheb Ambedkar Writings and Speeches (1979), Vol. I, *Annihilation of Caste*, pp. 57–58.

Dr. Babasaheb Ambedkar Writings and Speeches (1979), Vol. I, *Evidence before the Southborough Committee*, pp. 249–250.
Dr. Babasaheb Ambedkar Writings and Speeches (1979), Vol. I, *Ranade, Gandhi and Jinnah*, pp. 222–223.
Dr. Babasaheb Ambedkar Writings and Speeches (1982), Vol. II, *On Village Panchayats Bill*, p. 106.
Dr. Babasaheb Ambedkar Writings and Speeches (1990), Vol. VIII, pp. 193–194.
Dr. Babasaheb Ambedkar Writings and Speeches (1990), Vol. VIII. *Pakistan or Partition of India*, pp. 30–33.
Dr. Babasaheb Ambedkar Speeches and Writings (1994), Vol. XIII, p. 62.
Dumont, L. (1970). *Homo Hierarchicus: The Caste System and its Implications*. Chicago: The University Press, p. 107.
Dumont, L. (ed.) (1970). *Religion, Politics and History in India: Collected Papers in Indian Sociology*. The Hague: Mouton Publishers, p. 108, 133.
Dutt, R. P. (1948). 'Right Wing Social Democracy in the Service of Imperialism (Der rechte Flügel der Sozialdemokratie im Dienst des Imperialismus)', *For A Lasting Peace, For A People's Democracy*, #21.
EPW Research Foundation. (2003). 'Current Statistics', *Economic and Political Weekly*, 38(1), 6.
EPW Research Foundation. (2012). *India: A Pocket Book of Data Series*. New Delhi: Academic Foundation.
Freitag, S. (1991). 'Crime in the Social Order of Colonial North India', *Modern Asian Studies*, 25, 227–241.
Frykenberg, R. (2005). 'The Emergence of Modern Hinduism as a Concept and as an Institution', in Gunther-Diez Sontheimer and Herman Kulke (eds.), *Hinduism Reconsidered*. New Delhi: Manohar.
Frykenberg, R. (2009). *Construction of Hinduism at the Nexus of History and Religion*. New Delhi: Critical Quest, pp. 3–12.
Fuller, C. J. (1977). 'British India or Traditional India? An Anthropological Problem', *Ethnos*, 42(3–4), 95–121.
Gellner, E. (1983). *Nations and Nationalism*. Oxford: Basic Blackwell, chapter I, p. 18.
Geras, N. (1994). 'Democracy and the Ends of Marxism', in Parry Geraint and Moran Michael (eds.), *Democracy and Democratization*. London: Routledge.
Ghose, A. K. (2015). 'Services-led Growth and Employment in India', in *Labour, Employment and Economic Growth*. New Delhi: Cambridge University Press, pp. 21–56.
Ghosh, S. (1989). *India and the Raj 1919–1947: Glory, Shame and Bondage* (Vol. 2). Calcutta: Prachi Publications, Chapters II and III.
Giddens, A. (1976). 'Introduction', in Max Weber (ed.), *The Protestant Ethic and the Spirit of Capitalism*. London: Routledge (1992, Reprint).
GoI. (2016). 'Report of the Expert Committee on Land Leasing', NITI AAYOG Govt. of India New Delhi, March 31.
Goody, J. and Goody, J. R. (1976). *Production and Reproduction: A Comparative Study of the Domestic Domain* (No. 17). Cambridge: Cambridge University Press.
Gould, H. (1986). 'The Hindu Jajmani System: A Case of Economic Particularism in Approaches to Culture and Society. Selected Articles, 1945–1985', *Journal of Anthropological Research*, 42(3), 269–278.
Gour, H. S. (1919). *The Hindu Code*. Calcutta: Butterworth & Co (India), Ltd.
Government of India. (1944). 'Reconstruction Committee of Council (1944)', Record of the First Meeting of the Policy Committee No. 3C (Public Works and Electric

Power), held at Delhi on 23 September 1943. Magazine, Government of India, File No. 1(4): 45.

Government of India. (2016). *Economic Survey 2015–16*. New Delhi: Ministry of Finance.

Govt. of Maharashtra. (1979). Dr. Babasaheb Ambedkar: Writings and Speeches (Vol. 1). Bombay.

Govt. of Maharashtra. (1982). Dr. Babasaheb Ambedkar: Writings and Speeches (Vol. 2). Bombay.

Govt. of Maharashtra. (1989). Dr. Babasaheb Ambedkar: Writings and Speeches (Vol. 6). Bombay.

Govt. of Maharashtra. (1990). Dr. Babasaheb Ambedkar: Writings and Speeches (Vol. 9). Bombay.

Guru, G. (2009). 'The Rejection of Rejection: Foregrounding Self Respect', in G. Guru (ed.), *Humiliation*. New Delhi: Oxford University Press.

Guru, G. (2012). 'India's Liberal Democracy', in Arjun Appadurai and Arien Mack (eds.), *India's World: The Politics of Creativity in Globalized Society*. New Delhi: Rain Tree.

Hanumantha Rao, C. H. (1980). *Technological Change and Institutional Change in India*. New Delhi: Macmillan & Co.

Haque, T. (1996). *Sustainability of Small Holder Agriculture in India*. New Delhi: Concept Publishing Company.

Haque, T. and Sirohi, A. S. (1986). *Agrarian Reforms and Institutional Changes in India*. New Delhi: Concept Publishing Company.

Hobsbawm, E. (1990). *Nations and Nationalism since 1780*. Cambridge: Cambridge University Press, pp. 102–130.

Hunt, A. (ed.). (1980). *Marxism and Democracy*. London: Lawrence and Wishart.

Inden, R. (1990). *Imagining India*. Oxford: Blackwell, p. 30; for more details, see Said, E. (1978). *Orientalism*. New York: Vintage Books.

Indian Public Finance Statistics 2015–2016, Ministry of Finance Department of Economic Affairs Economic Division. http://dea.gov.in/sites/default/files/IPFSpercent 20Englishper cent202015-16.pdf.

Inkeles, A. (1966). 'Modernization of Man', in Myron Weiner (ed.), *Modernization*. New York: Basic Books, pp. 152–155.

Institute for Human Development. (2014). *India Labour and Employment Report 2014*. New Delhi: Academic Foundation.

Jadhav, N. (1991). 'Neglected Economic Thought of Babasaheb Ambedkar', *Economic and Political Weekly*, 26(15), 980–982.

Jaffrelot, C. (2003). *India's Silent Revolution: The Rise of the Lower Castes in North India*. New Delhi: Orient Blackswan.

Jaffrelot, C. (2005). 'Analysing and Ethnicising Caste to Eradicate it More Effectively', in *Dr. Ambedkar and Untouchability: Analysing and Fighting Caste*. London: C. Hurst and Co., pp. 31–51.

Jaffrelot, C. (2005). *Dr. Ambedkar and Untouchability: Fighting the Indian Caste System*. New York: Columbia University Press.

Jatava, D. R. (1965). *The Social Philosophy of B. R. Ambedkar*. Agra: Phoenix Publishing House, p. 106.

Jenkins, R. (1999). *Democratic Politics and Economic Reforms in India*. Cambridge: Cambridge University Press.

Jodhka, S. S. (2000). '"Prejudice" without "Pollution"?: SCs in Contemporary Punjab', *Journal of Indian School of Political Economy*, 12(3), 381–402.

Jodhka, S. S. (2002). 'Caste and Untouchability in Rural Punjab', *Economic and Political Weekly*, 37(19), 1813–1823.

Jodhka, S. S. (2006). 'Beyond "Crises": Rethinking Contemporary Punjab Agriculture', *Economic and Political Weekly*, 41(16), 1530–1537.

Joshi, B. R. (1982). *Democracy in Search of Equality: Untouchables Politics and Social Change*. New Delhi: Hindustan Publishing.

Kamble, B. N. (2001). 'Socio-Economic Development of the Scheduled Castes, with Special Reference to Agricultural Landless Labourers in Maharashtra', *Artha Vijnana*, 45(1 & 2), 208–232.

Keer, D. (1962). *Dr. Ambedkar: Life and Mission*. Bombay: Popular Prakashan, pp. 72–80.

Keer, D. (1994). *Dr. Ambedkar: Life and Mission*. Bombay: Popular Prakashan.

Khusro, A. M. (1958). 'Economic and Social Effects of Jagirdari Abolition and Land Reforms in Hyderabad', Dept of Publication and University Press, Osmania University, Hyderabad.

Kohn, H. (1924). *A History of Nationalism in the East*. London: George Routledge and Sons Ltd., p. 56.

Kolli, R. (2009). 'Corporate Sector in Indian National Accounts', *The Journal of Income and Wealth*, 31(2), 89–104.

Kolli, R. and Sinharay, A. (2011). 'Share of Informal Sector and Informal Employment in GDP and Employment', The Association of Research in National Income and Wealth: Annual Conference. Hyderabad: Centre for Economic and Social Studies.

Krishnan, P. S. (2016). 'Dalit Suicides: Socio-Historical Facts and Remedial and Corrective Measures: A Note', *Indian Express*, January 29, 2016.

Kuber, W. N. (1991). *Ambedkar: A Critical Study*. New Delhi: People's Publishing.

Kumar, D. (1962). 'Caste and Landlessness in South India', *Comparative Studies in Society and History*, 4(3), 337–363.

Kumar, D. (1985). 'Private Property in Asia? The Case of Medieval South India', *Comparative Studies in Society and History*, 27(2), 340–366.

Laxminarayana, K. (2017). 'Why Rupanwal Commission is a Travesty', *Economic and Political Weekly*, 52(46).

Lewis, O. and Barnouw, V. (1956). 'Caste and the Jajmani System in a North Indian Village', *The Scientific Monthly*, 83(2), 66–81.

Lobo, J. C. H. (1983). *Dr. B.R. Ambedkar: The Champion of Social Democracy in India*. Bangalore, India: Hilerina Publications, p. 14.

Maddison, A. (2001). *The World Economy: A Millennial Perspective*. Paris: OECD.

Madheswaran, S. and Attewell, P. (2010). 'Wage and Job Discrimination in the Indian Urban Labour Market', in Sukhadeo Thorat and Katherine S. Newman (eds.), *Blocked by Caste: Economic Discrimination in Modern India*. New Delhi: Oxford University Press, pp. 123–147.

Manjit, S. (2012). 'Preference for Migrant Agricultural Labour in Punjab', *Economic and Political Weekly*, 47(29), 27–28.

Marginson, S. (2007). *Globalization and Higher Education*. www.oecd.org/edu/research/37552729.pdf.

Marx, K. and Engels, F. (1977). *Selected Works* (Vol. I). Moscow: Progress Publishers, pp. 494–499.

Mehrotra, S. R. (1971). *The Emergence of Indian National Congress*. New Delhi: Vikas Publications, p. 248.
Mencher, J. P. (1974). 'The Caste System Upside Down, or the Not-so-Mysterious East', *Current Anthropology*, 15(4), 469–493.
Ministry of Finance. (2016). *Economic Survey 2015–16*. New Delhi: Government of India.
Ministry of Human Resource Development, Government of India National University of Educational Planning and Administration (NUEPA). (2015). *Education for All: Status and Trends*. New Delhi.
Mishra, S. N. (ed.). (2010). *Socio-Economic and Political Vision of Dr. BR Ambedkar*. New Delhi: Concept Publishing Company.
Mohanty, B. B. (2001). 'Economic Development of Scheduled Castes in Rural India: Rhetorics and Realities', *Artha Vijnana*, 45(1 & 2), 35–49.
Murdia, R. (1975). 'Land Allotment and Land Alienation: Policies and Programmes for Scheduled Castes and Tribes', *Economic and Political Weekly*, 1204–1214.
Nadkarni, M. V. (2007). 'Does Hinduism Lack Social Concern?', *Economic and Political Weekly*, 1844–1849.
Naik, A. K. and Tagade, N. (2018). 'Poverty and Inequality in Maharashtra: Intergroup Differentials and Its Determinants', *Journal of Social Inclusion Studies*, 4(1), 151–168.
Nair, G. (2016). 'Bitter Aftertaste of Beef Ban; "Choice", Caste and Consumption', *Economic and Political Weekly*, 51(10).
Nancharaiah, G. (1988). *Land and Caste*. Himalaya Publishing House.
Office of the Registrar General of India. (2011). *Census of India (2011)*. New Delhi: Government of India.
Omvedt, Gail (1982). *Caste, agrarian relations and agrarian conflicts* in Sociological perspectives of land reforms, edited by Sheo Kumar Lal, In All-India Seminar on Sociological Perspectives of Land Reforms (1980: University of Jodhpur). Agricole Publishing Academy.
Omvedt, G. (1994). *Dalits and the Democratic Revolution: Dr. Ambedkar and the Dalit Movement in Colonial India*. SAGE Publications India.
Pai, S. (2012). *Developmental State and the Dalit Question in Madhya Pradesh: Congress Response*. Routledge India.
Pallithanam, F. T. (ed.). (2007). 'Rekindling Hope? Access, Retention and Development of Land: A Dalit Perspective', Andhra Pradesh Social Watch Report, Hyderabad.
Panitch, L. and Leys, C. (eds.). (1999). *Global Capitalism versus Democracy, Socialist Register*. London: Merlin Press. Published in India by K P Bagchi & Company, Culcutta.
Papola, T. S. (2014). 'Economic Diversification and Labour Market Dynamics in Rural India', *Indian Journal of Agricultural Marketing*, 28(3), 18–33.
Patankar, B. and Omvedt, G. (1979). 'The Dalit liberation Movement in Colonial Period', *Economic and Political Weekly*, 409–424.
Patnaik, U. (2007). 'The Republic of Hunger and Other Essays', Three Essays Collective.
Planning Commission. (2013). *Press Note on Poverty Estimates, 2011–12* (No. id: 5421). New Delhi.
Przeworski, A. (1985). *Capitalism and Social Democracy*. Cambridge: Cambridge University Press.

Puri, H. K. (2003). 'Scheduled Castes in Sikh Community: A Historical Perspective', *Economic and Political Weekly*, 38(26), 2693–2701.

Radhakrishna, R. (2015). 'Well-being, Inequality, Poverty and Pathways Out of Poverty in India', *Economic and Political Weekly*, 50(41), 59–71.

Radhakrishna, R. and Chandrasekhar, S. (2008). 'Overview: Growth: Achievements and Distress', in R. Radhakrisnan and I. Gandhi (eds.), *Indian Development Report*. New Delhi: New Oxford University Press.

Radhakrishna, R. and Raju, D. S. R. (2015). 'Well-being of Agricultural Households in Post Reform India', *The Indian Economic Journal*, 63(3), 329–347.

Radhakrishna, R. and Raju, D. S. R. (2016). 'Well-being of Agricultural Households in Post-reform India', in C. Ramasamy and K. R. Ashok (eds.), *Vicissitudes of Agriculture in the Fast growing Indian Economy: Challenges, Strategies and the Way Forward*. Mumbai: Academic Foundation, pp. 151–174.

Radhakrishna, R., Ravi, C., and Reddy, B. S. (2010). 'Can We Really Measure Poverty and Identify the Poor When Poverty Encompasses Multiple Deprivations?', *Indian Journal of Human Development*, 4(2), 281–300.

Radhakrishna, R., Ravi, C., and Reddy, B. S. (2013). 'Assessment of Well-being in Multidimensional Perspective in Post-reform India', *Indian Economic Review*, 129–166.

Radhakrishna, R. and Ray, S. (eds.). (2005). *Handbook of Poverty in India: Perspectives, Policies, and Programmes*. Oxford University Press.

Ramachandran, V. and Jandhyala, K. (eds.). (2014). *Cartographies of Empowerment: The Mahila Samakhya Story*. New Delhi: Zubaan.

Rao, C. H. (1998). 'Agricultural Growth, Sustainability and Poverty Alleviation: Recent Trends and Major Issues of Reform', *Economic and Political Weekly*, 1943–1948.

Rao, P. N. and Suri, K. C. (2006). 'Dimensions of Agrarian Distress in Andhra Pradesh', *Economic and Political Weekly*, 41(16), 1546–1552.

Rao, R. (1993). *Babasaheb Ambedkar*. New Delhi: Sahitya Akademi.

Rao, S. (n.d.). 'Student Suicides in Elite Higher Educational Institutions', An Unpublished Paper. Center for Zakir Hussain studies, Jawaharlal Nehru University.

Rao, V. M. (2007). 'Sustainability of Indian Agriculture: Towards an Assessment', ISEC, eSocialSciences, Working Paper, August.

Rege, S. (2006). 'Baby Kondiba Kamble; Jine Amuche', in *Writing Caste/Writing Gender*. New Delhi: Zubaan, pp. 194–226.

Rege, S., Tak, D., Thosar, S., and Aranha, T. (2009). *Isn't This Plate Indian? Dalit Histories and Memories of Food*. Gender Studies: Student Project Series. Pune: Krantijyoti Savitribai Phule, Women's Studies Center.

Report submitted to Andhra Pradesh High Court in the context of Public Interest Litigation (2013).

Revathi, E. (1998). 'Farmers' Suicide: Missing Issues', *Economic and Political Weekly*, 33(20), 1207–1207.

Revathi, E. (2014). 'Liberalizing Lease Market: The Andhra Pradesh Land Licensed Cultivators Act', Working Paper No. 135, Centre for Economic and Social Studies, July.

Rodrigues, V. (2017). 'Ambedkar as a Political Philosopher', *Economic & Political Weekly*, 52(15), 101.

Roy, D. M. (1932). 'Touchability and Untouchability', *Land Holders Journal* (Vol. I, Issue VI), Calcutta: Macson Press, pp. 380–386.

Roy, M. N. (1971). *The Future of Indian Politics*. Calcutta: Minerva Associates.
Rudolph, L. and Rudolph, S. (1967). *The Modernity of Tradition*. Chicago: University of Chicago Press, p. 36.
Rudra, A. (1981). 'Against Feudalism', *Economic and Political Weekly*, XVI(52), 2133–2146.
Saha, P. and Verick, S. (2016). 'State of Rural Labour Markets in India', in *Dynamics of Rural Labour Relations in India*. Hyderabad: National Institute of Rural Development and Panchayati Raj (NIRD & PR).
Satyanarayana, A. (1993, January). 'Land, Caste and Dominance in Andhra Pradesh', *Proceedings of the Indian History Congress*, 54, 641–644.
Seal, A. (1968). *The Emergence of Indian Nationalism*. Cambridge: Cambridge University Press, pp. 8, 38–97; see also Brown, J. (1984). *Modern India: The Origins of an Asian Democracy*. New Delhi: Oxford University Press.
Sen, A. K. (1962). 'An Aspect of Indian Agriculture', *Economic Weekly*, 14(4), 243–246.
Sen, P. (1986). 'The 1966 Devaluation in India: A Reappraisal', *Economic and Political Weekly*, 21(30).
Shahare, M. L. (1991). 'Dr. B. R. Ambedkar: An Eminent Educationist', in Sudarshan Agarwal (ed.), *Dr. B.R. Ambedkar, the Man and His Message: A Commemorative Volume*. Prentice-Hall.
Shergill, H. S. and Singh, G. (1995). 'Poverty in Rural Punjab: Trend Over Green Revolution Decades', *Economic and Political Weekly*, 30(24 & 25), A80–A83.
Shetty, S. L. (2003). 'Growing Inequality: A Serious Challenge to the Indian Society and Polity', Dr. V. K. R. V. Rao Memorial Lecture, Annual Conference of the Indian Association for Research in National Income and Wealth. Bangalore: Institute for Social and Economic Change.
Shukla, V. and Mishra, U. S. (2014). 'Is the Recent Reduction in India's Poverty Inclusive?', *Economic and Political Weekly*, 49(47), 70–75.
Shulman, D. (1985). 'Reconsidering Hinduism', in G.D. Sontheimer and Herman Kulke (eds.), *Hinduism Reconsidered*. New Delhi: Manohar, pp. 7–10.
Sinha, A. (1978). 'Legal Loopholes: To Landlords' Rescue', *Economic and Political Weekly*, 1758–1760.
Sinha, C. (2007). 'Images of Motherhood: The Hindu Code Bill Discourse', *Economic and Political Weekly*, 49–57.
Source Material. (1982). *Dr. Babasaheb Ambedkar and the Movement of Untouchables* (Vol. 1). Education Department, Government of Maharashtra.
Sreenivasulu, Y. (2015). *Functioning of Land Lease Market in Different Agro-Climatic Settings in India*. New Delhi: Serials Publication.
Srinivas, M. N. (1952). *Religion and Society among the Coorgs of South India*. Bombay, Calcutta, New Delhi, Madras, Lucknow, London, and New York. Oxford, London: Asia Publishing House.
Srinivas, M. N. (1956). 'A Note on Sanskritization and Westernization', *The Journal of Asian Studies*, 15(4), 481–496.
Srinivas, M. N. (1966). *Social Change in Modern India*. Hyderabad: Orient Longman Ltd., p. 3, 91.
Srinivas, M. N. (1970). *Social Change in Modern India and other Essays*. Bombay: Asia Publishing House, pp. 5–6.
Srinivasulu, K. (2002). *Caste, Class and Social Articulation in Andhra Pradesh: Mapping Differential Regional Trajectories*. London: Overseas Development Institute, p. 3.

Stokes, E. (1978). *The Peasants and the Raj: Studies in Agrarian Society and Peasant Rebellion in Colonial India*. New Delhi: Vikas Publishers, pp. 19–23.

Suryanarayana, M. H. (2001). 'Scheduled Castes, their Disadvantages and Deprivation: A Rural All-India Profile', *Artha Vijnana*, 43(1&2), 84–97.

Swamy, A. (2010). *Land and Law in Colonial India* (No. 2011–03). Department of Economics, Williams College.

Swayampakula Subbaramayya and vs Swayampakula Venkatasubbamma. (1941). On 5 February, Madras High Court.

Tagade, N., Naik, A. K., and Thorat, S. (2018). 'Wealth Ownership and Inequality in India: A Socio-religious Analysis', *Journal of Social Inclusion Studies*, 4(2), 1–18.

Thapar, R. (1966). *A History of Indian* (Vol. I). Middlesex: Penguin Books, p. 19; for more details see Wink, A. (1986). *Land and Sovereignty in India*. Cambridge: Cambridge University Press, pp. 214–220.

Thapar, R. (1998). 'Imagined Religious Communities: Ancient History and the Modern Search for a Hindu Identity', *Modern Asian Studies*, 23(2), 203–223.

Thomas, J. J. (2012). 'India's Labour Market during the 2000s: Surveying the Changes', *Economic and Political Weekly*, 39–51.

Thomas, J. J. (2015). 'India's Labour Market during the 2000s', in K. V. Ramaswamy (ed.), *Labour, Employment and Economic Growth in India*. New Delhi: Cambridge University Press, pp. 21–56.

Thorat, S. (2001). 'Caste and Economic Discrimination: Theory and Evidence on Rural Labour Market', *Artha Vijnana*, 43(1 & 2), 123–146.

Thorat, S. (2005). 'Caste System and Economic Discrimination: Lessons from Theories', in *Reservation and Private Sector: Quest for Equal Opportunity and Growth*. New Delhi: Institute of Dalit Studies and Rawat Publications, pp. 66–88.

Thorat, S. (2006). *Ambedkar's Role in Economic Planning, Water and Power Policy*. Shipra Publications.

Thorat, S. (2009). *Dalits c India: Search for a Common Destiny*. SAGE Publications Ltd.

Thorat, S. and Attewell, P. (2010). 'The Legacy of Social Exclusion: A Correspondence Study of Job Discrimination in India's Urban Private Sector', Sukhadeo Thorat and Katherine S. Newman (eds.), *Blocked by Caste: Economic Discrimination in Modern India*. New Delhi: Oxford University Press, pp. 35–51.

Thorat, S., Banerjee, A., Mishra, V. K., and Rizvi, F. (2015). 'Urban Rental Housing Market', *Economic & Political Weekly*, 27, 47–53.

Thorat, S. and Dubey, A. (2012). 'Has Growth Been Socially Inclusive during 1993-94-2009-10?', *Economic & Political Weekly*, 47(10), 43–53.

Thorat, S. and Kumar, N. (2008). *In Search of Inclusive Policy: Addressing Graded Inequality*. New Delhi: Rawat Publications.

Thorat, S. and Lee, J. (2010). 'Food Security Schemes and Caste Discrimination', Sukhadeo Thorat and Katherine S. Newman (eds.), *Blocked by Caste: Economic Discrimination in Modern India*. New Delhi: Oxford University Press, pp. 287–310.

Thorat, S. and Madheswaran, S. (2018). 'Graded Caste Inequality and Poverty: Evidence on Role of Economic Discrimination', *Journal of Social Inclusion Studies*, 4(1), 3–29.

Thorat, S. and Newman, K. S. (eds.). (2010). *Blocked by Caste: Economic Discrimination in Modern India*. New Delhi: Oxford University Press.

Thorat, S. and Tagade, N. (2018). *Maharashtratil Vishamta ani Garibi: Sampattik Vishamta va Jatiya Bhedbhavacha Prabhav* (Inequality and Poverty in Maharashtra: Impact of Wealth Inequality and Caste based Discrimination). Pune: Sugava Prakashan.
Times of India. (1943). 'Urgency of Industrialisation of India', 26th October.
UGC Regulations on Prevention of Caste based Discrimination/Harassment/Victimi zation and Promotion of Equality in HEIs. (2012).
UNDP. (2010). *Human Development Report*. New York: United Nations Development Programme.
Valmiki, O. (2003). *In Jhootan*. Kolkatta: Samya, p. 35.
Various Reports of Census of India, 1901–2011.
Various Reports of National Sample Survey, 1954–55 to 2012–13.
Various Reports of National SC/ST Commission.
Various Reports of Planning Commission.
Vijay, R. (2012). 'Structural Retrogression and Rise of "New Landlords" in Indian Agriculture: An Empirical Exercise', *Economic and Political Weekly*, 47(5), 37–45.
Vyas, V. S. (2007). 'Marginalized Sections of Indian Agriculture: The Forgotten Millions', *The Indian Journal of Labour Economics*, Institute of Development Studies, Jaipur, Rajasthán, India, 50(1).
Walton, M. (2012). 'Inequality, Rents and Long-Run Transformation of India', Monograph No. 26. Bengaluru: Institute of Socio-Economic Change.
Washbrook, D. (1993). 'Economic Depression and the Making of "Traditional" Society in Colonial India 1820–1855', *Transactions of the Royal Historical Society*, 3, 237–263, p. 85.
Weber, M. (1958). *The Religion of India*. Glencoe: The Free Press, pp. 48–51.
Weber, M. (2009, Reprint). *The Religion of India: The Sociology of Hinduism and Buddhism*. Translated and Edited by Hans H. Gerth and Don Martindale. New Delhi: Radha Publications, p. 112.
Wiser, W. (1936). *The Hindu Jajmani System*. New Delhi: Munshiram Manohar Lal Publishers Pvt. Ltd.
World Bank. (2016). *World Development Indicators*. Washington, DC: World Bank.

Index

Note: Page numbers followed by 'n' refer to notes.

Taylor & Francis eBooks

www.taylorfrancis.com

A single destination for eBooks from Taylor & Francis with increased functionality and an improved user experience to meet the needs of our customers.

90,000+ eBooks of award-winning academic content in Humanities, Social Science, Science, Technology, Engineering, and Medical written by a global network of editors and authors.

TAYLOR & FRANCIS EBOOKS OFFERS:

- A streamlined experience for our library customers
- A single point of discovery for all of our eBook content
- Improved search and discovery of content at both book and chapter level

REQUEST A FREE TRIAL

support@taylorfrancis.com

Routledge Taylor & Francis Group   CRC Press Taylor & Francis Group

For Product Safety Concerns and Information please contact our EU representative GPSR@taylorandfrancis.com
Taylor & Francis Verlag GmbH, Kaufingerstraße 24, 80331 München, Germany

www.ingramcontent.com/pod-product-compliance
Ingram Content Group UK Ltd.
Pitfield, Milton Keynes, MK11 3LW, UK
UKHW020147200926
475702UK00016B/2592
9780367508630